Venture Capital Funding

Global and Indian Experiences

Venture Capital Funding

Global and Indian Experiences

Vandana Panwar

Assistant Professor,
Department of Management Studies,
Takshilla Institute of Engineering and Technology, Jabalpur

New Century Publications
New Delhi, India

NEW CENTURY PUBLICATIONS
4800/24, Bharat Ram Road,
Ansari Road, Daryaganj,
New Delhi – 110 002 (India)

Tel.: 011-2324 7798, 4358 7398, 6539 6605
Fax: 011-4101 7798
E-mail: indiatax@vsnl.com ≡ info@newcenturypublications.com
www.newcenturypublications.com

Editorial office:
LG–7, Aakarshan Bhawan,
4754-57/23, Ansari Road, Daryaganj,
New Delhi – 110 002

Tel.: 011-4356 0919

First Published: **September 2009**

ISBN: **978-81-7708-222-7**

Published by New Century Publications and printed at Salasar Imaging Systems, New Delhi.

Designs: Patch Creative Unit, New Delhi.

PRINTED IN INDIA

Contents

Foreword

Economic development in India depends critically on the efficient allocation of financial capital to its best uses. But as the subprime crisis in the United States illustrates, developing appropriate institutions is a difficult problem for even a developed economy. In fact, the subprime crisis can be traced to a systematic failure of financial intermediaries in the performance of a key function—the screening of potential borrowers for credit risk. Mortgage brokers, mortgage banks and government sponsored institutions all conspired to make transactions that lined the pockets of individual players but at the cost of the people as a whole. The failure of the global system and consequent global financial crisis, which has adversely affected India, is the consequence.

Those on the left who use the financial crisis to argue against further deregulation of the Indian financial system should look carefully at the source of the crisis, which was the willingness of government sponsored enterprises—Fannie Mae and Freddie Mac in particular—to buy toxic waste then repackage and sell into the private sector. Without the implicit guarantee of the U.S. government, it is unlikely that these institutions could have gotten away with their outrageous behaviour. Thus, government intervention into the mortgage market is at the root of the subprime crisis. But those on the right who want no regulation are equally deluded. The fall of Lehman Brothers is, in part, the consequence of deregulation of capital requirements by the U.S. Securities and Exchange Commission. The changes allow Lehman to leverage 33 to 1, a condition Lehman uses to expand its balance sheet by loading up on subprime mortgages.

Thus, simplistic, knee jerk solutions are not the answer. What is needed is careful, reasoned analysis that determines what works and what doesn't work. Here Vandana Panwar's work on venture capital finds its usefulness. Understanding this important segment of the financial system is important to regulators so as to develop rational regulation that harnesses the power of the private sector without allowing the self-dealing that distort the system toward instability. Finding this balance isn't easy, but it is crucial for a well function financial system.

While understanding VC sector is critical for rational regulation, it is just as important for the investor. An understanding of the information structure and function of VC funding will enable the investor to evaluate the likely outcome of a particular VC based on an understanding of how the VC works. Indeed, the essential idea of the market is that the private investor better understands the system than does the government regulator. Using an understanding of VC financing the private investor can and should enter private contracts that prevent excessive risk taking while at the same time allow new businesses to gain capital needed for growth. The balance between risk and return requires an understanding of how the VC works if the private investor is not to make mistakes, perhaps very costly. And the VC manager, seeking to avoid mistakes and seeking to provide an investment vehicle that can attract financial capital will also want to understand theory and practice of the VC. Managers will often depend more on experience than book learning, and that is a good thing. But experience uninformed by theory, is experience that can be mislead by novel situations. Understanding the theory, studying the case studies provided by Vandana's study will serve managers well.

Vandana's book fills a slot in the book shelf that regulators, investors and VC managers will want to fill. And the book is well written interesting and a joy to read.

August 14, 2009

Christopher Erickson, Ph.D.
College of Business Administration
New Mexico State University
Las Cruces, NM, USA

About the Book

Venture capital funding is an increasingly important area for entrepreneurial ventures in both industrialized and developing countries. Venture capital has become especially important in India in developing information technology (IT) sector.

Venture capital is a form of equity financing in which the investor actively participates in the venture being financed. Although the concept as such is very old, a formal market for venture capital in the US started only after World War II. A venture capital firm manages funds provided by investors and directs them to the most promising ventures, mainly in the form of equity.

This volume, which includes 13 case studies, provides an exhaustive account of the theory and practice of venture capital firms. The reader will gain insight into the operation of venture capital funding in India. The book examines in detail the contracts between venture capital firms and entrepreneurs to determine what provisions are included in these contracts that help in decision-making such as appraisal, screening, self-selection, monitoring, incentivizing and divestment. Experiences of other countries in managing venture capital operations are also explained in the book.

About the Author

Dr. Vandana Panwar is presently Assistant Professor in the Department of Management Studies, Takshilla Institute of Engineering and Technology, Jabalpur, Madhya Pradesh. After having graduated in Economics (Honours), she did her M.A. in Public Administration and Post-graduate Diploma in Business Management. Subsequently, she pursued doctoral programme in management and earned her Ph.D. degree from Nirma University of Science and Technology, Ahmedabad, Gujarat in 2005. She is also a visiting faculty at College of Materials Management, Jabalpur. Under a student exchange programme, she visited College of Business Administration, New Mexico State University, Las Cruses, USA.

Preface

Venture capital is a form of equity financing in which the investor actively participates in the venture being financed. Although the concept as such is very old, a formal market for venture capital in the US started only after World War II. A venture capital firm manages funds provided by investors and directs it to the most promising ventures, mainly in the form of equity. The venture capitalist is responsible for managing investor's funds, provides financial and strategic assistance to the recipient company and actively participates in its management. The support continues until the venture materializes, at which stage an outside investor might be interested in acquiring the company, or the venture might be able to go public. Returns are then distributed back to the original investors.

Venture capital funding is an increasingly important source for entrepreneurial ventures in both industrialized and developing countries. Venture capital financing has become especially important in India in developing information technology sector.

India does have a number of strengths for venture fund development: an enormous number of small businesses, public equity market, low wages not only for physical labour but also for trained engineers and scientists, a home-grown software industry that became a significant player internationally in the mid-1990s. Experiencing rapid growth, some Indian software firms became significant successes and were able to list on the U.S. NASDAQ. Finally, beginning in the 1980s, but especially in the 1990s, a number of Indian engineers who had emigrated to the U.S. became entrepreneurs and began their own high-technology firms. They were extremely successful, making them multimillionaires or even billionaires, and some of them became venture capitalists or angel investors. So there was a group of potential transfer agents. The Indian venture capital industry has grown rapidly with well over 100 venture capital firms today.

This volume, which includes 13 case studies, provides an introduction into the theory and practice of venture capital firms. By studying these examples, the reader will gain insight into the operation of venture capital funding in India. The book examines in detail the contracts between venture capital firms and entrepreneurs to determine what provisions are included in these contracts that help in decision-making such as appraisal/screening, self-selection, monitoring, incentivizing and divestment.

The book is organised into 8 chapters.

Chapter 1 is introductory in nature, explaining the concept of venture capital and the processes involved in decision-making.

Chapter 2 provides a primer on the theory of capital market imperfections, and how asymmetric information can lead to finance constraints. It also reviews the concepts of venture capital financing and its theoretical aspects.

Chapter 3 reviews the private equity environment and development of venture capital in some developed and developing countries.

Chapter 4 deals with the historical background of venture capital in India, its structure and legal framework. It further explains the current status of venture capital in India.

Chapter 5 describes the research methodology, research questions hypotheses, research design, sample and data collection.

Chapter 6 presents the 13 case studies.

Chapter 7 describes the results of the study.

Chapter 8 presents the conclusions of the study, limitations, implications, prospects of venture capital in the new millennium, recommendations and directions for future research.

I place on record my deep sense of gratitude to Professor T.R. Bishnoi and Professor Christopher Erickson for motivating me to undertake this work and helping me at every stage of its completion. I am grateful to Dr. Anup K. Singh, Director, Institute of Management for enriching the substance of the book. Thanks are also due to Professor I.M. Pandey, IIM Ahmedabad for lending his treasured material and meaningful suggestions. My special appreciation is for Ms. Seema Pandya for her support and encouragement. Finally, I thank the most important people in my life: My parents and brothers, my husband and daughter Ananya.

August 20, 2009 Vandana Panwar
Jabalpur

Acronyms/Abbreviations

APIDC	Andhra Pradesh Industrial Development Corporation
CCPS	Convertible Cumulative Preference Shares
CEO	Chief Executive Officer
CVCF	Canbank Venture Capital Fund
EPS	Earnings Per Share
GIDC	Gujarat Industrial Development Corporation
GIIC	Gujarat Industrial and Investment Corporation
GSFC	Gujarat State Financial Corporation
GSFS	Gujarat State Financial Services Ltd.
GVCF	Gujarat Venture Capital Fund
GVFL	Gujarat Venture Finance Limited
ICDs	Inter Corporate Deposits
IDBI	Industrial Development Bank of India
IPOs	Initial Public Offerings
IRR	Internal Rate of Return
IVCM	International Venture Capital Management
LAN	Local Area Networking
NASDAQ	National Association of Securities Dealers Automated Quotation System
NCD	Non-Convertible Debentures
NRIs	Non-Resident Indians
OCCPS	Optionally Convertible Cumulative Preference Shares
OCDs	Optionally Convertible Debentures
OIIDCO	Orissa Industrial Infrastructure Development Corporation
P/E	Price Earning Ratio
PBDIT	Profit Before Depreciation, Interest and Tax
PBID	Profit Before Interest and Depreciation
PBT	Profit Before Tax

R&D	Research & Development
ROI	Return on Investment
SEBI	Stock Exchange Board of India
SFCDs	Secured Fully Convertible Debentures
SIDBI	Small Industries Development Bank of India
TDB	Technology Development Board
TDICI	Technology Development and Industrial Corporation of India
U.K.	United Kingdom
U.S.	United States
VC	Venture Capitalist
VCC	Venture Capital Company
VCFs	Venture Capital Funds
VDIS	Voluntary Disclosure Income Scheme
WAN	Wide Area Networking
YTN	Yield-to-Maturity

1

Venture Capital: An Introduction

1.1 Importance of Venture Capital

Venture capital funding is an increasingly important source for entrepreneurial ventures in both industrialized and developing countries. Venture capital financing has become especially important in India in developing information technology sector (Nasscom, 2000).

India has a history of state-directed institutional development with the exception that government is avowedly hostile to capitalism; government control over economy and the bureaucracy had a reputation for corruption. Such an environment would be considered hostile to the development of an institution like venture capital.

India does have a number of strengths for venture fund development: an enormous number of small businesses, public equity market, low wages not only for physical labour but also for trained engineers and scientists, a home-grown software industry that became a significant player internationally in the mid-1990s. Experiencing rapid growth, some Indian software firms became significant successes and were able to list on the U.S. NASDAQ. Finally, beginning in the 1980s, but especially in the 1990s, a number of Indian engineers who had emigrated to the U.S. became entrepreneurs and began their own high-technology firms. They were extremely successful, making them multimillionaires or even billionaires, and some of them then became venture capitalists or angel investors. So there was a group of potential transfer agents (Dossani, 2001).

Despite the importance of venture capital to the Indian economy, little is known about the decision process that Indian VCs use to determine which proposals receive equity funding. The only Indian study we could access was conducted at a time when the Indian venture capital industry was in its infancy, with only 13 venture capital firms in existence (Pandey, 1996). The Indian venture capital industry has grown rapidly and matured since then, with well over 100 venture capital firms today.

Venture capital is a form of equity financing in which the investor actively participates in the venture being financed. Although the concept as such is very old, a formal market for venture capital in the U.S. started only after World War II. A venture capital firm manages funds provided by investors and directs it to the most promising ventures, mainly in the form of equity. The venture capitalist (VCs) is responsible for managing investor's funds, provides financial and strategic assistance to the recipient company and actively participates in its management. The support continues until the venture materializes, at which stage an outside investor might be interested in acquiring the company, or the venture might be able to go public. Returns then are distributed back to the original investors.

Venture capital arrangements are information-intensive. The venture capitalist must be an expert in both management and finance, and in the specific industry to which the venture belongs. In addition, he must be involved in the detailed operations of the recipient company. Theoretically, such arrangements can be most rewarded in environments where uncertainty and asymmetry of information most prevail. It is precisely such environments that traditional methods of financing, e.g. banks loans or public capital markets, fail to accommodate well. This implies that young companies, which operate in a highly uncertain environment, might face prohibitive costs in obtaining external capital. If such companies were able to obtain venture capital, however, their financial constraints could be significantly relieved.

The theory of capital market imperfections, the subject matter of another chapter, predicts that, in the presence of asymmetric information and conflicts of interest, some firms will be unable to obtain external finance at the cost of funds set in centralized securities markets. Then (Sahlman, 1990; 1994a) the structure of venture capital well suited to address the problems of informational asymmetry and agency costs that are most pronounced in high-tech industries and young firms. A major issue in the design of venture capital contracts is moral hazard and adverse selection.

Venture capital arrangements help reduce informational asymmetry and the associated principle-agent problem, it would be a potential alternative asymmetry for traditional methods of finance, especially in other high-risk environments, such as emerging markets and developing countries. Several researchers, (Sagari 1991a), point to venture capital as a viable source for financing development.

Since venture capital is based on equity financing rather than debt, financing development avoids financial instability typically associated with debt financing. The world debt crisis provided the need for alternative forms of financing that will promote growth and development while maintaining order and stability.

1.2 Venture Capital Investment Process

The evaluation of the proposed ventures is the most crucial aspect of the operation of VCFs. Because the investment will generally be in small firms with a direct involvement of the venture capitalists, and because these firms will be new without past performance, venture evaluation cannot be subjected to a very high degree of quantitative analysis (Poindexter, 1976). This is borne out by the venture evaluation experiences in the developed countries like USA (Poindexter, 1976; Tyebjee and Bruno, 1984; Macmillan, Siegal and Subba Narasimha, 1985). In this section we'll try to answer-What evaluation criteria are being used by the venture capitalists in a developing country like India, particularly when the venture capital activity is in its infancy?

1.3 Processes Involving Venture Capital Investment

According to Tyebjee and Bruno (1984), the venture capital investment activity is a sequential process involving five steps, namely

1. Deal origination.
2. Screening.
3. Evaluation or due diligence.
4. Deal structuring.
5. Post–investment activities and exit.

1.3.1 Deal Origination: How does a venture capitalist learn about potential ventures? In generating a deal flow, the VC investor creates a pipeline of deals or investment opportunities that he would consider for investing in. Deals may originate in various ways: referral system, active search system, and intermediaries. Referral system is an important source of deals. Deals may be referred to VCFs by their parent organizations, trade partners, industry associations, friends etc. Another deal flow is active search through networks, trade fairs, conferences, seminars, foreign visits etc. Intermediaries is used by venture capitalists in developed countries like USA, is certain intermediaries who match VCFs and the potential entrepreneurs.

1.3.2 Screening: Venture capital is a service industry, and VCFs generally operate with a small staff. VCFs, before going for an in-depth analysis, carry out initial screening of all projects on the basis of some broad criteria. For example, the screening process may limit projects to areas in which the venture capitalist is familiar in terms of technology, or product, or market scope. The size of investment, geographical location and stage of financing could also be used as the broad screening criteria.

1.3.3 Evaluation or Due Diligence: Once a proposal has passed through initial screening, it is subjected to a detailed evaluation or due diligence process. Most ventures are new and the entrepreneurs may lack operating experience. Hence, a sophisticated, formal evaluation is neither possible nor desirable. The venture capitalists, thus rely on a subjective, but comprehensive, evaluation. VCFs evaluate the quality of entrepreneur before appraising the characteristics of the product, market or technology. Most venture capitalists ask for a business plan to make an assessment of the possible risk and return on the venture. Business plan is the single most important document to be prepared by seekers of venture capital. It contains detailed information about the proposed venture. The evaluation of ventures by VCFs in India includes:

- Preliminary evaluation: The applicant required to provide a brief profile of the proposed venture to establish prima facie eligibility.
- Detailed evaluation: Once the preliminary evaluation is over, the proposal is evaluated in greater detail. VCFs in India expect the entrepreneur to have:- Integrity, long-term vision, urge to grow, managerial skills, commercial orientation.
- VCFs in India also make the risk analysis of the proposed projects which includes: Product risk, Market risk, Technological risk and Entrepreneurial risk. The final decision is taken in terms of the expected risk-return trade-off.

1.3.4 Deal Structuring: Once the venture has been evaluated as viable, the venture capitalist and the investee company negotiate the terms of the deal, viz., the amount, form and price of the investment. This process is termed as deal structuring. The agreement also includes the protective covenants and earn-out arrangements. Covenants include the venture capitalist's right to control the venture company and to change its management if needed, buyback arrangements, acquisition, making initial public offerings (IPOs), etc. Earned out arrangements specify the entrepreneur's equity share and the objectives to be achieved.

Venture capitalists generally negotiate deals to ensure protection of their interests. They would like a deal to provide for a return commensurate with the risk; influence over the firm through board membership; minimizing taxes; assuring investment liquidity; the right to replace management in case of consistence poor managerial performance.

The investee companies would like the deal to be structured in such a way that their interests are protected. They would like to earn reasonable return, minimize taxes, have enough liquidity to operate their business and remain in commanding position of their business.

There are a number of common concerns shared by both the venture capitalists and the investee companies. They should be flexible, and have a structure which protect their mutual interests and provides enough incentives to both to cooperate with each other.

1.3.5 Post-investment Activities and Exit: Once the deal has been structured and agreement finalized, the venture capitalist generally assumes the role of a partner and collaborator. He also gets involved in shaping of the direction of the venture. This may be done via a formal representation on the board of directors, or informal influence in improving the quality of marketing, finance, and other managerial functions. The degree of the venture capitalist's involvement depends on his policy. It may not, however, be desirable for a venture capitalist to get involved in the day-to-day operation of the venture. If a financial or managerial crisis occurs, the venture capitalist may intervene, and even install a new management team.

Venture capitalists generally want to cash-out their gains in five to ten years after the initial investment. They play a positive role in directing the company towards particular exit routes. A venture may exit in one of the following ways:

- Initial Public Offerings (IPOs).
- Acquisition by another company.
- Purchase of the venture capitalist's shares by the promoter or purchase of the venture capitalist's share by an outsider.

The secondary, over-the counter (OTC) market which specializes in the trading of shares of SMEs, play a critical role in exit through IPOs and acquisitions.

1.4 Venture Appraisal Procedures and Practices

The most important aspects of the operations of a venture capital are its appraisal system, methods of providing financial and management support, disinvestment mechanisms and marketing and promotional efforts.

Venture appraisal is the most crucial aspect of a VCF's operations. Out of hundreds of venture proposals that come to a VCF, only a few, 10 percent would be funded. Venture capitalists require extraordinary skills of judging ventures or projects and entrepreneurs. The evaluation of the man behind the venture is the first step in the appraisal process. Once the credentials of the entrepreneur have been established, the technical aspects of the venture are evaluated. A venture capitalist can get the potential of the project appraised by inside or outside experts. The services of experts can also be hired for evaluating the market and technical risks of the project. The advantage in getting projects appraised by outside experts is that the venture capitalist gets an objective and unbiased opinion.

The venture capitalists in India focus on evaluation of both the entrepreneur and the project. Generally, the VCF requires a comprehensive business plan from the applicant company for the consideration of its screening committee. The plan would include information about the project in terms of cost, technology, market, and promoter and in case of existing companies, past financial performance. After initial clearance by the screening committee, the proposal is subjected to an elaborate and exhaustive scrutiny with promoters and is supplemented by site visits. The technical appraisal is entrusted to experts in the field, whenever necessary.

In developed countries, such as the USA, a lot of importance is given to the evaluation of the entrepreneur. The venture capitalists check the applicant's credentials from the potential customers, key suppliers, bankers, auditors, previous employers etc. In addition to technical skills, the traits which they look for in the applicant include marketing expertise, financial planning and control skills, leadership and motivation.

The evaluation of the entrepreneur assumes far greater importance in India, especially in view of the fact that the philosophy of "hands-on management" has not been seriously accepted and practiced. Managers of some VCFs in India feel that they could tolerate technical or market failure of the product but certainly not management failure. They consider a fair assessment of the commitment of the entrepreneur to the venture as being at least as important as evaluating the project itself. The evaluation criteria also differ depending on the nature of the funds requirements such as early-stage financing, expansion financing, management buyouts, and mergers and acquisitions.

1.5 Methods of Venture Financing

A prerequisite for the development of an active venture capital industry is the availability of a variety of financial instruments which cater to the different risk-return needs of investors. They should be acceptable to entrepreneurs as well. In developed countries, innovation in financial instruments is a distinct feature of venture capital. Venture finance, conceptually being risk finance, should be available in the form of quasi-equity (conditional or convertible loans). A straight or conventional loan, involving fixed payments, would be an unsuitable form of providing assistance to a risky venture. Venture capital is typically available in the following forms in India:

1.5.1 Equity: VCFs in India provide equity but generally their contribution does not exceed 49 percent of the total equity capital. Thus, the effective control and majority ownership of the firm remains with the entrepreneur. They buy shares of an enterprise with an intention to ultimately sell them off to make capital gains. Equity helps new enterprises since it puts no pressure on their cash flows as there is no obligation to pay dividends if the enterprise does not have liquidity. Once the enterprise becomes profitable, the venture capitalist can earn a high return through capital gains. Of course, it requires the existence of a stock market for the shares of small enterprises.

1.5.2 Conditional Loan: It is repayable in the form of a royalty after the venture is able to generate sales. No interest is paid on such loans. In India, VCFs charge royalty ranging between 2 to 15 percent; actual rate depends on other factors of the venture such as gestation period, cost-flow patterns, riskiness and other factors of the enterprise. Conditional loans were used by VCFs in India in the initial years of their operations in a big way. They faced a number of problems in implementing this method of financing. The major problems were the high cost for well-performing companies; difficulties in administrating the scheme, particularly ascertaining the sales volume to determine the amount of royalty; minority shareholding of the VCF since conditional loan is a subordinate instrument; and in spite of high cost to the entrepreneurs, the low return to the VCF compared to return from highly profitable ventures financed through equity.

1.5.3 Income Note: A unique way of venture financing in India- a hybrid security which combines the features of both conventional loan and conditional loan. The entrepreneur has to pay both interest and royalty on sales, but at substantially low rates. Income notes suffer from limitations similar to conditional loans. They do not promise high return to VCFs; could be expensive for profitable ventures and are difficult to administer.

1.5.4 Other Financing Methods: A few venture capitalists, particularly in the private sector, have started introducing innovative financial securities like participating debentures (introduced by TCFC), partially convertible debentures and cumulative convertible preference shares. CCPs are attractive as the shareholders do not have the right to vote. They are entitled to voting if they do not receive a dividend for two consecutive years. Both a convertible debentures and convertible preference shares require an active secondary market to be attractive securities from the investor's point of view. In India, venture capitalists and entrepreneur favour a financial package which has a higher component of loan because the promoters fear the loss of ownership and control to the financiers and also due to the traditional reluctance of financiers to share in the risk inherent in the use of equity.

1.6 Monitoring Support and Monitoring

The distinctive feature of venture financing is that VCFs not only provide finance but also managerial assistance to the entrepreneurs. The hands-on style is a form of supportive and direct involvement. It is generally practiced through the VCF's representation on the assisted firm's board. It also entails close and regular discussion between the venture capital fund manager and the entrepreneur on problems of technology, marketing and general management. The venture capitalists help a great deal in shaping the strategies, policies and practices and business plan of the entrepreneur's firm. He also assists in affecting prudent financial discipline. Some venture capitalists may choose to act passively. Under such hands-off style, they do not participate in management of the firm. A venture capitalist bases his assessment of the management on the evaluation of financial reports, which the entrepreneur sends to him periodically. He may choose to follow a middle approach between the hands-on and hands-off styles of management. He may identify key decision areas such as capital investment, appointments of key personnel etc. on which he may like the entrepreneur to consult him. He can also specify the kind of information which the entrepreneur has to regularly furnish to him.

Whether or not a venture capitalist is directly involved in the management of the assisted firm, he has to develop a sound monitoring system. It is needed not only to safeguard the capital of the venture capitalist, but also to help in improving the worth of investment through timely actions. New entrepreneurs require continuous monitoring and support because of their managerial inexperience. Monitoring becomes easy and more effective if the venture capitalist also takes active participation in the management of the enterprise.

The management support by VCFs in India is not total and continuous; it is generally provided at the start-up stage. The relationship between the venture capital financier and the entrepreneur in India is not yet that of partners; it is still a relationship of a leader and a borrower. Most entrepreneurs do not want any interference from the venture capitalists. Venture funds like TDICI and Indus-VCF realize the poor quality of management in small enterprises and, therefore, are wedded to a hands-on management approach. A number of the new private sector entrants including CFC, TCFC, etc. also consider management participation as necessary.

1.7 Divestment Mechanisms

The objective of a true venture capitalist is to sell off his investment at substantial capital gain but most venture funds in India aim to operate on commercial lines along with satisfying their development objectives. Public sector venture funds invariably have some developmental objectives and they would also like to disinvest their holdings at adequate return with a view to recycle their funds.

The disinvestment options generally available to venture capitalists in developed countries are the promoter's buy-back, initial public offers (IPO), sale to other VCFs, in OTC sale, management buyouts etc. A few of them are effectively feasible in India:

1.7.1 Promoter's Buy-out: The most popular disinvestment route in India is promoter's buy-back. This route is suited to Indian conditions because it keeps the ownership and control of the promoter intact. The obvious limitation, however, is that in a majority of cases the market value of the shares of the venture firm would have appreciated so much after some years that the promoter would not be in a financial position to buy them back. In India, the promoters are invariably given the first option to buy back equity of their enterprises.

1.7.2 Initial Public Offers (IPO): The benefits of disinvestment via the public issue route are, improved marketability and liquidity, better prospects for capital gains and widely known status of the ventures as well as market control through public share participation. This option has certain limitation in the Indian context. The promotion of the public issue would be difficult and expensive since the first generation entrepreneurs are not known in the capital markets. Further, difficulties will be caused if the entrepreneur's business is perceived to be an unattractive investment proposition by investors. Also, the emphasis by the Indian investors on short-term profits and dividends may tend to make the market price unattractive. Yet another difficulty in India until recently was that the Controller of Capital Issues (CCI) guidelines for determining the premium on shares took into account the book value and the cumulative average EPS till the date of the new issue. This formula failed to give due weightage to the expected stream of earnings of the venture firm. Thus, the formula would underestimate the premium. The government has now abolished the Capital Issues Control Act, 1947 and consequently, the office of the Controller of Capital Issues. The existing companies are now free to fix the premium on their shares. The initial public issue for disinvestment of VCF's holdings can involve high transaction costs because of the inefficiency of the secondary market in a country like India. Also, this option has become far less feasible for small ventures on account of the higher listing requirement of the stock exchanges. In February 1989, the Government of India raised the minimum capital for listing on the stock exchanges from Rs. 10 million to Rs. 30 million and the minimum public offer Rs. 6 million to Rs. 18 million.

1.7.3 Sale on the OTC Market: An active secondary market provides the necessary impetus to the success of venture capital. VCFs should be able to sell their holdings, and investors should be able to trade shares conveniently and freely. The OTC Exchange in India was established in June 1992. The Government of India had approved the creation of the Exchange under the Securities Contracts (Regulations) Act 1989. It has been promoted jointly by UIT, ICICI, SBI Capital Markets, Canbank Financial Services, GIC, LIC and IDBI. Since this list of markets (who will decide daily prices and appoint dealers for trading) includes most of the public sector venture financiers, it should pick up fast, and it should be possible for investors to trade in the securities of new small and medium size enterprises.

The other disinvestment mechanisms such as the management buy-outs or sale to other venture funds are not considered to be appropriate by VCFs in India.

2

Theory of Venture Capital

The theory of capital market imperfections explains that asymmetric information is the main reason for adverse selection and moral hazard in financial markets. As a result, sometimes, new firms are subject to severe financial constraints and therefore unable to raise fresh capital for their projects. Venture funds often fill this gap by financing such projects. These venture capital funds deal with asymmetric information problem through optimal financial contact.

2.1 Theory of Capital Market Imperfections

Theory of capital market imperfections usually implies that, for some firms, equilibrium demand for capital exceeds supply, and that such firms will be unable to obtain external finance at the competitive cost of capital. This outcome, according to the theory, is due mainly to the asymmetry in information between "buyers" and "sellers" in the market Akerlof (1970).

2.1.1 Asymmetric Information: Asymmetric information refers to a situation in which one party of a contract has access to relevant information not available to other party (ies) of the contact. Amit at el. (1998) refers it as a "hidden information". This situation obviously is common to almost all markets and has been affecting economic behaviour throughout economic history.

Probably the earliest document phenomenon resulting from asymmetric information is the law of bad money, sometimes referred to as Gresham's Law; bad money drives out good Rasmusen, (1990). Consider an economy in which gold currency is the medium of exchange. Suppose there are two types of gold currency: type a, which is 100 percent gold, and type b, which is, say, only 50 percent gold, and the two are equally circulated. The two types however are observationally indistinguishable except to their owners. When owners of type a currency come to the marketplace to buy goods (sell currency) they will not be able to buy the true worth of their money. The reason is that merchants are not able to distinguish the two types of currency, Hence they will price it at the average value, i.e. as if it contains only 75 percent gold. Owners of type a currency, therefore, will refuse at this value. But owners of type b will, since at the average value they will end up with positive profits. Thus type b currency will remain in circulation but type a won't. Hence, bad currency drives out good currency. In anticipation of such an outcome, merchants would consider any traded currency to be of type b.

The scenario just described shows how asymmetric information affects economic behaviour of merchants before any trade transaction or contract is enforced. This is called "adverse selection". The effect of asymmetric information after the contract enforced is called "moral hazard". These will be reviewed in turn below. Various other papers implicitly recognized the importance of informational issues. For example, MacMillan, Zemann, and Narasimha (1987) provide a valuable discussion of how capitalists screen new projects.

2.1.2 Adverse Selection: Adverse selection results when goods of varying quality are exchanged while one side of the market can observe the quality of the goods but the other side knows at best its distribution (Masttesini, 1993). In this situation low-quality goods tend to dominate the market; i.e. low-quality goods drive out high-quality ones. The work of Stiglitz and Weiss (1981) and Myers and Majluf (1984) establish the framework for analyzing the connections between informational asymmetry and capital market imperfections. The idea is simple, and follows the same logic described above.

2.1.3 Credit Markets: Consider credit markets. Suppose there are two types of borrowers, good risk borrowers and bad risk borrowers. If lenders are able to distinguish the two types, they will charge each group the profit maximizing rates of interest. Bad borrowers will pay higher rates to compensate for their risk. But suppose that lenders are unable to identify the two groups, i.e. asymmetric information exists; borrowers know their type but lenders don't. In this case lenders might not find it profitable to charge the average rate of interest. Since this average is higher than what goods borrowers believe they should pay, they have an incentive to drop out of the market, leaving only bad-risk borrowers. In this case the probability of default will rise and thus expected profits for lenders will decline. To avoid this outcome, lenders will find it more profitable to keep the interest rate low and thus ration credit. Hence, credit rationing stems as an equilibrium result of asymmetric information between lenders and borrowers. Stiglitz and Weiss (1983; 1987) extend the model to include multi-period relationships and multi-group of borrowers, respectively.

Bester (1985) argues that rationing in credit markets can be eliminated if banks compete by choosing collateral requirements and the rate of interest to screen borrowers. The use of collateral in Bester's model induces self-selection in the market and thus the equilibrium attained separates borrowers of different risk. However, this result is possible only if strong regularity assumptions are imposed (Mattesini, 1993). Stiglitz and Weiss (1992) show that credit rationing may persist even though lenders can simultaneously vary collateral requirements and interest rates.

2.1.4 Equity Markets: Myers and Majluf (1984) examine the effects of asymmetric information on public equity markets. Suppose that a firm has an investment opportunity, with potential return either "high" or "low", depending on the state of the world. The firm has to issue equity to finance the investment. Managers know the true state but outside investors don't. Suppose that managers observe the good state and thus decide to issue equity. Investors therefore will value the firm based on the expected return; that is, the average return of the good state and the bad state. But at the average the firm's value will be less than its true value. If the difference between true and average values is sufficiently large, the firm will be better off not issuing equity and thus foregoing up a good investment opportunity due to asymmetric information. If managers observe instead the bad state, the issue will be overvalued because the true value of the issue is now less than the average assigned by outside investors. In this case the firm will be better off issuing equity. Rational investors will therefore consider the issue as a signal of the bad state and, thus, will value it at its (low) value. That is, any issue is considered as "bad news" to the market.

Myers and Majluf note that the above result is sensitive to a variety of parameters. For example, the return in the good state might be unusually high such that the overall value of the firm might still be higher after the issue, even if the issue is priced at the average value. In this case managers will not pass up the good opportunity, and thus will always decide to issue equity. This also might happen if investors believe that the good state is more likely to occur than the bad state, i.e. the probability of the good state is 0.5. But, in general, the model shows the possibility of adverse selection in the public equity market because of asymmetric information between managers and outside investors.

2.1.5 Moral Hazard: Moral Hazard arises between two parties when one party is able to affect the quality of the good or service exchanged, while the other party cannot monitor perfectly. Amit at el. (1998) explains this type of informational asymmetry as a "hidden action" where one party to a transaction cannot observe relevant actions taken by the other party (or at last can not legally verify these actions). The difference between adverse selection and moral hazard is that, in the former, the informed party knows only the quality of the good (or service) exchanged but cannot alter it; in the latter the informed party can affect the quality of the good or service exchanged. This distinction is rather approximate; in some cases adverse selection can be modelled as a special case of moral hazard (Kreps, 1990). The allocation of the funds and the learning process are subject to moral hazard, Bergemann (1998)

In terms of game theory, adverse selection can be modelled as an incomplete information game, in which each player knows his type, or equivalently his payoff function, but does not know with certainty the type of the other player. Moral Hazard, on the other hand, can be modelled as a game with imperfect information, in which the move of the other player is not observed (see, e.g., Gibbons, 1992). As Harsanyi (1976; 1995) shows, games with incomplete information can be modelled as games with complete but imperfect information, which is another way to show that adverse selection can be viewed as a sort of moral hazard problems.

Moral hazard in debt contracts is well documented in many writings, including Townsend (1979), Stiglitz and Weiss (1981) and Williamson (1986), among others. Stiglitz and Weiss build their formal analysis on the result derived by Rothschild and Stiglitz (1970); namely, that as the variance of a random variable rises, the expected value of any convex function of it also rises. An inverse relationship holds for concave functions. They show that, in a debt contract, the borrower's return function is convex in the project's return, while the lender's function is concave. Hence the borrower's expected return rises as the project becomes more risky, i.e. as the variance of the project's return rises, while that of the lender declines. Moral hazard problems, therefore, are inherent in debt contracts.

Given the conflict of interest between the lender and the borrower, as the former raises the interest rate, the borrower will have stronger incentives to choose riskier actions. The reason is that higher interest rates make bankruptcy more likely, other things held constant. By choosing riskier actions both very high and very low returns will be more likely. Since below a certain level of returns the borrower defaults anyway, increasing the likelihood of very high returns means higher expected returns for the borrower. Therefore, higher interest rates cause borrowers to choose riskier actions. But this means that expected returns for the lender might decrease. Hence, the lender cannot raise the interest rate indefinitely; beyond a certain level higher interest causes lower expected returns for the lender. If this critical level is below the market clearing level, demand for credit will exceed supply, and rationing is obtained as an equilibrium solution.

2.1.6 Capital Market Imperfections and Finance Constraints: Imperfections in credit markets and public equity markets imposes high costs for some firms to obtain external finance, especially firms for which lenders or investors do not have enough information to assess their quality. Such firms are therefore said to be "financially constrained". Establish firms with high net worth and large asset values can easily signal their creditworthiness to outside investors and therefore obtain external finance. On the contrary, young firms with small assets and low net worth do not have tangible evidence of their creditworthiness and hence will find difficulties in raising capital.

Trester (1997) argues that the problem of an entrepreneur dissipating the firm's assets can be mitigated if the investor has no option to declare default and seize the assets.

Calomiris and Hubbard (1990) present a model in which two types of capital markets coexist: a "perfect" market or a market in which information between borrowers and lenders is symmetric, and imperfect market, in which asymmetric information prevails. The authors then show that firms with significant financial resources and reputation will be able to access the perfect market, while firms with low internal resources will approach the imperfect market, holding investment opportunities constant. That is, well-known will be able to finance their investment, just as predicted by the Neoclassical theory, while less-known firms will be rationed and thus their investment spending remains limited to their internal funds. These firms are not able to access the market for external funds and hence subject to financial constraints due to imperfection mentioned above.

2.2 Theory of Venture Capital

This section is a review of studies on venture capital, general description, analysis of venture capital arrangements and related issues.

2.2.1 Introduction: Venture capital implies active investment in ventures where capital is provided through independent, professionally managed, dedicated pools of capital that focus on equity or equity linked investments in privately held, growth companies. This definition includes professional venture capital, where venture capital funds are formal institutions managing pools of capital provided by limited partners. It also includes investors, sometimes called "angels", who act individually to provide capital and assistance to entrepreneurs as well as some forms of family business (Wetzel, 1983; Freear et al., 1994 and Poza, 1989).

The key terms found in most definitions of venture capital are; high-growth, high-risk, value addition by the venture capitalists, long-term gain, and absence of security or collateral for securing capital. Thus, we can provide the following definition of venture capital (Pandey et al., 1996):

"Venture capital is an investment, in the form of equity, quasi-equity and sometimes debt- straight or conditional (i.e., interest and principal payable when the venture starts generating sales), made in new or untried technology, or high-risk venture, promoted by a technically or professionally qualified entrepreneur, where the venture capitalist"

- expects the enterprise to have a very high growth rate,
- provides management and business skills to the enterprise,
- expects medium to long-term gains, and
- does not expect any collateral to cover the capital provided."

Venture capital organizations finance these high-tech, potentially high-reward projects, purchasing equity or equity-linked stakes while the firms are still privately held, Gompers (2001). The venture capital industry has developed a variety of mechanisms to overcome the problems that emerge at each stage of investment process. At the same time, the venture capital process is also subject to various pathologies from time to time, which can create problems for investors or entrepreneurs.

2.2.2 Venture Capital Cycle: The venture capital cycle starts with raising a venture fund; proceeds through the investment in, monitoring of, and adding value to firms; continues as the venture capital firm executes successful deals and returns to its investors; and renews itself with the venture capitalist raising additional funds.

Venture capital funds act as financial intermediaries between investors and entrepreneurs. Investors supply funds as limited partners to VC and venture capitalist act as general partners while supplying funds to the entrepreneurs. The limited partnership is governed by several conditions, among which following are noteworthy: (a) a fund's life must have an agreed-upon date of termination; in the United States, in most cases, this life being set a ten years, (b) the transfer of limited partnership units is restricted, so they cannot be easily bought and sold like registered securities, (c) withdrawal from the partnership prior to the termination date is prohibited and (d) Limited partners cannot participate in the active management of a fund if their liability is to be limited to the amount of their commitment. (Sahlman, 1990).

General partners are responsible for managing the funds and directing them to the most promising ventures. They are typically experienced in particular industries (e.g. pharmaceuticals, semiconductors, etc.). Usually they contribute a small percentage (1 percent) of committed capital (Sahlman, 1990). Their compensation is based on the total committed capital as well as on realized gains on the fund.

This compensation has two components. The first component is monetary compensation paid to fund managers. The venture capitalist may also receive private benefits from certain activities, Gompers and Lerner (1996).

Once a venture capital fund has been established, the venture capitalist must identify investment opportunities, arrange deals with entrepreneurs, monitor the investments, and ultimately achieve some return on his capital. The venture capitalist usually invests in recipient companies in the form of convertible preferred stock; that is, preferred stock that can be converted into common stock. The financing process is done in stages, and the amount of capital given at each stage is sufficient only to reach the next stage. Venture capitalists take an active role in the recipient companies through memberships on boards of directors, Lerner (1995). To avoid losses, venture capitalists form a portfolio by investing in several companies at one time.

The venture capitalist continues his financial, managerial and marketing support until the venture materializes. At this stage, an outside investor (e.g. a large company) might be interested in acquiring the recipient company, or the recipient company might go public. Returns from selling the company are then distributed to the limited partners, and the venture capitalist starts raising a new venture capital fund.

Black and Gilson (1998) argue that the health of the venture capital market depends fundamentally on a vibrant public market that allows new firms to issue shares.

2.2.3 Venture Capital Arrangements: In an environment of uncertainty and informational asymmetry, the venture capitalist faces the problem of identifying the most promising venture, where adverse selection is common at this stage. Even after a contract between the venture capitalist and the entrepreneur is signed, possible conflicts of interest between the two parties present serious difficulties for the venture to develop and mature; such problems are usually referred to as moral hazard problems. The following discussion will analyse how the venture capital industry developed its practices and arrangements to minimize these problems.

A. Sharing: Venture capital is structured around a basic theme of sharing. Investors are limited partners, and the venture capital fund finances entrepreneurs through equity. Both parties, therefore, have in essence the same objective. This structure dramatically reduces possible conflicts of interest and associated moral hazard (Milgrom and Roberts, 1992). Sharing extends even to the employees of venture-backed company's employees are granted stock in the company, thereby giving them a stake in its success" (Kunze, 1990). Another form of sharing is syndicating investments by more than one venture capitalist. In addition to pooling more resources and capital, syndication helps spread the risk among the venture capitalist. It also brings together more expertise and support (Lerner, 1994b). Bygrave and Timmons (1992) note that syndication also helps to share information and thus reduce uncertainty. Debt contracts, in contrast, suffer from inherent conflicts of interests between the borrower and the lender. Since the entrepreneur has to pay fixed payments regardless of the performance of the project, he will be better off choosing risky actions, exposing the lender to the risk of default, as Stiglitz and Weiss (1981) show: This leads to serious moral hazard problems and agency costs.

B. Monitoring and Assistance: Sharing has important consequences. One is that it creates incentives for the capital provider to monitor and assist his partner (Davis, 1992). Given the venture capitalist's stake in the venture, the better the quality of assistance to the entrepreneur, the better the likelihood that the venture will succeed, and therefore, the higher the expected value of his stake. It is also noted that the financial contribution that the venture capitalists make may be less valuable than the business expertise and contracts they contribute to small ventures (Sagari, 1992). Value addition by venture capitalists is done in a variety of ways: contributes / provides the margin of success over failure, not merely a money manager for investors' funds but also a full partner with the entrepreneur, sharing a mutual goal of creating a valuable company, spend about half their time monitoring and assisting their portfolio investments, building the investor group, reviewing and helping to formulate business strategy, and filling in the management team. (Bygrave and Timmons, 1992;Kunze, 1990; Gorman and Sahlman, 1989)

Sapienza (1992) found that the average value-added by venture capitalist, as perceived by both venture capitalists and entrepreneurs, is significantly positively related to the level of innovation and performance of these companies. The frequency of contact between the two, as well as value-added, is significantly negatively correlated with the stage of the venture. The assistance provided by venture capitalist is particularly useful for small, highly innovative ventures. Venture capitalists who focus on early-stage investments are more willing to exercise control and spend more time over the project than other venture capitalists. Provision of money alone appears to play a necessary but far-from sufficient condition to promote economic growth and resilience; evidence is mounting that venture capitalists do add value.

Such a degree of involvement by venture capitalists would be inconceivable from traditional financiers. Combining harmony of interests with monitoring and assistance, venture capital structure helps to overcome the high-risk and informational asymmetries associated with typical ventures.

C. Selection Criteria: Venture Capital funds' decision-making has been the focus of a large and growing body of research (Tyebjee 1984; MacMillan 1985; MacMillan 1987; Robinson 1987; Timmons 1987; Sandberg 1988; Hall and Hofer 1993). While a comprehensive review is beyond the scope of this study, we summarize the most import factors relevant for investment decision of Venture funding as identified by select studies.

Sharing also affects the selection criteria of ventures. The type of information and criteria that venture capitalists look after when selecting a company reflects their preferences as active investors and shareholders. As equity holders, venture capitalists would profit most from fast-growing companies, as this would translate into higher value of their equity. The bias of venture capitalists towards small and innovative companies, therefore, is not accidental. For example, venture capital funds directed an average of 60 percent of total annual disbursements to high-tech ventures (Venture Capital Journal 1998). This preference can be compared to that of commercial bankers (Sagari, 1992, and Rosman and O'Neill, (1993). Since bankers invest mainly through lending, they usually target mature, well-established companies whose financial histories reflect their viability as good borrowers. This sharp difference in preferences between venture capitalists and commercial bankers has a significant impact on market growth and development.

Tyebjee (1984) argued that decision criteria can be reduced to only two dimensions—expected return and risk. The attractiveness of the market and the product's differentiation are related to the expected return. A capable management team and resistance to environmental threats indicate a lower level of risk. As expected, VCs are risk-averse and profit-oriented in their decision-making and, moreover, they are willing to invest in risky deals if offset by the profit potential.

Tyebjee and Bruno (Tyebjee 1984) study attempted to ascertain the factors, which influence the investment decisions of VCFs in the US. They found five categories of decision criteria: market attractiveness, product differentiation, managerial capabilities, environmental threat resistance, and cash-out potential. Using a linear regression model, the authors found that the perceived risk was influenced by managerial capabilities and the resistance to environmental threat while the expected return was strongly influenced by market attractiveness, followed by a highly differentiated product. Cash-out potential did not have any impact on the perceived risk and the expected return of a venture.

VCs, when confronted with these results, disagreed (Tyebjee 1984). In particular, two significant variations were observed: a) That managerial quality has a much higher impact on the selection process and b) that the management quality considerably affects both expected return and risk.

MacMillan, Siegal and Subba Narasimha (1985) carried out a two-step study, interviewed of 14 VCs and identified 27 criteria of evaluating venture investment. Then they grouped these criteria in six groups: entrepreneur's personality, entrepreneur's experience, product characteristics, market characteristics, financial considerations and composition of venture team. They then tested the model with a questionnaire mailed to a sample of 150 VCs in the US. The analysis revealed that, out of 10 criteria most frequently rated as essential, six related to the entrepreneur's personality and experience. Goslin and Barge (1986) reported similar results. They found that the most important characteristics of the entrepreneur were management experience and marketing experience.

Venture capital research has not been limited to the U.S. Using the method of MacMillan (1985) et al., Ray (1991) and Ray and Turpin (1993) analyzed the investment activities of venture capital firms in Singapore and Japan, respectively. Both in Singapore and Japan, the entrepreneur's personality and experience were found to be the most important aspects and financial considerations as the least important in the evaluation of the venture investment. Similarities among the top criteria used in the US, Singapore, and Japan were: entrepreneur's sustained intensive efforts, his familiarity with the target market and his ability in evaluating and reacting well to risk. US and Singapore VCs also gave top consideration to demonstrated leadership and at least 10 times returns in five to 10 years while, for Japanese VCs, market growth rate, liquid investment and creating a new market were additional significant factors.

Despite a number of similarities, the study by Ray (1991) revealed some significant differences between the US and Singapore. Singapore's VCs gave more importance to the creation of a new market and having acceptance in the established market. Ray argued that, given its small domestic market and the tradition of new market developments through exports, it is probably easy for entrepreneurs in Singapore to create new export markets. The US has the largest domestic markets in the worlds, therefore, creation of a new market and the acceptance of the venture in existing markets were not important considerations for US VCs.

As in Singapore, VCs in Japan are significantly concerned about the creation of new markets. Also, Japanese VCs, contrasted with their US counterparts, have a narrow range of criteria for rejecting a proposed venture investment. Most VCs in Japan relied heavily on outside specialists in evaluating products, technology and markets. The VCs relied heavily on their own intuition, however, in appraising all aspects of a proposal including finance and production. Ray (1991) found a similar pattern for Singapore.

Pandey (1996) in the study to evaluate criteria being used by the VCs in India, found that out of the top five criteria, most frequently rated as essential, four relate to the entrepreneur's personality, viz., integrity, urge to grow, long-term vision and well-thought strategy to remain ahead of competition. The sample consisted of nine VCs. Pandey concluded that VCs in India consider the entrepreneur's integrity and urge to grow as the most important critical aspects of venture evaluation, but a very low priority to the high-tech component of the product, untapped market, and venture returns. As noted above, these results are suspect since the data were gathered when the Indian venture capital industry was extremely immature.

A close examination of the VC decision literature discussed above yields some generalizations. It appears that VCs use four broad categories of information when judging the attractiveness of a particular venture proposal: (a) entrepreneur/team characteristics, (b) product/service attractiveness, (c) market conditions and (d) financial returns if proposed venture is successful. Since the prior studies use statistical techniques to aggregate into broad categories, it must be remembered that each category is composed of a number of finer-grained criteria. For example, market attractiveness is composed of market size and growth among other information factors.

D. Staging Capital Commitment: Another essential feature of venture capital is staging the commitment of capital to portfolio ventures (Sahlman, 1988, 1990, 1994 b). Gompers (1995) examines the role of staged investment as a monitoring device. It has also been used as an instrument to implement the optimal investment path, Neher (1997). This feature is closely related to equity financing. In a sharing contract with asymmetric information (i.e. without monitoring), the entrepreneur always has an incentive to under-report profits (Bolton and Scharfstein, 1990). This entails the investor receiving a smaller share of the profits, thus increasing his own. By staging capital, such incentive is inhibited, since the entrepreneur has to return to the venture capitalist to obtain capital for the next stage of the project. The mechanism, furthermore, encourages the entrepreneur to optimize his efforts to convince the venture capitalist to continue his support; so not only do venture capitalists monitor entrepreneurs, but they also adopt procedures like staging the commitment of capital to further reduce informational asymmetry and align the incentives of the entrepreneurs to meet their goals.

Staging the commitment of capital also helps reduce the uncertainty typically surrounding small ventures. As time passes, the venture capitalist is able to gather more information about the team, the market, the environment and the project, thus reducing major risks and uncertainty considerable (Sahlman, 1988). Moreover, by staging the commitment of capital the venture capitalist gains the option to abandon and to revalue the project as new information arrives.

E. Adverse Selection: Several studies, e.g. Sahlman (1990, p. 512), Amit et al. (1990a, 1990b, 1998) and Peterson (1992), expressed concerns about adverse selection in the venture capital market. Given the relatively high costs of obtaining venture capital. Such costs would greatly affect the type of entrepreneurs seeking venture capital. For the venture capital market to operate with minimum efficiency, benefits of venture capital must outweigh its costs.

2.2.4 Costs and Benefits of Venture Capital: Prior to striking a deal, the venture capitalist must value the entrepreneur's project. Based on this valuation venture capitalist would buy shares in the venture and hence provides capital to the entrepreneur. In the presence of asymmetric information, the venture capitalist cannot perfectly distinguish high-quality entrepreneurs and/or ventures from low-quality ones. This is especially true for early-stage ventures. Such ventures usually have no product revenues, a partial or emerging management team, a less than fully demonstrated technology and undemonstrated market potential (Coopers and Lybrand, 1993). Uncertainty in such cases is tremendous and thus informational asymmetry could affect the venture capitalist's valuation of the venture. This is usually translated in high discount rates, up to 70 percent for start-up companies (Sahlman, 1990). High-quality entrepreneurs would view such valuation to be less than what they deserve and hence have an incentive to drop off the market, seeking capital from other sources.

Another potential source of adverse selection is dilution of ownership. By involving a venture capitalist, the entrepreneur looses some, frequently substantial, control rights over the venture. For some, the motivation for being an entrepreneur is actually to control their destiny (Kunze, 1990). Dilution of ownership therefore can be viewed as a non-pecuniary cost that the entrepreneur has to pay to obtain venture capital.

Further, entrepreneurs who have strong confidence in their quality and project might generally prefer to have full control over the venture, since in this case they will enjoy all returns if the project is successful. However, if the entrepreneur expects the projects to fail, he will be better off involving a venture capital to deteriorate. Venture capitalists, in anticipation of such results, would expect every applicant to be low quality; at the extreme, the venture capital market might break down.

The venture capital market exists, however, for certain reasons. Factors that help reduce adverse selection can be classified into two categories. One category includes factors that create incentives for high-quality entrepreneurs to remain in the market in spite of the costs involved. The other includes those that create incentives for venture capitalists to back entrepreneurs of unknown quality or believed to be of the low-quality type.

On the entrepreneur's side, there may be many high-quality entrepreneurs that do not have sufficient resources to run their ventures on their own. Traditional sources of capital, such as banks, are usually reluctant to provide capital to such ventures because of high risks involved. Hence such entrepreneurs have no choice but to look for venture capital, either through formal venture capital funds or informal "angels", as a source for external capital. Further, if the entrepreneur were risk-averse, he would involve the venture capitalist under the risk-sharing property of equity financing. Amit et al. (1990a, 1990b) show that sufficiently high incentives for risk sharing would induce some high-quality entrepreneurs to accept the average bid by the venture capitalist.

Many high-quality entrepreneurs, although innovative and productive, lack the required experience in management, marketing, and financial planning. In this case the entrepreneur might be willing to accept venture capital in compensation for the experience and contracts of the venture capitalist. Warne (1988) shows that, if assistance cannot be acquired separately through a competitive market and in presence of asymmetric information, entrepreneurs would be willing to pay more for venture capital than for a loan without assistance.

A related factor is the reputation that the entrepreneur would get by obtaining venture capital. Such reputation helps the entrepreneur to obtain further capital in the further at a lower cost than otherwise. For example, venture-backed IPOs are generally better valued than non-ventured backed IPOs. Hence an entrepreneur might forego the initial high costs in return for relatively low-cost capital from other sources of capital.

Finally, staging capital commitments might induce high-quality entrepreneurs to apply for venture capital but deter those of low quality. The point is similar to Flannery's (1986) explanation of a firm's choice to issue short-term debt. Flannery argues that, when issuing debt is costly, high-quality firms can sometimes effectively signal their true quality to the market by issuing short-term debt, while low-quality firms will issue only long-term debt. It is also similar to Hermalin's (1986) argument that more-able workers will sign short-term contracts to signal their ability. A similar argument can be presented for the venture capital market.

On the venture capitalists side, venture capitalists add value to their portfolio ventures. This added value might compensate for the entrepreneur's low ability. Further, the venture capitalist usually has enough control over the venture to replace the management or, if necessary, assumes the responsibilities of the CEO.

Staging capital also allows the venture capitalist to back an entrepreneur even though the quality of the latter is not fully known prior to the engagement of the former. Barry (1994) notes that the venture capitalists "make a relatively small commitment initially and only commit additional funds after the entrepreneurs have been able to demonstrate in deed rather than words the promise made to attract funds". Hence, the venture capitalist, if necessary, can use the option to abandon to deny funding an entrepreneur found to be of poor quality.

2.3 Optimal Contract

Chan (1983) develops a model that explains the existence of venture capital as a financial intermediary. The emergence of such an intermediary induces a Pareto preferred allocation, leading investors to a higher welfare state.

Warne (1988) explores why venture capital provides capital and assistance jointly, when they are available separately in competitive markets. According to the author, if there are joint economies in the provision of capital and assistance, then there is a clear advantage to venture capital. Such economies of scope may be justified by elimination of duplicate monitoring by the entrepreneur if capital and assistance are provided separately. Another reason is the fixed costs of investigating the project and the entrepreneur. One might add the possible moral hazard problems that may arise between the financier as a principal and the consultant as an agent.

Chan et al. (1990) develop an agency model in order to explain why venture capital contracts combine a risky claim for the venture capitalist with disproportionate control and contain explicit covenants permitting passage of control to the venture capitalist following a poor performance by the entrepreneur. The authors therefore develop a two-period agency model, in which both the venture capital and the entrepreneur have the skill to control production, but the latter's skill is unknown to both at the time of contract signing. Interim information arrival reveals this skill to both parties and is used to determine who controls second period production.

Admati and Pfleiderer (1994) develop a model of financial contracting with multiple investment decisions, and show how conflicts of interest and informational asymmetries can be effectively resolved by an inside investor. By 'inside investor" they mean an investor who "observes the private information about profitability, and becomes involved in making the subsequent investment decisions". Admati Pfleiderer set up a multi-period model in which an entrepreneur seeks outside capital to finance a project. One way to obtain capital is through venture capital, where the venture capitalist provides all the capital needed for the first period. Admati and Pfleiderer then examine the financial contract that leads to an optimal decision concerning continuation or abandonment of the project each period. The authors find that the optimal contract is a fixed-fraction contract. In this contract the venture capitalist obtains a fraction of the total payoffs, and finances that same fraction of future investments. The authors show that this is the only contract that induces optimal continuation in all circumstances.

Bowden (1994) follows a cooperative-game approach to examine conditions for existence of a Pareto-optimal contract between the venture capitalist and the entrepreneur. These include that the entrepreneur is (a) more risk-averse, or (b) more optimistic (has different expectations) than the venture capitalist.

2.4 Relationship between External Investors and Venture Capitalists

Venture capitalists act as agents for the limited partners, who choose to invest in entrepreneurial ventures through an intermediary rather than directly. In such situations, conflicts arise between the agent and the principal, which must be addressed in the contracts and other mechanisms that govern their relationship (Sahlman, 1990).

In the venture capital industry, the principle–agent problem is likely to be particularly difficult. There is inevitably a high degree of information asymmetry between the venture capitalists, who play an active role in the portfolio companies, and the limited partners, who cannot monitor the prospects of each individual investment as closely. The contractual provisions attempts to resolve the agency problem, the operating cost problem, and the resolving simultaneously.

2.4.1 Agency Costs: Venture capitalists have many opportunities to take advantage of the people who invest with them. To a degree, the agency problem is exacerbated by the legal structure of limited partnerships, which prevents limited partners from playing a role in the management of the venture-capital partnership.

Contracts are designed with several key provisions to protect the limited partners from the possibility that the venture capitalists will make decisions against their interests. First, the life of a venture-capital fund is limited; the venture capitalist cannot keep the money forever. The investors also preserve the right not to invest in any later fund managed by the same venture capitalists. Second, the limited partners preserve the right to withdraw from funding the partnership by reneging on their commitments to invest beyond the initial capital infusion. Third, the compensation system is structured to give the venture capitalists the appropriate incentives, Gompers (1996).

Gompers and Lerner (1999a) examine the nature of venture capitalists' incentive compensation in 419 venture partnership agreements and "offering memoranda" for funds formed between 1978 and 1992. They find that compensation for older and larger venture capital organizations is more sensitive to performance than the compensation of other venture groups. The profit participation and other aspects of the contract encourage the venture capitalist to allocate the management fee to activities that will increase the total value of the portfolio. Fourth, the mandatory distribution policy defuses potential differences of opinion about what to do with the proceeds from the sale of assets in the portfolio. The general partners cannot choose to invest in securities that serve their own private interests at the expense of the limited partners. Finally, the contract addresses obvious areas of conflict between the venture capitalist and the limited partner. Thus, the venture capitalist is often explicitly prohibited from self-dealing. Also, the venture capitalists are contractually required to commit a certain percentage of their effort to the activities of the fund.

2.4.2 Operating Costs: Two kinds of operating costs deserve analysis when discussing venture capital i.e. taxes, and operating costs. With respect to taxes, partnership gains are not subject to partnership-level taxation. The limited and general partners report the realized gains and losses on their individual tax returns. Second, securities can be distributed without triggering immediate taxable income for the recipient. Thus a limited partner who receives stock in a portfolio company can defer recognizing the gain (or loss) until that security is sold. Third, the venture capitalists do not incur taxable income when they receive their carried interest in the partnership: they report taxable income only as gains and losses are realized on the underlying securities. Finally, the partnership's compensation scheme can be structured to allocate losses to those who can make best use of them.

2.4.3 Resolving the Problems: The final component of this analysis of the economic relationship between the limited partners and the venture capitalists is an examination of how limited partners decide which venture capitalists to back. Filtering out the 'good' from the 'bad' venture capitalists is extremely important. 'Good' venture capitalists have the skill and intention to generate high risk-adjusted rates of return for the limited partners. Actual rates of return depend on factors such as capital markets, competition among venture capitalists, and the market for innovation.

In sum, the relationship between the limited and general partners in a venture-capital fund is fraught with agency problems. The limited partners structure a contract that creates incentives for mutual gain, and they specifically forbid certain obvious acts of self-interest like buying stock in portfolio companies at prices less than those paid by the fund. The limited partners then expend resources to monitor the fund's progress, often through special committees.

2.5 Venture Capitalist-Entrepreneur Relationship

The relationship between the limited partners and the venture capitalists shares several elements with that between the venture capitalists and the entrepreneurs. First, each relationship entails staging the commitment of capital and preserving the option to abandon. The limited partners insist on a limited life for the fund and the venture capitalists invest in stages related to the attainment of specific goals by the venture.

The compensation schemes are similar as well. The venture capitalists have strong incentives to create value because they share in the profits of the fund. The entrepreneurs receive a significant share of the value they help create. Also, in both cases, there are defined mechanisms in place to achieve liquidity. The limited partners insist on distributions of investment returns. The venture capitalists build into their stock-purchase agreements a number of mechanisms for achieving liquidity, such as the right to demand redemption of their convertible preferred stock.

Finally, the venture capitalist and entrepreneur alike face serious consequences if they fail. Entrepreneurs will be denied access to capital, their equity participation will be retracted, and their reputations damaged. Similarly, venture capitalist will find capital more difficult and cost to rise and their reputations will suffer as well, though their penalties are modest in comparison with those confronting entrepreneurs. The optimal contract is a time-varying share contract, which provides inter-temporal risk sharing between venture capitalist and entrepreneur. The share of the entrepreneur reflects the value of a real option, which is based on the control of the funds, Bergemann (1998). In both cases, however, the multi-period nature of the game creates strong incentives to perform well and to forego opportunistic behaviour.

Finally, relationship financing, including monitoring and the occasional replacement of the management improves the efficiency of the financial contract and the entrepreneur's allocation of the funds Bergemann (2002). The entrepreneur also drives private non-pecuniary benefits from having some control over the firm whereas the venture capitalist demands disproportionately higher control rights than the size of his equity investments. The entrepreneur is compensated for a greater loss of control through better terms of financing, ability to extract higher rents from asymmetric information, and improved risk sharing, Kirilenko (2001).

2.6 Venture Capital and Economic Development

When growth and development are targets, directing funds to innovative, small companies with high growth potentials is a clear choice. According to Schumpeter (1942), a driving force for growth is innovation. Venture capitalists are able to explore territories and break barriers that traditional financiers, because of the lack of information and high risks, are unable to explore. Scherer (1984) finds that it is small companies, rather than larger ones, that are more able to create innovations. Normally, such firms have little or not enough cash flow to support debt obligations; high quality information on their activities and prospects may be impossible or very costly to obtain externally, and their level of capitalization is very low. These factors create serious moral hazard and adverse selection problems that cannot adequately be dealt with through debt contracts. He suggests the model of venture capital to those who in practice attempt to solve some of the financial problems of the developing world.

Other writers have also suggested the venture capital model for development, including Klein (1990), Gibson and Blake (1992) and Lenzi (1992). It is worth noting, however, that establishing venture capital institutions in less developed countries is not a trivial task. A successful venture capital market requires well defined property rights, an effective legal system, positive social attitudes towards sharing, as well as entrepreneurial activities, and an efficient mechanism for venture capitalists to cash out their investments, such as a functioning market for public securities and/or mergers and acquisitions.

2.7 Venture Capital and Financial Stability

When equity financing is discussed, one cannot ignore its link to financial stability. The reason is that the "financial instability" hypothesis, advanced by Hyman Minsky (1982), is built on the widespread use of debt in current capitalist economies. The financial fragility hypothesis, however, is not confined to advanced capitalist economies. The world debt crisis is a practical example of how financial instability affects developing countries as well (Felix, 1994). Although Minsky provides a compelling theory of aggregate economic performance, he apparently provides no remedy for financial instability. Capitalism is inherently unstable.

Venture capital is one form of equity financing that combines the advantages of sharing and reducing the failures usually associated with public equity markets. Some writers provide policy recommendations toward expanding the size and scope of the venture capital industry. Bygrave and Timmons (1992) provide policy recommendations for expanding the venture capital industry in the U.S. Sagari (1992) explores government policies towards risk capital in different developing countries, and points to the necessary ingredients for venture capital to grow in such countries.

Adopting such policies would extend the use of equity financing in the economy and, hence, help mitigate financial instability. Venture capital thus is a compelling option to investment and development financing which inhibits the "thrust towards fragility" emphasized by Minsky. Financial instability, therefore, need not be inherent in market economies.

2.8 Summing Up

Adverse selection and moral hazard arising from asymmetric information can severely limit access to capital for some firms. For such firms, investment is sensitive to availability of financial resources, and would be strongly correlated with their internal funds holding investment opportunities constant [Lucas (1978), Fazzari et al. (1988), Carpenter (1992), Whited (1991; 1992), Hoshi et al. (1991), Morgan (1991), Fazzari and Peterson (1993), Schaller (1993), Weinberg (1994), and Jovanovic (1982)]. Despite the criticisms, these findings tend to support the hypothesis of capital market imperfections.

Venture capital arrangements address principle-agent problems and thus attenuate, though not eliminate, the implications of asymmetric information for investment decisions. They also point to the costs and benefits of obtaining venture capital. Venture capital is not without costs, and one can see when venture capital would have net benefits and when it would have net costs. For example, for a risk-neutral entrepreneur with high net worth and a low-risk project, costs of venture capital might be prohibitive. On the other extreme, a risk-averse entrepreneur with limited resources and a relatively high-risk project might find venture capital as the only source of capital. Between these extremes it is difficult to draw a line, and it is very likely that cases for which venture capital is a net benefit will not be constant over time.

Therefore, based on the above literature it is important to study the method of venture funding and its outcomes and implications. The particular issues are appraisal/screening, self-selection, monitoring, incentivizing, disclosure compliance. It is a study of venture funding and its final outcome of contract.

3

Development of Venture Capital: Global Experiences

In this chapter, we shall briefly review the private equity environment and development of venture capital in some developed and developing countries. The brief profile of venture capital industry in selected countries is detailed below. It covers the distribution profile of VCFs, volume of funds available, investment strategy, and divestment.

3.1 Private Equity Environment

In the private equity environment, emerging market companies are competing and winning globally. Fortune 500 has ranked China first in the top 50 emerging companies followed by South Korea, India, Mexico, Russia etc. According to the World Development Indicators, Capital markets are growing quickly. Amongst the four countries, China had the maximum market capitalization of 2500 billions US$ in 2006. Russia ranks second with market cap of 1200 billion US$. India and Brazil having the market cap of 1000 and 700 billion US$ respectively.

3.2 Venture Capital in USA

In the United States of America, venture capital has contributed immensely to the growth of the economy. It has made significant contribution to the development of the computer and semi-conductor industry. It has also helped in the implementation of very large scale integration technology. While venture capital was instrumental in the development of American economy, its institutionalization did not begin until after World War II. Prior to that, it was a common practice for wealthy individuals, syndicates organized by investment bankers or by a few families to make venture investments. The institutionalization process was facilitated by the formulation of American Research and Development Corporation (ARDC) in Boston in 1946, passing of Small Business Investment Company (SBIC) Act in 1958 as a vehicle of small business financing and the substantial tax incentives provided to those investing their funds in VCFs.

ARDC, started by Georges Doriot, was the first successful venture capital firm. Its first investment worth US$ 61,400 in 1957 was in the shares of Digital Equipment Corporation, a new company, which grew phenomenally in terms of sales, number of employees and market worth in its shares. Doriot's philosophy was to build creative men and their companies. For him capital gains were the reward of this philosophy, not a business goal. The objective of this company was to seek out creative men with a vision of things to be done, help breathe life into new ideas and process and products with capital, and with more than capital with sensitive appreciation for creative drive.

The creation of Small Business Investment Companies (SBICs) as a means of small business financing in 1958 gave the real impetus to the development of the venture capital industry in the USA. The purpose of the SBIC Act was to establish government-controlled venture capital funds for developing new and early stage business and they proved to be very effective during the sixties and seventies. Even today, when large venture capital organizations dominate the US venture industry, SBICs, in their new and modified form, are the major source of its growth.

The venture capital industry in the USA has been growing ever since its inception. Its growth was, however, accentuated after 1978 when the capital gains tax was reduced from 49 to 29 per cent. The rate was brought down to 20 per cent for individuals in 1981. These resulted in substantial returns to investors; the venture capital was able to attract capital without difficulty. This coincided with the emergence of the very large scale integration which substantially reduced the cost of computer chips and gave a boost to the computer industry.

Although the venture capital finance is made available to all enterprise in the USA, the high technology businesses have received large funds over the years. Most of the venture capital investments in the USA are confined to high-technology, high-risk and rapidly changing businesses. Substantial venture capital has been invested in the fields of information, communications, genetic engineering, medical electronics, biotechnology and artificial intelligence. In volume terms, the USA dominated the venture capital business with a pool of about US$ 30 billion in 1991, having increased from US$ 16.3 billion at the end of 1984 (OECD, 1986).

VCFs in the US can be categorized into four main groups (Clarke, 1987):

1. Private venture capital firms (PVCFs);
2. Small business investment companies (SBICs);
3. Subsidiaries of finance corporations; and
4. Subsidiaries of non-finance corporations.

PVCFs include family firms and institutionally funded independent private partnerships and are the most dominant source of venture capital. They account for about 60 per cent of the venture capital industry's capital; and they are very experienced and sophisticated investors. Institutionally-funded private firms are generally organized as limited partnership where venture capitalist, in his capacity as general partner, is responsible for the management of the partnership. For their management, general partners are compensated in the form of an annual management fee-generally 2.5-3 per cent of the capital invested and a percentage, quite often 20 per cent of the net long-term capital gain.

SBICs, created under the SBIC Act 1958, have access to government loans in addition to private committed capital. They are of two types: equity-oriented SBICs which account for about 8 per cent of the venture capital and mostly provide equity capital and debt-oriented SBICs: Subsidiaries of finance and non-finance corporations account for about 17 per cent of the venture capital.

In the USA, expansion-stage financing is much higher than the seed stage or the later stage of acquisition or buyout financing. This indicates the interest and objectives of the venture capitalists in associating with a business/product which has been successfully developed and pre-tested. Also, their goal is to make large financial returns. Thus, profits are made by structuring the transaction in a certain way. Analysis is focused much more on meeting the requirements of the transaction than on evaluating the long-term prospects of the company and strategic objectives.

According to Thomson Reuters and the National Venture Capital Association (NVCA), Venture capital performance showed positive returns across all investment horizons 3 years and longer for the period ending December 31, 2008. However, with the exception of the 20 year horizon, most categories experienced quarter over quarter and year over year declines.

Turmoil in the broader capital markets caused the one-year all venture private equity performance index (PEPI) [1] to decline significantly to -20.9 percent, a 18.8 percentage point decrease from the period ending September 30, 2008. The slowed exit markets in 2008 have driven lower one-year return numbers throughout 2008. The next largest consecutive quarterly change occurred in the three-year time horizon where all venture PEPI decreased by 2.1 points quarter-over-quarter to 4.2 percent. Five-year and ten-year performance posted similar declines from the previous quarter, decreasing 2.0 and 1.6 percentage points, respectively. Twenty-year performance was showed no change from the previous quarter at 17.0 percent.

Venture returns across all horizons outperformed public market indices, NASDAQ and the S&P 500, through December 31, 2008. The next year is expected to be challenging for the venture capital industry as the shuttered

IPO window and lower M&A valuations will take a toll on performance numbers in the short term. Additionally, the roll-off of the positive 1999 return figures is expected to drive the longer term performance figures down as well.

However, it is believed that venture capital will continue to perform well relative to other alternative investments and once the exit market improves, so too should return numbers.

3.3 Venture Capital in Europe

In Europe, venture capital started in the eighties. A number of European countries now have venture capital firms which are members of the European Venture Capital Association (EVCA) founded in 1983. In spite of these developments, about three-fourths of the venture capital investment in Europe is confined to three countries, namely the UK, France and the Netherlands.

The slow growth of venture capital in Europe in the initial years can be attributed to a number of factors. For example, it is suggested that 'financial institutions, equity markets and company law have all evolved differently in these countries, with the result that venture capital along United States, or United Kingdom lines has scarcely developed (OECD, 1986). The government policy in the USA has been to create a climate conducive to risk-taking and entrepreneurship, and deregulating markets and reducing taxes rather than providing special incentives for the financing of SMEs as was the case in a number of European countries.

In the late eighties, Europe witnessed a fast growth of venture capital due to changes in public policy and the economic conditions. The creation of over-the-counter (OTC) or secondary stock exchanges gave further impetus to the development of venture capital. For example, the venture capital pool increased from US$ 8.95 billion in 1986 to US$ 29 billion in 1990, slightly more than 80 percent of the size of the US venture capital (Bygrave and Timmons, 1992).

Private equity and venture capital provides investment

opportunities to institutional and professional investors. The vast majority of these private equity and venture capital investors, called limited partners. The major source of funds in Europe is bank which contributes approximately about 20 per cent of the capital, followed by government agencies, corporate investors, pension funds and insurance companies. Other than the United Kingdom, no other country has sources of funds like the United States, i.e. 25 per cent of the capital comes from the pension funds. They do not manage the funds that they have invested in, and do not intervene at the level of the investee company. However, they regularly assess the quality of the investments made on their behalf.

Of the € 79bn funds raised in 2007, € 60bn (76.0 percent) was allocated to buyouts and € 10.3bn (13.1 percent) to venture and growth capital. Venture capitalists in Europe focus on industrial products, consumer products, computer products and other electronic products. Owing to growing emphasis on development of technology, West Germany, United Kingdom, France and to a lesser degree, the Netherlands and Italy, have invested heavily in Research and Development.

A significant development vis-à-vis venture capital in Europe is the establishment of a Pan-European network of VCFs by twelve companies including Bosch, Fiat, Olivetti, Petrofina, Philips, Pirelli and Volvo. This network has created a holding company with US$ 30 million funds for investing in European VCFs.

Different type of investors were roped in for raising funds in Europe for the period 2003-2007. Pension funds had the largest share of 23 percent in the total funds raised. Next came the banks and the insurance companies having a share of 15.6 percent and 9.9 percent respectively. The other investors consisted of government agencies, private companies, corporate investors, capital markets, academic institutions etc.

The geographical origin of funds raised in Europe during 2003-2007 depicts that approximately three-fourth of the funds was raised by the Europeans and the balance by USA and rest of the world. Half of the total venture capital investment in Europe is invested in the United Kingdom. The Netherlands and France are the next largest players in the industry followed by Belgium and West Germany. The countries in Western Europe have started playing greater roles in this area, with exceptional growth resulting in Italy and Scandinavia. This has increased the start-up activities in Europe. On per capita basis, the number of start-ups in Western Europe is almost equal to the US.

The only difference is that the US started these 30 years back and Europe has been a new entrant. The Gross National Product of 12 Countries of European Community is over US$ 4 trillion, approximately equal to that of the US. Thus, there are tremendous opportunities for the growth of Venture Capital industry in the economy of Europe.

Investments by European private equity and venture capital firms amounted to €73.8bn in 2007, and approximately 5,200 European companies received private equity investments. About 85 percent of these companies have fewer than 500 employees. Studies show that between 2000 and 2004 European private equity and venture capital financed companies created 1 million new jobs, which translates to a compound annual growth rate of 5.4 percent per year (eight times the EU25 total employment rate of 0.7 percent). Between 1997 and 2004, the average employment growth in buyout-financed companies was 2.4 percent, compared to 30.5 percent for venture-backed companies.

PE/VC fund investors have a long-term commitment horizon of generally ten years, which stems from contractual agreements which bind PE/VC funds to their investors. On this basis, PE/VC funds should not be considered as short-term investors, which imply holding periods of less than one year, as their average holding periods in investee companies is four years. More concretely, PE/VC firms also distinguish themselves from short-term investors by the way they manage their investments. Short-term investors take advantage of market trends but do not influence the way the underlying companies operate, unlike private equity and venture capital.

The private equity industry is regulated on a national basis in most EU member states. Private equity houses deal almost exclusively with sophisticated, 'professional' investors. These investors are able to understand and accept the risks and rewards of investing in the asset class. This is largely reflected in the type and level of regulation across Europe. In addition, although there is no harmonized framework for private equity at the European Union level, a number of EU legislative measures in place indirectly affect the industry, such as MiFID, UCITS, the Pension Funds Directive, and the Capital Requirements Directive.

The European industry believes in high professional standards that are crucial to a stable, long term relationship with institutional investors and regulators. They are also vital to increasing overall transparency and trust in the asset class. For nearly three decades, the industry has worked to create the most advanced professional standards of any alternative asset class anywhere in the world. The European private equity industry has already enacted IFRS and US GAAP compatible valuation and reporting guidelines, management principles for private equity houses and OECD-inspired guidelines for the corporate governance of portfolio companies.

3.4 Venture Capital in United Kingdom

3.4.1 Historical background: The early stirrings of the UK Venture capital industry began in 1930s. The UK has the largest venture capital industry outside the USA and it accounts for about two-thirds of total VC investments in the European Community (OECD, 1986). In the past, the growth of new business in Britain had been hampered by the "equity-gap". There was a need for a steady and growing supply of venture capital to finance entrepreneurial talent (Lorenz, 1985).

The venture capital industry had invested only £ 10 million

(pounds) in 1979 but the amount had increased to £ 284 million in 1984. It had made significant contribution in creating hundreds of new enterprises and in catalyzing the spirit of entrepreneurship. There are estimated to be well over a hundred of venture capital firms in UK having provided venture funds to thousands of companies. In 1988, for example, funds worth Rs. 37,000 million to over 1,500 companies were provided by the UK venture capital industry (Cottrell, 1989). The following reasons are attributed for the rapid growth of the UK venture capital industry (Mason, 1987; Kitchen, 1988):

- The demonstration effect of the high profitability of venture capital in the USA (e.g. the flotation of Apple Computer).
- The establishment of regional venture capital organizations such as Investors in Industry.
- Tax incentives to individuals investing in entrepreneurial companies.
- The establishment of the Unlisted Securities Market (USM) and the Business Expansion Schemes (BES). BES is designed to motivate private investors, through large tax exemptions, to invest in shares of private, unquoted companies.
- The growth in the number of management buyouts, which has created a demand for equity finance.
- The increased involvement of merchant banks, providing venture capital to small, growing companies with a view to obtaining future fee-earning work from them.
- The "bandwagon" effect.

Historically, the small firms in the UK have received equity finance from the investment trusts. But in the post-war periods, investments trusts started investing in large, quoted companies at the cost of the small, risky companies. The most important source of equity finance for new firms during the 1960s and early 1970s was Investors in Industry or 3i. 3i was established in 1945 by the Bank of England and the major clearing banks with the purpose of supplying long-term finance to growing firms. About two-thirds of financing go to small firms. They provide finance in the form of loans and equity investments.

It was in the later part of the 1980s that a large number of private venture funds emerged in the UK. A number of factors, such as tax incentives, establishment of the unlisted securities market (USM), and encouragement to investment trusts etc. contributed to this development.

The UK is an excellent example of a country where a number of tax incentives have been initiated specifically to give a fillip to the venture capital investment. In fact, it has been found in the UK that investors are motivated more by the potential tax breaks than by the quality of investments. It is estimated that only 2 percent of the BES total investments are invested in the high-tech sector, and 6 per cent in the young or very young start-up companies (OECD, 1986).

The UK's USM was established in 1980 with highly flexible rules to admit start-ups. It operates on the same basis as the regular stock market, but with liberal regulations for trading the shares. For example, USM requires 10 per cent of a company's shares to be offered in the primary issues before they can be traded; in the listed market the requirement is 25 per cent. The establishment of USM boosted venture activity since it made it much easier for entrepreneurs and venture capitalists to realize their capital gains. The UK experience has, however, shown that most business which obtained the USM listings were at the larger end of the SME scale. This necessitated the introduction of a third market in 1987 for smaller companies and with ever easier listing requirements than demanded by the USM.

Yet another policy change in the UK giving encouragement to venture capital was the liberalization of rules regarding investment trusts and investment companies in 1981. It was made easier for these companies to invest in unlisted securities which encourage a large number of them to enter the venture capital business.

3.4.2 Investment Activity: Worldwide investment by UK-based private equity firms reached £ 31.6 billion in 2007, a strong increase on the already impressive total of £ 21.9 billion in 2006 (BVCA Report, 2007). The UK private equity business has become truly global. Private equity firms based in the UK now invest considerably more by volume in continental Europe, the US and elsewhere than they do in the UK itself. The UK is increasingly seen as the gateway to Europe and, as the increasing asset flows to destinations outside Europe, a world capital for private equity. It reflects a depth of knowledge built up over decades, a favourable regulatory environment and unparalleled access to capital. At the same time, the UK industry continues to support enterprise in its home market.

The British Private Equity and Venture Capital Association (BVCA) established in 1984 is the industry body for the UK private equity and venture capital industry. In 2007 there were 214 members that represent the overwhelming number of UK-based private equity and venture capital providers and their advisers. The BVCA has over 25 years of experience representing the industry, which currently accounts for 46 percent of the whole of the European market, to government, the European Commission and Parliament, the media, regulatory and other statutory bodies at home, across Europe and around the world.

The number of companies financed rose from 1,630 in 2006 to 1,680 in 2007. Total investment by BVCA members in UK companies continues to increase, with UK companies absorbing £ 12 billion in 2007, compared to £ 10 billion in 2006. At the same time, the rate of growth of investment in continental European companies continues to increase, rising from £ 10 billion to £ 14 billion. As a consequence, the proportion of investment in UK companies has fallen to 38 percent in 2007 from 47 percent in 2006.

Deals in continental Europe were larger than in the UK,

with the average deal size at £ 56 million compared to £ 9 million in the UK. The average deal size in US companies is £ 54 million. The share of assets invested in the world, including the US, rose to 18 percent last year from 7 percent in 2006.

BVCA members raised £ 29.3 billion in independent funds in 2007, a 15 percent fall from the £ 34.3 billion raised in 2006. The percentage raised from overseas sources increased to 75 percent, at £ 22 billion. North American investors committed the greatest amount of funds: £ 12.2 billion, or 42 percent of the total, compared with 37 percent of the total in 2006. The second-largest investor base was the UK at £ 7.3 billion, or 25 percent of the total funds raised, down from 28 percent in 2006.

Overseas MBO and MBI deals attracted the greatest amount of investment: £14.8 billion, or 75 percent of the total. This represented a sizeable increase from 66 percent in 2006. Overseas investment in expansion deals also increased by 28 percent to £ 4.6 billion, while overseas early stage investment fell by 34 percent from £380 million to £ 249 million, this was still considerably higher than the 2005 total of £ 95 million. And the total number of early-stage companies receiving funding actually rose from 78 in 2006 to 82 in 2007. This rise is mainly attributable to funding for 'other early-stage' companies, rather than for start-ups, which saw a marked decrease in funding. The number of 'other early-stage' companies receiving funding rose from 32 in 2006 to 59 last year. In the UK, MBOs and MBIs also dominate the investment activity at £ 7.7 billion or 64 percent of the total. This proportion has remained fairly constant over the last three years.

Venture Capital investors continue to finance a significant number of early stage companies, both in the UK and abroad (584 in total for 2007, as compared to 578 for 2006), which accounts for 35 percent of all companies that received funding by BVCA members in 2007. The amount of investment, however, declined from a total of £ 1.3 billion in 2006 to £683 million in 2007.

Expansion deals rose to £ 3.8 billion, or 32 percent of the total, a small increase on the previous two years. Early stage financing fell to £ 434 million, or 4 percent of the total, which is a considerable decline from 9 percent of the total in 2006.

3.4.3 Investment in UK by Industry: Consumer services were the single most active sector with £6.1 billion worth of deals, 51 percent of the UK total. Financials also rode the wave of a buoyant economy in the latter part of 2006 and first half of 2007, with £1.6 billion of deals. Its share of the total rose from 6 percent to 13 percent.

The biggest fall in investment was among industrial groups. Commodities attracted a great deal of interest. There were £ 277 million of oil and gas deals in 2007, compared to just £ 41 million in 2006. In addition, there was £ 67 million worth of basic material deals, compared with £ 29 million in 2006.

3.4.4 Regional Investment: London and the South East continue to dominate the UK investment landscape, attracting 42 percent of all UK investment. In total, there were £ 8.2 billion worth of deals in London and the South East, involving 554 companies.

In London alone, 334 companies absorbed £ 5.7 billion, a considerable rise on the £ 4.3 billion in 2006. This represents 48 percent of the total invested, compared to just 35 percent in 2005, reflecting the fact that larger companies are increasingly headquartered in London, where the benefits the capital offers are seen to outweigh the costs of doing business. The importance to companies of being close to London and its financial expertise and sources of funding are evident.

The proportion of investment flowing to other regions was largely static or in mild decline with the exception of the East Midlands, which increased its share from 4 percent in 2006 to 7 percent. More than £800 million was invested in total in the East Midlands. Yorkshire and the Humber saw the biggest decline with only £499 million of investment, compared to

£ 1.2 billion the year before – its share of the total fell from 12 percent to 4 percent. However, the comparison is skewed by an unusual number of large deals in the region in 2006.

The North West was the most active region outside the South East and London with 154 companies receiving investment totalling £ 600 million. The region accounts for 5 percent of all UK investment.

3.4.5 Sources of Funds: While pension funds remain the richest source of UK private equity investment capital, there has been a surge of interest by banks, funds of funds, government agencies and private individuals.

BVCA members raised £ 29.3 billion from third parties in 2007, a 15 percent fall from the £ 34.3 billion raised in 2006, possibly reflecting difficult economic conditions in the second half of the year. The proportion raised from UK sources fell from 28 percent to 25 percent—to £7.3 billion in total. Meanwhile, the percentage raised from overseas sources increased to 75 percent of the total, or £ 22 billion. However, the proportions of funds raised from UK and overseas sources tend to fluctuate over the years relative to each other, and any comparisons do not necessarily indicate a trend. Pension funds are, again, the biggest allocators to private equity, providing £ 6.7 billion in funds, or 23 percent of the total. However, this was down from £ 10 billion in 2006 when they were 29 percent of the total.

Reduced allocations by pension funds were partly offset by increased flows from funds of funds, which contributed 21 percent of the whole, or £ 6.1 billion, up from 16 percent in 2006. It is likely that pension funds have chosen to make allocations to private equity increasingly through funds of funds, which can offer greater diversification.

Investment from banks rose sharply, from £ 3.5 billion to £ 5.6 billion. Banks now provide 19 percent of the total funds raised by BVCA members, up from 10 percent in 2006. Overseas banks have shown particular interest in UK-based funds, contributing £ 4.4 billion, or 15 percent of the total.

This represents a significant increase from £ 1.3 billion in 2006 when they were just 4 percent of the total. Insurance companies invested £ 2.4 billion in 2007 and government agencies £ 3 billion. There was a drop off in interest by academic institutions.

North American investors again lead the pack in terms of fundraising, committing £ 12.2 billion, or 42 percent of the total, compared with 37 percent of the total in 2006. The next largest sources of investment were UK investors at £ 7.3 billion, or 25 percent of the total funds raised.

Across continental Europe, assets committed to UK-based funds were static or slightly down, with the exception of Germany, where funds committed increased from £ 919 million to £ 1 billion. Assets raised from Asian sources also fell slightly.

Of the funds raised by BVCA members in 2007, a full 90 percent—or £ 26.3 billion—was earmarked for buyouts, up from 85 percent in 2006. By contrast, funds raised for early stage investment fell from £ 1.24 billion to £ 830 million (although assets marked for technology companies rose) and funds raised for expansion decreased to £ 614 million, from £ 775 million.

3.4.6 Divestments: Private equity and venture capital firms generate returns for their investors by 'divesting' or 'exiting' part or their entire stake in a portfolio company. Divestments typically take place 3-5 years after the initial investment. There are a number of divestment types, the following being among the most common:

- **Trade sale:** A private equity firms sells its stake in a portfolio company to another company, often operating in the same sector.
- **Secondary sale:** A firm sells a stake in a portfolio company to another private equity firm.
- **Flotation:** A company is floated on the stock market and the shares are passed on to. investors or sold and the proceeds passed on at a later date.

A total of £ 13.6 billion was divested in 2007—or £ 12.8 billion stripping out the effect of increased BVCA membership numberswhich is comparable to the 2006 figure of £ 13.1 billion. The largest slice (28 percent) of divestments was derived from sales to other private equity firms. These sales, at £ 3.8 billion, have risen significantly as a percentage, from just 10 percent in 2006 to 28 percent in 2007. Trade sales also increased significantly, from £ 2.5 billion in 2006 to £ 3.6 billion last year, and the proportion of trade sales rose from 19 percent to 27 percent. The next highest divestment type was repayment of preference shares and loans, at £ 2.7 billion. There were relatively few flotations. Just £ 380 million, or 3 percent of the total divestments were IPOs, despite accounting for 11 percent of divestments in 2006. Write-offs amounted to £ 889 million, or 7 percent of the total.

3.5 France

During the 1970s and 1990s, most European countries adopted public policies aimed at encouraging development of the innovation process in order to remain internationally competitive in the specialized high-tech sectors. As in Germany, in France the policy to support venture capital is part of a wider program to support innovation and reduce comparative handicaps. For the last 30 years, French authorities have constantly sought to maintain an active policy in this field.

In France, Societes Financieres d'Innovation (SFI), with the fiscal advantage of setting 50 percent of their new investment against taxable income, was established in 1972. They were not highly successful. This lack of success could be attributed to the SFIs failing to attract the right sort of managers, and failing to appreciate the importance of a direct involvement in the management of supported companies. The French government introduced more tax incentives to revitalize the venture capital industry, which has led to the establishment of Fonds Commun de Placement a Risque in

1983. Investors receive tax-exempt capital gains at the end of five years.

Venture capital is the fast developing concept in France, with a number of genuine venture capital funds now in existence—mostly owned or supported by banks. Three of these funds are long-standing with experience of over 10 years; there are about 40 other sources of small company risk capital (Lorenz, 1985). The creation of the Second Marche in 1983 and development of financial instruments such as warrants and options have helped the growth of the French venture capital industry. Expansion capital dominates the French venture capital industry, accounting for as much as 65 percent of investment in recent years.

France ranked as Europe's third-largest venture-capital and private- equity market in 2001, after the UK and Germany, according to a report prepared by the international accounting firm PricewaterhouseCoopers and the UK private-equity investor. France was third in terms of total investment (US$ 3 bn) and the amount of technology investment in 2001 (US$ 1.1bn) and second (ahead of Germany, but still behind the UK) in terms of buyout investment (US$ 1.7bn) and funds raised (US$ 4.9bn). The market was much less buoyant than the previous year when US$ 5.2bn was invested and US$ 7.5bn was raised. France accounted for 18.14 percent of investment in Western Europe in 2001, 14.4 percent of funds raised, 13.25 percent of technology investment and 17.53 percent of buyout investment.

3.6 Netherlands

The Netherlands has a fast growing venture capital market. As in France, a number of the funds are owned or supported by banks and the government provides a lot of encouragement to the venture capital industry.

A special measure introduced by the government in 1981 to help provide risk capital for the small-business sector is the particulerie participatie maastschappijen (PPM Scheme).

PPMs are small-company investment funds where up to half the risk is indemnified by the government. PPMs can invest up to 40 percent of their investments outside the rather complex rules of the scheme (Lorenz, 1985).

The Government has established a number of PPMs which are giving a great boost to the venture capital industry. The establishment by the Amsterdam Stock Exchange in 1982 of the Parallel Market (a second tier market with lenient listing requirements) has given a further boost to the venture capital.

The NVP is the industry association of private equity firms in the Netherlands. The NVP was founded in 1984. It is a member of the Confederation of Netherlands Industry and Employers VNO-NCW and of the European Private Equity & Venture Capital Association (EVCA).

The venture capitalist firms uses money from pension funds and other large investors. During 2008, Dutch venture capitalists invested a total of € 23.3 billion in more than 1,300 companies, with 75 percent of these located in the Netherlands. These companies have a combined turnover of € 84 billion and have together almost 325,000 employees. 25 companies having solely foreign private equity firms as shareholders, have joint revenues of € 28.5 bn and 1,30,000 employees, of which 31,000 in The Netherlands. In total, private equity represents 19 percent of GDP and about 6 percent of total employment in the Dutch private sector.

The total amount of seed and start-up capital invested increased to € 228 million in 2008, up 66 percent from € 137 million in 2007, largely due to a small number of very large start-up investments in the energy sector. The increase in start-up financing, or venture capital, which began in 2006, continued in 2008 despite the economic conditions. A total of 41 percent of all investments on a company level were seed or start-up capital, compared with 47 percent in 2007. The current economic crisis had only a limited impact, as investors assess these companies largely in terms of their long-term perspective. Moreover, these types of investments are made without financing from banks.

Dutch venture capital firms continue to focus on small and medium-sized participations. As in previous years, almost 80 percent of the total number of investments was less than € 5 million in 2008. Dutch venture capital firms invested a total of € 1.8 billion in private equity in 2008. This is half the amount invested in the record year 2007 and a 25 percent drop compared with 2006. There were virtually no buy-outs with a private equity investment of more than € 50 million in 2008. First of all, the economic recession sparked considerable uncertainty about the future of companies, which made it difficult for sellers and buyers to reach agreement on the acquisition price. Secondly, the financing from banks linked to these private equity investments was extremely scarce.

The average invested sum per company was € 6.3 million in 2008. The drop compared to the previous year, when the average stood at € 9.9 million, was due to the absence of large buy-outs. Domestic and foreign private equity firms together invested € 2.7 billion in private equity in Dutch companies, compared with € 5.4 billion in 2007. Foreign parties continue to show an interest in medium-sized and large takeovers in the Netherlands.

Of the total number of private equity investment, 58 percent were made in the health and biotechnology sectors, communications, computer and consumer electronics and energy and environment. Thus these innovative sectors accounted for the largest number of investments and 30 percent of the total amount invested. The investments in energy and environment more than doubled to € 180 million. Many sectors faced a drop in the invested sums, but the biggest drop, of 80 percent, was seen in the business and industrial products and services sector.

Dutch parties divested a total sum of over € 1 billion. The largest sums in divestments were secondary buy-outs, or sales to other private equity firms. These accounted for 30 percent of the total divestments. Multinationals and other strategic parties accounted for another 30 percent of total divestments.

The public capital market played no role as an exit channel in 2008. The private equity firms generally have healthy portfolios. However, as in other sectors, these companies are also affected by economic recession. Private equity firms have shown themselves to be active shareholders and support companies to help them weather the current storm. There are, for the moment, few investments for which provisions have been taken or that have resulted in bankruptcies: around 7.5 percent of the cost of the divestments.

A private equity firm works together with companies on their future. 49 percent of private equity investments is made in sold-off, non-core activities of large companies. These are generally business units that had to fight for the attention of the parent company top executives and were at the back of the line when investment budgets were distributed. Some of these companies include: Bols, Daalderop, Gazelle, IHC Holland Merwede, Mosa, Raet, Wavin. 17 percent of the investments is related to (a lack of) company succession. Examples include: Bever Zwerfsport, Grozette, and Peijnenburg.

Private equity creates employment growing at the majority of the companies (57 percent). Employment remains unchanged at 25 percent of companies. Two-thirds of the companies expands the number of products and/or opens new branches. Dutch private equity firms attracted € 1.8 billion in new funds in 2008. Private equity has become a fixed part of the investment portfolio of many banks and pension funds. In addition, we have seen a sharp increase in private investors, such as families and wealthy individuals, who invest their capital in funds they may or may not have founded themselves. This group is choosing alternative investment methods over traditional ones, partly as a result of the market conditions.

3.7 Germany

BVK is the association of private equity and venture capital companies operating in Germany and is based in

Berlin. It was founded on 8 December 1989 after a merger of the original BVK and the German Venture Capital Association (DVCV). It has 315 full members (private equity and venture capital companies) and 97 associate members (e.g. law firms, auditors, etc.) as of January 2009 (Table 3.1).

Table 3.1: Facts and Figures of German Venture Capital

(€ billion)

	2007	2008
Capital under management	31.9	35.1
Fundraising	5.7	1.9
Investments (industry statistics)	7.5	6.4
Investments (market statistics)	10.6	8.4
Portfolio	27.1	31.9
Portfolio companies	6,279	6,409

Source: BVK Annual Report, 2008

The companies employed a total of 1,900 employees in 2008, 1,125 of which were professionals/investment managers. Total assets under management by companies amounted to € 35.1 billion by the end of 2008. Fundraising by German private equity firms in 2008 reached € 1,945 million, marking a massive downturn by two-thirds compared to the previous year figure of € 5,662 million. It came from institutional and private investors. At 49 percent, the majority of new funds came from Germany. The most important sources for capital were industrial companies, which provided about 30 percent of funds.

Investments by Germany-based private equity and venture capital firms reached € 6.4 billion, after € 7.5 billion in 2007. The number of companies being financed remained largely stable at 1,194 after 1,175 in the previous year. The total portfolio volume at year-end amounted to € 31.1 billion, with the number of private equity firms in portfolio reaching 6,409.

About € 8.4 billion were invested in Germany, about 21 percent less than in 2007, as € 10.6 billion was invested. Private equity firms in Germany invested about € 5.9 billion of that amount, while additional € 2.5 billion came from foreign private equity firms.

About 76 percent, investments mainly focused on buy-outs. Buy-out investments totalled € 4,826 million and remained below the previous year-07 volume of € 6,173 million. At the same time, the number of transactions fell to 130 from 157 in the 2007.

Seed and start-up investments were largely unaffected by the financial and economic crisis. At € 439 million (7 percent) they were up slightly against previous year levels of € 427 million. The number of companies receiving funding increased from 483 to 592.

Investments in expansion financing also saw an increase. At € 877 million (14 percent) they exceeded previous year levels (€ 639 million) by 37 percent. This increase is mainly due to the rise in expansion finance for buy-out companies as part of their activities, up from € 89 million to € 240 million. In 2008, many buy-out companies furnished their portfolio companies with new equity to insulate them against the impacts of the financial and economic crisis. About 4 percent of investments were attributable to turnaround funding and replacement capital.

Industries with the highest inflow of capital were business and industrial products (24 percent), chemicals and materials (17 percent), construction (13 percent) and consumer goods and retail (9 percent). Germany-based private equity firms invested a total of € 621 million in high-tech companies and € 1,293 million in cleantech companies. The industries with the largest number of financed companies were business and industrial products (210 companies), computer and consumer electronics (181) and life sciences (176).

3.7.1 Geographical Distribution of Investments: Investment by private equity firms based in Germany may have declined from € 7,452 million in 2007 to € 6,393 million, but the volume of funds invested by these company's in Germany increased from € 5,480 million to € 5,923 million, while foreign investments dropped from € 1,972 million to € 470 million. In 2007, there were a number of larger buy-outs abroad by Germany-based companies, which was not the case in 2008. As a result the proportion of foreign investments fell from 26 percent to 7 percent.

Of the € 5,923 million invested in Germany, almost half (48 percent) was accounted for by the German state of North Rhine-Westphalia, which was home to a number of larger buy-out transactions. This was followed by Bavaria with 15 percent, the state of Hesse with 10 percent and Baden-Württemberg with 9 percent. These four states continue to top the list of investments into German companies (market statistics) when the origin of the funding private equity firm is not relevant. The majority of companies were funded in Bavaria (238 companies) and Baden-Württemberg (231), followed by North Rhine Westphalia (113), Schleswig-Holstein (106) and Berlin (66).

3.7.2 Initial and Follow-on Investments: Of the € 6,393 million invested by private equity firms based in Germany in the course of 2008, € 4,020 million i.e. 63 percent were invested in 388 companies, which received funding for the first-time. Further € 1,455 million were invested as part of follow-up investments.

3.7.3 Syndication of Investments: The volume of syndicated funding amounted to € 3,833 million, which marks a syndication ratio of 60 percent based on the volume. Compared to 2007, there was a marginally higher proportion of investments with co-investment partners.

3.7.4 Divestments: The volumes stated for exits refer to the initial investments at cost and do not consider any changes in value. The volume of divestments by private equity firms based in Germany (industry statistics) almost halved compared to the previous year, down from € 2,909 million to € 1,557 million. This is mainly attributable to the increasingly dramatic situation on capital markets as well as clear signs of restraint in the M&A market which made the successful sale of interest either difficult or impossible. As a result the number of companies German private equity firms divested from either in full or in part fell from 697 to 575. German companies reported divestments of € 1.6 billion. Trade sales dominated at 35 percent, sales to other private equity firms 30 percent and divestment by IPO/sale of quoted equity 9 percent. While the number of trade sales dropped from 89 to 74, sales to private equity firms increased from 10 to 29. Total losses were down from € 139 million and 151 companies to € 118 million and 136 companies. As a result of declining share prices both declined the number of exits by IPO (from 7 to 3) and through the sale of shares (from 34 to 10).

3.8 Other European Countries

There are many other countries in Europe where venture capital activity is picking up. Belgium, for example, its real GDP growth rate was 2.8 percent in 2007, which is above the Eurozone average (2.1 percent). Belgium independent funds have set a new record of fundraising, focusing mainly on their domestic market. Belgium is attracting a certain interest from foreign investors. Syndications are emerging as a new trend, trade sales and secondary deals were a major exit route in 2007. Sweden has an inactive venture capital industry until the eighties due to double taxation and very high tax rates. It created an OTC market in 1983 and has now introduced favourable tax laws. These factors along with a highly educated population and high level of entrepreneurship have given a boost to venture capital. Today, Sweden has set a positive trend for invested amount for the first three quarters 2008 and the amount invested in venture companies has already reached all time high. Its private equity investments in percent of GDP was highest at 1,195 percent in 2007 (EVCA Year book 2007). Medical technology, biotechnology and IT attracted the most number of investments. Total amount received from divestments was 10932 MEUR.

3.9 Private Equity in Asia

The concept of venture capital in the sense of risk or start-up capital is quite old in Asia. This sort of capital has been available for establishing new business, and financing later developments, by friends, relatives and family members for centuries. The history of modern venture capital in Asia and the Pacific region goes back to the sixties when Japan started SBICs (Small Business Investment Companies). Australia was the next to launch venture capital in the seventies followed by Hong Kong, Singapore, South Korea and Taiwan in the beginning of the eighties. Towards the mid-and late eighties, many other Asian countries started venture capital activities.

A number of countries in Asia, at the government policy level, define venture capital in terms of technology financing. For example, in India, Taiwan and Korea, tax and other incentives are given to venture capitalists only when finance is provided for high-tech ventures. In practice, most Asian venture capitalists, however, follow a flexible and broad approach to venture capital. Venture capitalists supply funds to new, high risk, not necessarily high-tech, ventures, and also extend management, marketing and financing skills to the assisted firms. In the Asian context, the concept of venture capital may be defined as investment in the form of equity, quasi-equity and/or conditional loan, made in new, unlisted, high risk or high-tech, firms started by technically or professionally qualified entrepreneurs, where venture capitalists (a) expect the enterprises to have rapid growth, (b) provide management assistance to assisted firms, expect medium to long-term capital gains, and (c) do not require any collateral to cover the capital provided (Pandey and Jang, 1996).

3.9.1 Venture Capital Industry in Asia: Table 3.2 gives the overview of the venture capital industry in Asia, includes the no. of venture capital funds/companies, No. of venture capital professionals and the VC under management in US$ million. Japan and China (People's Republic) has the largest number of venture capital funds/ companies in Asia with 232 and 200 companies respectively. Korea, Hong Kong, and Taipei are having 180,177, 165 companies and Vietnam having the minimum VC companies i.e. 7.

Japan is having the highest no. of 1531 venture capital professionals among all the VC countries in Asia. Hong Kong, Singapore, Korea and Taipei are having 631, 509, 483 and 437 professionals in their VC industry.

The venture capital investment by the management is maximum in Hong Kong, Japan and Singapore with 26,019; 21,515 and 9,754 million US$.

Table 3.2: Overview of the Venture Capital Industry in Asia

Country	No. of Venture capital funds/companies	No. of Venture capital Professionals	VC under Management (US$ million)
China	200	360	6,044
Hong	177	631	26,019
Indonesia	31	105	153
Japan	232	1531	21,515
South Korea	180	483	6,251
Malaysia	41	95	811
Philippines	18	59	291
Singapore	117	509	9,754
Taipei	165	437	6,261
Thailand	16	58	580
Vietnam	7	21	114

Source: Asia Venture Capital Journal, The 2003 Guide to Venture Capital in Asia.

3.9.2 Supply of Venture Capital: Private equity in Asia showed a measure of resilience, despite enduring a year of extreme turbulence in the financial industry. In the 12 months ending December 2008, US$ 47.8 billion of fresh capital is known to have come into the region. This, compared to the US$ 40.9 billion for 2007, is a growth of 16.8 percent (Asia Private Equity Review, 2009). A fundraising and investment environment that was barely affected by the subprime fallout of 2007 is now showing definite impact from the collapse of leverage supply, free-falling stock markets, and shrinking investor confidence. Paradoxically, though, Asia is now relatively shining even brighter as an investment destination compared to the black mood in Western markets.

3.9.3 Capital Pool: The growth of venture capital in Asia has been quite impressive in the past twelve years. There has been an increase of 337 percent since 1996. In the year 2008, there was a rise of 6900 million US$ as compared to the 1370 million $ in 2007.

3.9.4 Sources of Capital: 339 limited partners were known to have made 449 fund allocations in 2008, representing moderate increases of 7.2 percent and 5.9 percent respectively compared to those for 2007. Institutions from mainland China remain to be the most active players, the number of fund allocations made by them increased by 68.1 percent to 195. Institutional investors from USA known to have made only 45 allocations, representing a 43.8 percent decrease of that for 2007. Government-related agencies, which participated in almost a quarter of the fund allocation number, have emerged as the most active investor group.

The largest two source of venture capital are Corporations and Banks, accounting for about 463 percent and 236 per cent of the total supply of venture capital in 2001. The next two sources which contributed venture capital are government agencies and insurance companies. It is noticeable that in a number of Asian countries, banks and insurance companies are owned or significantly controlled by the government Pension funds provided slightly more than one-tenth of the venture capital. In the USA, pension funds provide more than one-third of the venture capital while the role of government is quite negligible. In Europe, on the other hand, banks provide almost one-third of the venture capital, the contribution of pension funds being slightly more than ten per cent. Government also contributes towards the venture capital in a small measure (about five per cent).

The patterns of the venture capital sources in the Asian and Pacific countries show little variation. Corporations are the largest source of venture capital in majority of the economies and then comes the Banks. While, Government agencies are the largest sources in Malaysia (39 percent) and Banks are the largest sources in Thailand (36 percent). The differences in the venture capital sources between the Asian countries are due to unique regulatory conditions and financial markets. In most Asian countries, government agencies and government-owned banks, insurance companies and financial institutions have played a much larger role than in the USA and the developed European countries.

3.9.5 New Capital Commitment: The steadily deteriorating situation through 2007 and 2008 meant that Asia Pacific's overall private equity pool had still not made its long expected breakthrough the US$ 200 billion ceiling by the end of 2008. Total capital under management remained just under at slightly above US$ 198 billion although the US$ 200 billion mark may in fact have been reached subsequently. However, the substantial expansion of the pool in the period 2005-2007, when each year saw some US$ 20-30 billion added to the capital under management total, is unlikely to be replicated, at least until the next boom cycle in the global macro economy.

Asian private equity aggregate fund pool surged to US$ 253.9 billion by the end of 2008. The number of funds contribuung to the fresh fund pool in year 2008 was 178, a slight 11.0 percent decrease compared to the 200 record in 2007. The average fund size has increased by 31.2 percent to US$ 268.4 million, from US$ 204.5 million recorded for 2007.

Perhaps surprisingly, new funds raised also do not yet show the worst effects of the financial crisis. The overall total raised in the first half of 2008 was almost US$ 24.4 billion – a half-year figure that compares favourably with FY 2007's total of almost US$ 55 billion.

China was the main venue for much of this fundraising,

with almost US$ 12 billion raised in 2007, an almost 131 percent increase on 2006, and raising holding up well in first half of 2008 at over US$ 8.8 billion by end June. Hong Kong closely tracked the motherland at almost US$ 16 billion raised by FY 2007, up 55.4 percent on 2006, and just under US$ 8 billion added in the first half of 2008.

India, another hot market, showed good and apparently sustained growth with over US$ 6.3 billion raised in 2007, almost US$ 2 billion more than the previous year, and a further US$ 3 billion raised in first half 2008.

Singapore performed even better in rate of increase during 2007, with over US$ 4 billion delivering an almost 189 percent up tick on 2006. However, the fall off in fundraising there to just US$ 126 million in first half of 2008 could be a taste for where all markets highly exposed to the global recession are headed. Certainly, Australia, which saw over US$ 6.5 billon raised in 2007, over US$ 2 billion up on 2006, saw only a shade over US$ 1.1 billion raised in the first half of 2008. And both Japan and Korea showed the totals of new funds raised actually shrinking—the latter down by over 83 percent to just US$ 919 million in 2007, and only US$ 262 million by end June 2008.

The closure of the KKR Asian Fund–Kohlberg Kravis Roberts's debut Asian vehicle–at US$ 4 billion, of CVC Capital Partners Asia Pacific III at US$ 3.5 billion, Pacific Equity Partners Fund IV at US$ 3 billion, and Affinity Asia Pacific Fund III at US$ 2.8 billion were all representative of the glut of fundraising during 2007.

3.9.6 Investments: The investment figures show the true story of the regional environment over the past 18 months–though the data argues that the impact has not been as bad as it could have been, at least over the first half of 2008. Private equity investment in Asia Pacific reached an all-time high in 2007 at nearly US$ 87.3 billion, up on an already record-breaking total of almost US$ 62 billion in 2006. Deal making then fell back to just under US$ 35 billion in the first half of

2008–which still exceeds 2005's full-year total of just under US$ 30 billion (Table 3.3).

Arguably, then, the industry has reached a scale that it is not going to retreat from, and a down year under the new dispensation is still far above the region's historical private equity performance. Nonetheless, the second half of 2008 may call for some revised assumptions, as the sheer speed of changes is in itself causing many potential vendors to delay making decisions until future prospects are clearer.

Table 3.3: Investment Breakdown by Country from January to September 2008

Investee Country	Amt. Invested US$ million	No. of Deals	(Disclosed)	No. of Investees
China	10,762	288	(229)	284
Japan	9,530	169	(124)	169
India	8,695	244	(207)	237
Australia	4,520	97	(68)	91
South Korea	2,452	24	(20)	24
Singapore	2,348	24	(17)	23
Taiwan	1,451	18	(15)	18
Indonesia	955	2	(2)	2
Hong Kong	941	11	(10)	11
Philippines	788	5	(5)	5
Malaysia	381	10	(7)	10
Mongolia	300	1	(1)	1
Pakistan	230	6	(2)	6
Vietnam	213	36	(16)	36
Thailand	93	12	(11)	12
New Zealand	68	19	(9)	19
Macau	20	1	(1)	1
Sri Lanka	4.	2	(1)	2
Tonga	n/d	1	(0)	1

Source: Asian Venture Capital Journal, October 7, 2008 Volume 21 Number 37.

US$ 46.3 billion in deal value had been transacted, virtually the same compared to the US$ 46.9 billion for 2007.

789 transactions were known to have been completed in 2008, a 13.0 percent decline compared to 907 in 2007. The average deal size has increased to US$ 66.4 million in 2008, compared to the US$ 57.6 million.

3.9.7 Investment Strategy

A. Stages of Financing: Asian countries generally focus on the buy-outs (MBO/MBI/LBO), Expansion/Growth capital and PIPE financing, although a small percentage of venture capital does go for the start-up/early stage and Mezzanine/Pre-IPO financing. During 2007-2008, 72 billion US$ were invested in Buy-outs stage in Asia, 35 billion US$ in Expansion/Growth capital stage and 25 billion US$ in PIPE financing. The venture capital industry has invested 12 billion US$ in Start-up/Early Stage and 8 billion US$ in Mezzanine/Pre-IPO stage. In some Asian countries, however, the venture capital firms have made large investments for seed and start-up financing. They include India, Korea, Philippines, Taiwan and Sri Lanka.

Asian countries generally focus on the second and third stages of financing (expansion and start-ups), although a small percentage of venture capital does go for the first stage-seed and Mezzanine financing. Cumulatively, until 2001, 66.52 percent of all the venture capital investment in Asia went for expansion, start-up 35.7 percent and about 21.7 percent to turnarounds.

In some Asian countries, however, the venture capital firms have made large investments for seed and start-up financing. They include Pakistan (100 percent), Sri Lanka (65.5 percent), India (64 percent), China (44 percent) and Malaysia (33 percent).

From the general pattern of investment by financing stages, it is clear that in Asia, venture capital has evolved more as development capital, than as true venture capital. The preferences of venture capital firms are expansion and growth financing rather than seed and start-up financing. This seems to be a global phenomenon. Even the American and European venture capital firms lacks an urge to invest in start-ups (Bygrave and Timmons, 1992).

The cumulative venture capital investment in Asia and Pacific. Venture Capital investments are made mostly in financial services with an investment of approximately 45 billion US$. Investment in other industries like-transportation/distribution, Telecommunication, manufacturing is between 10-12 billion US$.

Table 3.4 shows that the Asian and Pacific countries distribute the venture capital investment mostly in their domestic territory. Thailand investing (95 percent), Korea and Malaysia (92 percent), Japan (87 percent), and China (86 percent) in their domestic geographic region. Hong Kong and Singapore are the two economies that distribute more in other Asian economies than in their domestic geographic region. The Asian and Pacific countries distribute in Non-Asian countries but the distribution is very negligible.

Table 3.4: Venture Capital in Asia: Disbursement by Geographic Region

Country	Domestic (percent total)	Other Asia (percent total)	Non Asia (percent total)
China	86	13	1
HongKong	11	85	4
Indonesia	60	16	24
Japan	87	5	8
South Korea	92	6	2
Malaysia	92	7	1
Philippines	80	16	4
Singapore	15	64	21
Taipei, China	79	7	14
Thailand	95	4	1
Vietnam	80	20	0

Source: AVCJ

176 divestment processes initiated by investors, a 60.2

percent decrease compared to 442 for the same period in 2007. US$8.6 billion has been returned to investors for an aggregate invested capital of US$ 3.1 billion. Initial Public Offerings ('IPOs') and/or sales through the secondary market accounted for 64.2 percent of the divestment movements, while trade sales took up 31.3 percent. IPOs, however, only accounted for a mere 10.5 percent of the realized capital, while trade sales returned over US$ 7.6 billion to investors.

Number of Private Equity firms in Asia has increased by 30 percent during the last two years. Economies having more than 50 percent increase in the number of private equity firms are Sri Lanka, Pakistan, India, Vietnam and China having 125 percent, 80 percent, 68 percent, 60 percent, 53 percent change respectively.

China and Japan having the largest number of firms having 450 and 399 firms. Hong Kong, Australia and Korea having 294, 230 and 205 firms. Countries having less than 10 firms are Pakistan, Sri Lanka and Bangladesh i.e. having 9,9 and 2 firms.

Venture Capital Firms are skill-intensive. The venture capital management learns by experience; they do not have formal training. Generally, there would exist a general partner of each US$ 10-15 million capital under management. Given the average size of venture capital firms around the world in recent years-that is, US$ 40 to US$ 50 million. One can infer that most firms have three to five general partners (Bygrave and Timmons, 1992).

VCFs in the Asian countries are generally small. The average firm size in Asia has, however increased from US$ 4,368 million in 2001 to US$ 17,491 million in 2006. Within Asia, average firm sizes vary widely-from US$ 500 million in Thailand to US$ 12,000 million in Japan.

Two factors which provided impetus for the fast growth of venture capital in the USA and the UK were a favourable tax environment and the existence of the stock exchanges and other exit mechanisms for the small firms. A number of Asian countries provide tax incentives to boost venture capital investment. These tax incentives may be in the form of low income tax (Australia and Hong Kong), low or no capital gain tax (Australia, Hong Kong, China and India) and low or no tax on dividend income (Australia). Some countries provide tax incentives to VCFs, assisted-firms as well as investors investing in VCFs. Some countries such as Taiwan, Korea and India want to boost technological development and, therefore, provide tax incentives only if VCFs invest in high-tech firms.

Most Asian countries have stock exchanges with elaborate listing requirements but a few have well functioning, over-the-counter or second markets (Japan, India, Korea, Malaysia, New Zealand, Singapore and Indonesia). Private placement or sale to other parties as an exit route is used by VCFs in countries such as Indonesia, Pakistan, Philippines, Sri Lanka and Taiwan. Buyback by promoters is yet another exit route used in a few countries. Management buyouts are not a very popular method of exit in Asia.

Venture Capital in Asia is thought to be a relatively risky business due to cultural bias, poor infrastructure, and restrictive government policies (Stine,1990). Culturally, Asian entrepreneurs would like to have full control of finances and ownership of the enterprises. They are averse to outside ownership and interference. They are also able to mobilize financial support from families and friends in case of need. This culture has started changing on account of influence of the Western education on the new generation of entrepreneurs and investors. A number of Asian countries lack well-developed and well-functioning capital markets. There exist highly rigid regulations with regard to entry, exit and registration of enterprises on the stock markets. Once again, a change is visible in this regards. A number of countries have not only improved the functioning of the stock exchanges, but some of them have also established OTC markets. Governments of most Asian countries are also adopting liberal policies. They are becoming market-oriented and are deregulating their economies and reforming their financial sectors and fiscal systems. There thus seem to be sufficient incentives for the venture capital to grow faster in Asia.

3.10 Venture Capital in Japan

Japan is a developed country outside the Western countries which has the largest venture capital activity in Asia. At the start of 1993, Japan had 120 VCFs with a capital pool of ¥ 1,981 billion and cumulative investment of ¥ 694 billion (AVCJ, 1994-95).

Unlike European countries, Japan has not adopted the US model of venture capital. Three reasons can be attributed for this (Clarke, 1987): First, the large manufacturing companies in Japan have the ability to quickly adopt new technologies. They are capable of attracting capital as well as the best talent from academic institutions. They provide tough competition to small enterprises and consequently these cannot grow fast. Second, traditionally, large firms in Japan guarantee lifetime employment to young people recruited from schools and universities. Seniority is given the utmost regard and importance, and thus, reward and promotion are according to seniority. Small enterprises find it difficult to attract talented people since they are unable to promise lifelong employment. Third, the Japanese are averse to contractual business relations. Thus, it is difficult to form partnerships between strangers for the purpose of realizing capital gains. They believe in long relationships, and therefore, do not accord social sanction to the buying and selling of shares for capital gains. Small enterprises have, however, assumed importance in Japan in recent years.

The rapid technical changes have given new hope and scope to small businesses. Both capital and labour markets are no longer too hostile to them. Venture capital is needed by small enterprises to finance their risky projects. In 1974, the Ministry of International Trade and Industry (MITI) of Japan founded a Venture Enterprise Centre (VEC) which also collects information about venture business. In Japan, there is a strong relationship between 'venture' and 'advanced technology'. 'Venture' connotes scientific and technical effort and success more than commercial risk and reward. Thus, the proliferation of small, rapidly growing advanced technology companies is a recent phenomenon in Japan.

MITI in 1963 created small business investment companies-inspired by the US SBIC Act of 1958- to provide equity capital for small enterprises. Unlike in the US, where SBICs are private companies operating on commercial basis, Japanese SBICs are subject to a number of restrictions and, thus, their investment has remained small. Also, until recently, Japan has followed a rigorous stock exchange listing requirement. This inhibited small companies from growing fast and going public.

The ten largest venture capital firms in Japan are affiliated to huge securities houses or banks. Their investment policy is conservative. Bankers also lack the will and incentives to set up enterprises on their own.

In 2008, with the deterioration of American sub-prime mortgage crisis, the economic growth speed in various countries was slowed down; the stock market was dropped successively, which also affected the development of the venture investment industry.

In 2008, the newly raised funds in Chinese venture investment market reached to 14.55 billion US$, up by 14.6 percent compared with 2007. 191 organizations finished the fund raise with the average 76.1 million US$ venture funds in each organization.

It was inevitably cautious for Chinese venture investment organization to invest in 2008 with the influences of international financial crisis. The venture investment amounts totalled 4.85 billion US$ in the whole year in 500 projects. The investment amounts and quantities were decreased at average compared with 2007.

Because of the break-out of the international financial

crisis in the latter half 2008, the amounts of the newly raised venture investment funds exceeded that in 2007, but which varied in different quarters. The newly raised funds in the former half of 2008 reached to 10.86 billion US$, accounting for 74.6 percent of the total amounts in the whole year, but it only accounted for 25.4 percent in the latter half.

In 2008, with the potential influences of international financial crisis and the policy guides to expand the domestic demands issued by Chinese government, more and more venture investors broke through the previous investment concepts. They no longer cared all fields of the hi-tech industry and transferred their attentions to the traditional civil industries with the anti-periodic cnaracteristics. In 2008, the investments in the traditional projects were about 120 with 1.42 billion USD investment amounts, accounting for 24 percent. With the exhaustion of the traditional energy resources and highlights on the energy saving and the emission reduction, the investments in the energy resource and environmental protection were the focuses of the venture investment. In 2008, there were about 45 cases in Chinese energy resource and environmental protection industry, accounting for 9 percent of the total cases. The investment funds totalled 328 million USD. Five organizations including NewMargin Ventures and Tsing Capital etc. totally invested 50 million US$ in ET Solar Group Co., Ltd for the research and exploitations of the PV System. Wuxi Qiaolian (Group) Inc., jointly invested by Avenue Capital, NPEA Capital, Acer Technology Ventures and Tsing Capital, involved 70 billion US$ investment amounts for the researches and design of the wind power technologies. Because of the depression capital market in China, the stock right transformation became the major channel to exit the venture investment. The listed quantities dropped greatly.

3.11 Venture Capital in Developing Countries

Venture capital as a concept, except in a few Asian

countries, is not widespread in developing countries. Only a few of them have made serious attempts to establish venture capital firms. These VCFs have been generally set up by developed banks as subsidiaries or separately managed funds. Examples include Brazil where the state-owned National Development Bank has established BNDESPAR, a venture capital subsidiary. Ina few developing countries, commercial banks have also established VCFs. In the Philippines, a number of VCFs are closely affiliated to commercial banks. A similar situation exists in India and Argentina.

Private sector VCFs are generally absent in developing countries. They have, however, come up in some countries with the support of the International Finance Corporation (IFC) since 1978. Some examples are SOFINNOVA in Spain, VIBES in the Philippines, Brasilpai in Brazil, IPS in Kenya, KDIC in Korea and SEAVI in South East Africa. IFC has been instrumental in setting up these VCFs although its equity participation has been limited. IFC's support has provided as impetus for establishing private sector VCFs, but it is not a necessary condition for their successful establishment (OECD, 1986). Private sector VCFs have come up in countries such as Korea, Tiwan and Malaysia on their own initiatives. Korea is a noteworthy example where a number of companies have originated with the support of Korea Technology Advancement Corporation (KTAC)—a venture capital group which was set up in 1974 with the objective of investing in high-tech business, particularly by commercializing the R&D results from the Korean Advanced Institutes for Science and Technology.

Foreign venture capital firms are almost non-existent in the developing countries. Taiwan is an exception which has been able to attract foreign VCFs since the initiation of venture capital in 1983.

The development of venture capital in developing countries suffers from a number of drawbacks. A significant aspect is the paucity of funds. Development banks and commercial banks-promoters of VCFs in developing countries-lack the entrepreneurial approach. They are risk-averse and sceptical towards equity investment. They may also lack the flexibility, drive and managerial skills needed for venture financing. Some researchers have noticed in their studies the inefficient performance of the government-sponsored VCFs in first-round financing.

Further, a number of developing countries do not provide enough incentives for the development of venture financing. There are countries which discriminate against VCFs as their tax laws favour debt against equity. Also the aspect of disinvestment is important to venture capital since investors aim at making capital gain by selling off equity, but unfortunately the capital and money markets in most developing countries are either non-existent or ill-developed or non-functioning. The government of almost all industrialized countries provided and still extend some form of financial assistance as a source of venture capital. They also provide a number of tax incentives, and many of them have created second stock markets with easy listing requirements.

3.12 Summing Up

Perhaps, the most difficult aspect for the development of venture capital in developing countries is lack of the environment of entrepreneurship and risk-taking. It is a societal phenomenon and cannot be helped merely by tax and other incentives. Entrepreneurship should be encouraged and rewarded. "In a general sense, government and societies should not discourage as investor's ability to profit and accumulate wealth" (OECD, 1986). The government role is crucial in creating right commercial, financial and social environment for venture capital to be successful. In fact, based on the experience of developed countries, OECD (1986) has identified three areas where government action is required for the development of venture activity, namely, tax policy. disinvestment avenues and attitudes towards risk.

Note

1. The Private Equity Performance Index is based on the latest quarterly statistics from Thomson Reuters' Private Equity Performance Database analyzing the cash flows and returns for over 1266 US venture capital partnerships with a capitalization of $224 billion. Sources are financial documents and schedules from Limited Partner investors and General Partners. All returns are calculated by Thomson Reuters from the underlying financial cash flows. Returns are net to investor after management fees and carried interest.

4

Venture Capital in India

The venture capital system as practiced in the industrial countries, particularly the USA, does not exist in India. In the USA, given its highly progressive industrial environment and entrepreneurial culture, it is normal for an entrepreneur or inventor of a new product/process to set up a company to produce and market the product by obtaining finance through the sale of the company shares to VCFs which are readily willing to share the risk in return for future gains. India is emerging as a Global innovation centre with many opportunities in its basket. India has the ability to build market leading companies that serve both global and domestic markets. It is moving beyond supplier of low-cost services to higher-value products. Quality of entrepreneurship is also on the ascending curve. This chapter deals with the introduction of venture capital, its historical background, structure and legal framework in India. It further explains the current status of VC in India, including stages, industry, cities and finally the investment process.

4.1 Introduction

Starting and growing a business always require capital. There are a number of alternative methods to fund growth. These include the owner or proprietor's own capital, arranging debt finance, or seeking an equity partner, as is the case with private equity and venture capital.

Private equity is a broad term that refers to any type of non-public ownership equity securities that are not listed on a public exchange. Private equity encompasses both early stage (venture capital) and later stage (buy-out, expansion) investing. In the broadest sense, it can also include mezzanine, fund of funds and secondary investing.

Venture capital is a means of equity financing for rapidly-growing private companies. Finance may be required for the start-up, development/expansion or purchase of a company. Venture Capital firms invest funds on a professional basis, often focusing on a limited sector of specialization (e.g. IT, infrastructure, health/life sciences, clean technology etc.).

The goal of venture capital is to build companies so that the shares become liquid (through IPO or acquisition) and provide a rate of return to the investors (in the form of cash or shares) that is consistent with the level of risk taken.

With venture capital financing, the venture capitalist acquires an agreed proportion of the equity of the company in return for the funding. Equity finance offers the significant advantage of having no interest charges. It is "patient" capital that seeks a return through long-term capital gain rather than immediate and regular interest payments, as in the case of debt financing. Given the nature of equity financing, venture capital investors are therefore exposed to the risk of the company failing. As a result the venture capitalist must look to invest in companies which have the ability to grow very successfully and provide higher than average returns to compensate for the risk.

When venture capitalists invest in a business they typically require a seat on the company's board of directors. They tend to take a minority share in the company and usually do not take day-to-day control. Rather, professional venture capitalists act as mentors and aim to provide support and advice on a range of management, sales and technical issues to assist the company to develop its full potential.

Venture capital has a number of advantages over other forms of finance, such as:

- It injects long term equity finance which provides a solid capital base for future growth.
- Venture capitalist is a business partner, sharing both the risks and rewards. Venture capitalists are rewarded by

business success and the capital gain.

- Venture capitalist is able to provide practical advice and assistance to the company based on past experience with other companies which were in similar situations.
- Venture capitalist also has a network of contacts in many areas that can add value to the company, such as in recruiting key personnel, providing contacts in international markets, introductions to strategic partners, and if needed co-investments with other venture capital firms when additional rounds of financing are required.
- Venture capitalist may be capable of providing additional rounds of funding should it be required to finance growth.

4.2 History of Venture Capital in India

History of venture capital in India dates back to early 1970 when Government of India appointed a committee laid by Late Shri R.S. Bhatt to find out the ways to meet a void in conventional financing for funding start-up companies based on absolutely new innovative technologies. Such companies either did not get any financial support or the funding was inadequate which resulted into their early mortality. The committee recommended starting of Venture Capital industry in India. In mid 80's three all India financial institutions viz IDBI, ICICI, IFCI started investing into the equity of small technological companies.

In Nov 1988, Govt. of India decided to institutionalize Venture Capital Industry and announce guidelines in the parliament. Controller of Capital issues implemented these guidelines known as CCI for VC. These guidelines were very restrictive and following a very narrow definition of VC. They required Venture Capital to be invested in companies based on innovative technologies started by first generation entrepreneur. This made VC investment highly risky and unattractive. Nonetheless about half a private initiative were taken. At the same time World Bank organized a VC awareness seminar and selected 6 institutions to start VC investment in India. This included TDICICI (ICICI), GVFL, Canbank Venture Capital Fund, APIDC, RCTC and ILF (now known as Pathfinder). The other significant organizations in private sector were ANZ Grindlays, 3i Investment Services Limited, IFB, Jardine Electra.

After the reforms were commenced in 1991, CCI guidelines were abolished and VC Industry became unregulated. In 1995, Goverment of India permitted Foreign Finance companies to make investments in India and many foreign VC private equity firms entered India. In 1996, after the lapse of around 8 years, government again announced guidelines to regulate the VC industry. Though there were many shortcomings when these guidelines were at the starting point. These guidelines did not create a homogeneous level playing field for all the VC investors. This impeded growth of domestic VC industry. Lack of incentives also made Indian Corporate and wealthy individuals shy of VC funds. With the result, VC scene in India started getting dominated by foreign equity fund.

In 1997, IT boom in India made VC industry more significant. Due to symbiotic relationship between VC and IT industry, VC got more prominence as a major source of funding for the rapidly growing IT industry. Indian VC's which were so far investing in all the sectors changed their focus to IT and telecom industry.

The recession during 1999-2001 took the wind out of VC industry. Most of the VC either closed down or wound-up their operations. Almost all of them with the exception of one or two like GVFL changed their focus to existing successful firms for their growth and expansion. VC firms also got engaged into funding buyouts, privatization and restructuring. Currently, just a few firms are taking the risk of investing into the start-up technology based companies.

The above development of venture capital in India can be summarized into four phases. Phase I - Formation of TDICI in the 80's and regional funds as GVFL and APIDC in the early

1990. Phase II - Entry of Foreign Venture Capital funds (VCF) like Draper, Warburg Pincus between 1995-1999. Phase III - 2000 onwards, Emergence of successful India-centric VC firms like Helion, Infinity, Chryscapital, Westbridge, etc. Phase IV - (Current) Global VCs and PE firms actively investing in India.

A significant feature of venture capital financing in India, which is little recognized, is the support from commercial banks provided for small scale industries. The small scale industries in India run both the risks inherent in a venture capital project-the failure of management and the high risks in the venture.

4.3 Categories of Venture Capital Providers

The venture capital providers in India (other than the commercial banks' efforts as stated above) can be divided into following categories:

1. Specialized financial institutions and their financing schemes.
2. Funds promoted by state level institutions.
3. Funds promoted by public sector banks.
4. Private agencies.
5. Overseas venture capital funds.

4.3.1 Special Financial Institutions and Their Financing Schemes: In India, the Industrial Financial Corporations of India (IFCI), Industrial Development Bank of India (IDBI) and the Industrial Credit and Investment Corporation of India (ICICI) are the major three institutions, which are engaged in the financing of high tech new ventures. The difference and similarities between three schemes of IFCI, IDBI and ICICI are discernible from the objectives sought to be pursued under the broad characteristics of the schemes precisely explained below.

A. Risk Capital Scheme of IFCI: The IFCI began its equity financing through its Risk Capital Foundation (RCF) by providing risk capital assistance on soft terms to first generation entrepreneurs. The corporation envisages providing assistance to technologists and the professionals who do not have adequate resources of their own for contributing to equity capital of the industrial projects undertaken by them with a view to enlarging entrepreneurial base for wider dispersal of ownership and control of industry in the national interest. The corporation is continuing its efforts through the newly formed Risk Capital and Technology Finance Corporation Ltd. (RCTFC) set up in 1988 as a wholly owned subsidiary of the IFCI. RCTFC was established with an objective of providing financial support to such activities in the area of innovative technology, energy conservation and environmental pollution. Some of the projects financed under the new scheme of IFCI include development of artificial intelligence software, three Dimensional Computer animation, educational robots, hybrid seeds etc.

In addition to operating its own schemes, the RCTC also manages a Venture Capital Unit Scheme VECAUS-III (started in mid-1991) with a resource base of Rs. 30 crore with participation from the UTI. IFCI and World Bank in equal proportions.

B. Technology Development & Information Company of India Ltd. (TDICI) of ICICI: Encouraged by the response to technology financing, ICICI floated a separate company-Technology Development and Information Company of India (TDICI) in collaboration with UTI in 1988. Apart from Venture Capital financing TDICI activity profile includes technology consultancy services and technology escort services such as marketing, business management, export marketing and guidance for individual venture capital projects etc. TDICI makes investments in highly risky projects promising high return in future. It gives preference to companies, which are unable to raise public share capital and would not be financed by anyone else.

In addition to equity participation (up to a maximum of 49 percent) undertaken by typical venture capital companies,

TDICI offers the unique option of conditional loans. The entrepreneur neither pays interest on it nor does he have to repay the principal amount. If the venture succeeds, TDICI recovers back its investment in the form of royalty on sales which ranges between 2 percent to 8 percent. On the contrary, if venture fails to take off even after 5 years, TDICI will consider writing off the loan. TDICI usually has a nominee on the Boards of companies with whom it enters into long-term contracts. TDICI assists such venture projects in arranging working capital finance, recruiting senior executives. It also takes advice of the outside experts in taking various decisions. Some of the projects financed by ICICI include:

- Mastek a Bombay based software firm in which TDICI invested Rs. 42 lakh in equity in 1989 went public in 1992. It showed an annual growth of 70 percent to 80 percent in the turnover.
- Temptation Foods which exports frozen vegetables and fruits, went public in November, 1992. The TOICI invested Rs. 50 lakh in its equity.

C. Seed Capital Scheme or Venture Capital Fund of IDBI: IDBI's scheme is known as "Seed Capital Scheme" intended to help create a new generation of entrepreneurs who have the requisite traits of entrepreneurship but who lack financial resources to promote industrial ventures. The assistance is provided for meeting the risk capital requirements of entrepreneurs.

IDBI is doing well under the venture capital fund scheme by assisting the projects which are engaged in the promotion and development of indigenous technology that is new and untested in India. The financial assistance is provided under this scheme in the areas of chemical, software electronics, biotechnology, food products and medical equipment.

The project cost varies between Rs. 5 lakh to Rs. 250 lakh. IDBI provides assistance both for financing the cost of fixed assets as well as for meeting the operating expenses in the form of unsecured loans carrying a concessional interest rate of 6 percent p.a. during the early stages of development.

4.3.2 Funds Promoted by State Level Institutions: Funds promoted by state level institutions include:

A. APIDC-Venture Capital Ltd. (A-VCL): This is wholly owned by the Andhra Pradesh Industrial Development Corporation Ltd. It aims at specialising venture fund Management Company. It has been entrusted with the management of a fund, namely APIDC - Venture Capital Fund. It is established with a capital of 13.5 crore contributed by APIDC, IDBI, Andhra Bank and IOB and few small organisations. The A-VCL undertakes investments with the objective of bringing technological innovations in order to improve quality, reduce energy consumption, increase competition and enhanced exports.

B. Gujarat Venture Finance Ltd. (GVFL): The GVFL has been promoted by Gujarat Industries Investment Corporation Ltd., (GIIC) in association with Gujarat Lease Finance Corporation Ltd., Gujarat Alkalies and Chemicals Ltd. and Gujarat State Fertiliser Corporation Ltd. GIIC holds 40 percent of the equity capital of the GVFL and the rest is contributed by other three organisations. The GVFL is a fund management company, and presently acts as a trustee manager of a venture fund, namely (GVCF) Gujarat Venture Capital Fund, started in 1990. GVFL provides finance for innovations in technology leading to an improvement - in product quality and energy conservation, for launching new products based on imported technology.

4.3.3 Funds Promoted by Public Sector Banks: A good example is Canara Bank Venture Capital Fund (CVCF). This fund has been promoted by Canara Bank and its subsidiary Canbank Financial Services Ltd. (CANFINA). It was set up in 1989 as a trust. It provides finance in the form of equity, conditional loans, conventional loans or both. Its capital base is Rs. 24 crore. The Fund aims at providing financial support for commercial exploitation *of* new technologies, technology up gradation to improve quality etc.

4.3.4 Private Agencies: Venture capital funds set up in the private sector include 1. Credit Capital Venture Fund (CCVF), 2. 20th Century Venture Capital Fund, 3. India Investment Fund, 4. Indus Venture Capital Fund (IVCF) and (5) SBI Capital Venture, Capital Fund.

A. Credit Capital Venture Fund (CCVF): The Credit Capital Venture Fund (India) was established in 1986. It has a capital base of 10.8 crore. The principal shareholders are Credit Capital Finance Corporation, Bank of India, Asian Development Bank and Common Wealth Development Corporation. It finances ventures promising high returns with maximum assistance limited to Rs. 50 lakh. It also provides value added services in an advisory role and actively participates in marketing, recruitment and management affairs. Thus it helps the entrepreneurs to realise maximum returns. It has also launched 10 state funds of Rs. 10 crore each. It is now known as Lazard Credit Capital Fund (India) Ltd. (LCCVF).

B. 20th Century Venture Capital Fund: It was promoted by 20th Century Finance Ltd. and has a resource base of Rs. 20 crore. The fund aims at reviving the sick industries and help first generation entrepreneurs.

C. India Investment Fund: It is India's first private venture capital fund mainly subscribed by Non-Resident Indians (NRIs). The Fund is "an offshore company owned predominantly by NRI investors incorporated in early 1987. The fund provides equity or equity linked finance to new projects or often young as well as established Indian companies which can demonstrate a potential for sustained growth. The maximum assistance made available to one venture is limited to Rs. One crore. The principal investment objective of the fund is long term capital appreciation. Merchant Banking Division of Grindlays Bank has been retained as the advisers for the Fund which evaluates and recommends specific investment proposals. The fund follows hands off approach in making the investment.

D. Indus Venture Capital Fund (IVCF): This fund was

promoted by Shri T. Thomas, the former Director of Unilever. The Indus Venture Management Ltd. (IVML) has been entrusted with the management of (IVCF). IVCF has a capital resource of Rs. 21 crore contributed by IVML, the IDBI, IFCI, Deutsche Bank, International Finance Corporation (Washington) and a few other national and international organisations.

E. SBI Capital Venture Capital Fund: This fund has been set up by the SBI Capital Markets Ltd. to finance ventures through its "bought out deals". The objective behind the fund is to promote new capital issues by purchasing them when capital market is sluggish and disposing them off at times when market picks-up. The fund has a capital base of Rs. 10 crore.

4.3.5 Overseas Venture Capital Funds: Overseas Venture Capital Funds look for investment in areas ensuring high and guaranteed returns such as tourism, hospitals, air transport, information technology, communication, pharmaceutical, consumer durables, food processing industry, machinery components and textiles etc. Following are some of the examples where foreign venture capitalists have undertaken investments:

- Global insurance giant, AIG, has tied up with IL & SF to float a 150 million venture fund.
- IL & SF is also planning to launch a $ 100 million fund with the ADB.
- George, Sors has already floated the Indocean Fund.
- NIKKO Securities has tied up with Walden and San Francis Company to float a venture capital fund with a minimum capital of $ 50 million.

4.4 Structure of Funds in India

Given India's peculiar Regulations and investment environment, three main types of fund structure exist: one for domestic funds and two for offshore ones.

4.4.1 Domestic Funds: Domestic Funds (i.e. one which

raises funds domestically) are usually structured as: i) a domestic vehicle for the pooling of funds from the investor and ii) a separate investment adviser that carries those duties of asset manager. The choice of entity for the pooling vehicle falls between a trust and a company (India, unlike most developed countries does not recognize a limited partnership), with the trust form prevailing due to its operational flexibility.

4.4.2 Offshore Funds: Two are the common alternatives available to offshore investors: the "offshore structure" or the "unified structure".

A. Offshore Structure: Under this structure, an investment vehicle (an LLC or an LP organized in a jurisdiction outside India) makes investments directly into Indian portfolio companies. Typically the assets are managed by an offshore manager, while the investment advisor in India carries out the due diligence and identifies deals.

B. Unified Structure: When domestic investors are expected to participate in the fund, a unified structure is used. Overseas investors pool their assets in an offshore vehicle that invests in a locally managed trust, whereas domestic investors directly contribute to the trust. This is later used to make the local portfolio investments.

India is still a small portion of the overall PE Market in Asia. The size of the Asian PE market in the world is US$ 174.2billion. While the share of Indian private equity is just US$ 11.1 billion in Asian venture capital industry.

4.5 Guidelines for Venture Capital

A restricted definition of venture capital is followed in India for the purpose of tax concessions. The approved venture capital firms are eligible for tax exemption on the capital gains on equity investments. From 1996 until 2000, the Securities and Exchange Board of India (SEBI) was empowered to regulate only domestic funds, leaving a consistent edge to foreign investors. The SEBI (Venture Capital Fund) Regulations, 1996 clearly states that any company or trust proposing to carry on activity of a VCF shall get a grant of certificate from SEBI. Section 12 (1B) of the SEBI Act also makes it mandatory for every domestic VCF to obtain certificate of registration from SEBI in accordance with the regulations. In order to monitor (if not regulate) foreign investment in the VC sector the SEBI introduced a new set of regulations applicable to offshore funds, called the SEBI Regulations, 2000. Hence there is no way that an Indian Venture Capital Fund can exist outside SEBI Regulations. However registration of Foreign Venture Capital Investors (FVCI) is not mandatory under the FVCI regulations. (Source: Indian Venture Capital Journal, Volume 1/Issue 1 2005, Indian Private Equity: Venturing into India, p.34-38; Fenwick & West LLP [Greguras, Stafford and Gopalan 2006], 2006 Update on Structuring Venture Capital and Other Investments in India.)

4.5.1 SEBI Regulations, 1996: Under the VCF Regulations a venture capital fund can be established either in the form of a trust or a company. Though the guidelines (Refer: Appendix E) do not appear to make registration with SEBI mandatory, the institution has made its intention clear to regulate all domestic VCFs. According to the Government of India (GOI) guidelines (refer to Appendix), venture capital financing should be confined to the enterprises fulfilling the following conditions:

- Size: Total investment not to exceed Rs.100 million.
- Technology: New and relatively untried or very closely held or being taken from pilot to commercial stage or incorporating some significant improvement over the existing ones in India.
- Entrepreneur: Relatively new, professionally or technically qualified persons with inadequate resources or backing to finance the project.
- Aggregate minimum capital commitments from its investors should be Indian Rupees 50 million.
- A VCF cannot invest more than 25 percent of its aggregate Capital Commitments in any one Venture Capital

Undertaking (VCU).

These conditions do not apply if the financial assistance is provided for the revival of sick units. Venture capital excludes financing of enterprises engaged in trading, broking, investment or financial services, and agency or liaison work. A venture capital firm in India is required to invest at least 75 percent of its funds in venture capital activity, and must be managed by professionals.

4.5.2 SEBI Regulations, 2000 (Foreign Venture Capital Investment-FVCI): Foreign VC/PE players can invest in India either directly under the foreign direct investment (FDI) regime or may invest under the FVCI regime. While it is not mandatory to register with the SEBI as a FVCI, several benefits have been granted to registered users.

Investment Conditions/Restrictions

(a) FVCI is permitted to invest its entire corpus in a domestic SEBI VCF.

(b) While 2/3 of its investible funds must be placed in unlisted equity shares, the remaining third might be invested by the FVCI in:

- Debt or debt instruments of a VCU, in which the FVCI has equity.
- Preferential allotment of equity shares of a listed company, subject to a lock-in period of 1 year.
- Equity shares or equity linked instruments of a "financially weak, listed company" (i.e. eroding between 50 and 100 percent Year-over-Year).

The FVCI will have to appoint a domestic custodian and open a special, non-resident currency account at a bank.

FVCI's registered with the SEBI are entitled to benefits such as:

- Transfer of shares between residents and non-residents will not be subjected to the restrictive pricing guidelines existing for the FDI route.
- Exemption from both entry and exit pricing regulations (especially significant in case of strategic sale or buy-back

arrangement with promoters)

Taxation to be borne by Funds investing in India can range from 0 to 40 percent according to temporal and jurisdictional factors. Many Offshore and Domestic Funds choose the jurisdiction of Mauritius to take avail of the benefits applicable under the double taxation avoidance treaty (DTAT).

Under the India-Mauritius DTAT, any capital gain earned by a resident of India is exempt from tax in India. Further, the withholding tax (WHT) on dividend also gets reduced to 5 percent as against normal applicable WHT of 20 percent. In other words, there is no Indian tax on sales of shares in an Indian company by a Mauritius company.

4.6 Venture Capital in India: Objectives and Vision

Venture capitalists finance innovation and ideas which have potential for high growth but with inherent uncertainties. This makes it a high-risk, high return investment. Apart from finance, venture capitalists provide networking, management and marketing support as well. In the broadest sense, therefore, venture capital connotes financial as well as human capital. In the global venture capital industry, investors and investee firms work together closely in an enabling environment that allows entrepreneurs to focus on value creating ideas and allows venture capitalists to drive the industry through ownership of the levers of control, in return for the provision of capital, skills, information and complementary resources. This very blend of risk financing and hand holding of entrepreneurs by venture capitalists creates an environment particularly suitable for knowledge and technology based enterprises.

Scientific, technology and knowledge based ideas properly supported by venture capital can be propelled into a powerful engine of economic growth and wealth creation in a sustainable manner. In various developed and developing economies venture capital has played a significant developmental role. India, along with Israel, Taiwan and the

United States, is recognized for its globally competitive high technology and human capital. India has the second largest English speaking scientific and technical manpower in the world. Given such vast potential in IT, software and also in the field of service industries, biotechnology, telecommunications, media and entertainment, medical and health services and other technology based manufacturing and product development, venture capital industry can play a catalytic role to put India on the world map as a success story.

The notion of venture capital is catching up in India after it was introduced in the budget for the year 1986-87. A five percent cess was levied on all know-how import payments for the creation of a venture fund by IDBI. ICICI (Industrial Credit and Investment Corporation of India) also started venture capital activity in the same year. Many public and private sector firms have entered the venture capital industry now.

4.6.1 Supply of Venture Capital: The flow of new capital (fund raising) into venture funds in India has shown an upward trend. Venture Capital firms invested US$ 413 million over 67 deals in India during 2008. The VC investment activity during the period was significantly higher compared to 2007 which had witnessed 36 investments worth US$ 252 million and US$ 165 million invested across 28 deals in 2006. The total VC investments in 2008 were US$ 661 million (across 108 deals) as against the US$ 648 million (across 97 deals) during 2007. The largest investment of US$ 18 million was raised by Tutor Vista during Q3 '08.

Unfortunately, VC investments in the country have plunged 250 percent in the first half i.e. ending June 2009 in value terms. The number of deals dipped by 148 percent, with just 27 deals, invested US$ 117 million. This decline is due to the VC firms raising the bar with their investments risk. The due diligence is taking longer as they are scrutinizing every aspect of the companies they are looking to invest in.

4.6.2 Private Equity in India: India's growth in Private

Equity Investment during the last five years is more than astounding (approximately at 240 percent). Even more bewildering is their rise from a country that barely existed on the PE landscape as far as 1997. In 2005 the value of PE deals had increased by 75 i.e. their number rose up from 71 in 2004 to 146 in 2005 (with more than 10 deals over US$ 50 million).

According to the Asian Development Bank 2006, with more than 100 India-centric VCFs/PEFs and forecasts investment ranging between US$ 25-35 bn by 2011, India would stay on the map of all the major players in the Industry together with China.

Profitability of the deals is increasing as well, with a burgeoning share of divestments ranging in the 100 percent to 500 percent IRR area. Since 2004 some deals over the 500 percent IRR have appeared, signalling an extension not only in quantity but also in the quality/ critical mass of the deals. On the dim side a small intensification of negative range IRR is almost inevitable with the growing number of deals.

The reasons cited most commonly for deals "falling through" in India are differences over valuation, combined with the fact that family owned businesses are finding it difficult to "hand over rights" to a private equity firm in view of the availability of numerous funding options. The same applies to listed companies, as these are held under tight control, usually by the founders and act more like privately held firms.

In 2006, the geographical scope of players grew wider with a considerable attention from Japanese, Middle East and European Firms pitching their tents in India. Some of the new names include Mitsui, Sumitomo (Japan), Ishtamar and Abraj Capital (Gulf).

Acting as a magnet was 2005's sensational deal, when Warburg Pincus sold a chunk of its stake in cellular player Bharti Tele-Ventures for US$ 560 m. So far, Warburg (which invested US$ 300 m in Bharti between 1999 and 2000) has made US$ 1.1 billion selling two-thirds of its 18 percent stake in Bharti.

Some of the U.S. titans have freshly entered or are just about to make a move. Kohlberg Kravis and Roberts' (KKR) entry in India coincided with its 85 percent acquisition in Flextronics International—including its Indian operations—for US$ 900 m, in what became the biggest buy-out in the Indian IT space. At the same time the arms of Blackstone and Carlyle have opened their Indian funds and will strike their first deal in the nearest future.

4.6.3 Distribution of Investments by Deal Size: The distribution of investment by no. of deal shows the maximum no of deals in the investment range of amount from US$ 0-2 million to US$ 15 million and above. The maximum no. of deals is in the range of US$ 5-10 million i.e. the total no. of deals in this range were 20 during the year 2007. These investments are mostly related with the expansion and growth stage.

Then the range of US$ 0-2 million has total no. of 13 deals of early stage and the least no. of deals are in the range of US$ 15 million and above i.e. 3 deals.

4.6.4 Investment by Stage: The policy focus of venture capital financing in India is on financing the high-risk, high-tech, high-growth, small and medium size enterprises started by new entrepreneurs. Thus, a large portion of the venture capital funds are invested in start-ups.

With significant developments in 2005-06, there has been an increased focus by many funds on larger and mature deals. This included Private Issue of Public Equity (PIPE) deals- a sale of one or more publicly quoted shares to one or more private investors which almost tripled across sectors. Moreover, the share of PIPE to other type of deals advanced notably, as it came to cover 49 percent of all deals in 2006-Q1, whopping 67 percent in the second quarter and accounted for 70 percent of overall value of PE transactions (PIPE: Banking, Pharma, Auto components).

Buyouts were rather rare in 2005, only five deals with a

total value of US$ 185 m. The year 2006—especially the second half—was under the aegis of a buy-out boom, as Private equity players exploited the tumbling Price Earnings ratios to strike deals with advantageous valuations. Moreover, the buy-out boom was driven by the need for consolidation of most Indian industries, partly expressed by the mounting competitive pressure on Indian conglomerates, which prompted owners to focus on core business and hive off less central companies. Finally, the boom was driven by the opening up of enterprises, needy of capital and expertise to venture in the international market.

The Indian PIPE/Buyouts stage lags behind the world average and retains a rate of 44 percent of total investments (against a 51 percent average in the rest of the world). The stage harvesting above average amount of investments is the late one, bolstered by the rallying capital markets up until May 2006 and beating the world average by 8 percent (with approximately 25 percent of the investment).

In the year 2007, total number of deals were more than 300 with total amount invested approximately US$ 5648 million. About 67 percent of VC investments 2008 were in the early stage segment. During the same year, major PE investments were made in the expansion/growth stage, with an investment value of US$ 5.9 bn across 176 deals (contributed 61 percent of the total deals in value as against 41 percent in 2007). Start-up/ Early stage investments at US$ 1.4 bn across 57 deals, formed 15 percent of the total deals in value in 2008 against 16 percent in 2007.

Private Investment in Public Enterprises (PIPE) formed 13 percent of the total deals value in 2008 as against 32 percent in 2007. This was primarily due to the non-performance of the Public markets.

There was a marginal improvement in buy-out deals (9 deals totalling US$ 0.73 bn in 2008) by 1.5 percent as compared to the previous year. With the economy slowing and a liquidity squeeze happening, promoters who traditionally were reluctant in giving up controlling stakes, were now open to consider such opportunities.

Furthermore, out of the total investments of US$ 37.42 bn in the past 4 years, the total value of exits via Initial Public Offerings (IPO) totalled USD 16bn. With this situation of capital markets, some players have withheld their exit plans through IPO's and have explored alternative ways of exit such as trade sales, M&As, etc.

Going ahead, we foresee many fund managers performing poorly, specifically PE funds that were investing largely into PIPE deals and thus finding it difficult to raise money for subsequent funds. This would give an opportunity to emerging managers/first time managers. Some of the Indian Corporates that have made plans to enter the PE business are Aditya Birla Group, Tata Group, Reliance ADAG etc. Other PE funds that are currently raising funds are Avigo, CX partners, Tano, Lazard, etc.

The good news is some funds have already achieved their first or final close during Q1 2009. These are the funds that have a good track record and have mainly secured funding from existing and new investors.

The secondary transactions are gaining momentum in India. PE deals are currently available at steep discounts, as existing LPs want to limit their exposure to PE due to portfolio rebalancing or do not have the money to meet their unfunded commitments. With the fall in the public markets, the valuation of companies in unlisted segment have relatively come down, but the numbers of deals are happening at a slower pace as PE players are taking a conservative approach towards investments as they are waiting for the valuation expectations of the promoter to settle. "The Hedge fund" style of PE investments is also losing momentum. PE funds focusing more on traditional PE investments by providing value added services to the target company, such as working capital management, strategic value added, operating efficiency etc. As maximum numbers of deals are sub US$ 25 mio i.e. mainly Small and Medium Enterprises we would see more and more funds focusing on this segment while providing value added services to the portfolio company.

According to industry experts, the best opportunities in 2009 would be buying distressed units of large conglomerates and picking up stakes in non-cyclical sectors focused on domestic consumption.

4.6.5 Investment by Industry: In terms of sector-wise break-up, Pharma, healthcare and biotech emerged as the largest sector with 18.4 percent share of all PE investment, having received US$ 374 million in 19 deals during 2005. The Pharma sector has been long in the eye of private equity investors as it is extremely fragmented. The other significant sectors were IT & ITES with 12 percent of deal value, automotive with 9.6 percent and banking & financial services with 9.1 percent. A sector wise break-up is shown in the table 4.3 below. Especially poised for a growth trajectory are manufacturing, which experts predict will grow exponentially in the high-end region, as well as investments based on Infrastructure and Real Estate.

Information Technology and IT-Enabled Services (IT & ITES) industry retained its status as the favourite among VC investors during 2008. Led by the US$ 12 million investment by Bellwether and others into Chennai-based microfinance firm Equitas, BFSI emerged as the second largest (in value terms) for VC investments during the period.

During 2008 the financial sector received 23 percent of the total deal value, followed by telecommunications (11 percent), Infrastructure (10 percent), transportation & distribution (9 percent) and utilities (8 percent). The past trend of PE investment in India, i.e. diversified across various sectors continued in 2008. This could be one of the key reasons for global investors looking for attractive opportunities in India.

Other microfinance firms that attracted investments during 2008 included Kolkata-based Arohan Financial Services (which raised funding from Lok Capital and others) and

Guwahati-based Asomi Finance (IFC and Aavishkaar Goodwell).

During first half of 2009, with 14 investments worth about $ 75 million, Information technology (IT) and IT-enabled services (ITeS) companies accounted for about 52 percent of the deals (63 percent in value terms). Within IT and ITeS, online services firms retained their status as the favourites, accounting for over 57 percent of the investments (by volume) within the industry. Domestic demand driven sectors like financial services (especially microfinance), health and education also continued to attract the VC attention.

4.6.6 Investment in IT and ITES: India entered the map of international business map through off-shoring. Today, it is uncontested market leader in Business Process Outsourcing (BPO) and is rapidly progressing into the next phase of industry evolution—Knowledge Process Outsourcing (KPO).

Given India's 44 percent global market share for software and back-office service and a sector set to grow from US$ 6 bn to US$ 10 bn in revenues by 2010, there is plenty of opportunities for VCFs and PEFs. According to research conducted by Nasscom (the Indian IT industry entity) and McKinsey & Co, the ITES-BPO industry is growing at over 50 percent and has employed over 1.1m Indians in the year 2008. (Source: Indian Venture Capital Journal, Volume 1/Issue 1 2005, The BPO Opportunity, p. 08-19).

Coming trends for the BPO sector are: consolidation of Third party providers to gain economies of scale and the emergence of niche players with deep domain knowledge and expertise. Unlike BPO, which may be tagged as cheap labour outsourcing, KPO represents more of a high-end consulting business, and could be a trampoline for India Inc's large pool of low-cost English speaking, scientific, technical, academic and professional talent.

VC investment, bolstered by a regained market confidence, is thus likely to soar within the next years – especially in the early phase while buyouts are likely to occur within the near future, as valuations of IT companies are likely to pick-up with the rebound in the sector.

4.6.7 Investment by Geographical Area: Venture capital investments are also influenced by the geographical area or location of the entrepreneur's project. Table 4.1 shows the different location/ cities where the venture capitalists are interested in funding the projects. While companies based in South India attracted a higher number of investments, their peers in Western India attracted a far higher share of the pie in value terms. According to the IVCA report February 2008, the most attracting city for the PE investments is Mumbai having 109 deals, valuing US$ 5,995 million in 2007 which was 50 percent more than the no. of deals in 2006, Followed by Delhi/National Capital Region with 63 investments worth almost US$ 2.7 billion and Bangalore with 49 investments worth US$ 700 million.

Table 4.1: Top Cities Attracting PE Investments in India

	2006		2007	
City	No. of Deals	Value (US$ M)	No. of Deals	Value (US$ M)
Mumbai	69	1,780	109	5,995
Delhi/NCR*	41	395	63	2,688
Bangalore	40	1,525	49	685
Chennai	22	354	32	824
Hyderabad	17	492	41	1,380
Pune	10	1,114	-	-
Ahmedabad	-	-	14	492
Kolkata	-	-	12	339
*National Capital Region includes Noida & Gurgaon				

Source: IVCA Report, February 2008.

4.6.8 Liquidity Events: Venture Capital firms obtained exit routes for their investments in three companies during Q3 '08, the largest being ICICI Venture's reported sale of a 14 percent stake in discount retail chain Subhiksha to

PremjiInvest, the PE investment vehicle of Wipro Chairman Azim Premji, for US$ 56 million. Canbank Ventures-backed IT services firm Iteamic agreed to be acquired by US-based technology consulting company-Ciber for an undisclosed amount. Iteamic employed about 200 professionals and is expected to report revenues of US$ 7-8 million for fiscal 2009. Shopping search engine uGenie, backed by BlueRun Ventures, Sierra Ventures and Mentor Partners, was acquired by US-based self-publishing marketplace Lulu for an undisclosed amount.

4.7 Leading Private Equity/Venture Capital Funds in India

Some of the important members of the Indian Venture Capital Association that represent most of the active venture capital and private equity firms in India are given below. These firms provide capital for seed ventures, early stage companies, later stage expansion, and growth finance for management buyouts/buy-ins of established companies.

1. APIDC Venture Capital Limited.
2. Auto Ancillary Fund.
3. Canbank Venture Capital Fund Limited.
4. Gujarat Venture Capital Fund.
5. Gujarat Venture Capital Fund.
6. Industrial Venture Capital Limited.
7. Karnataka Information Technology Venture Capital Fund.
8. India Auto Ancillary Fund.
9. Information Technology Fund.
10. Tamil Nadu Infotech Fund.
11. Orissa Venture Capital Fund.
12. Uttar Pradesh Venture Capital Fund.
13. SICOM Venture Capital Fund.
14. Punjab Infotech Venture Fund.
15. National Venture Fund for Software and Information Technology Industry.
16. Bain Capital.
17. Baring Private Equity Partners India Ltd.

18. Beacon India Advisors Pvt. Ltd.
19. Canaan Partners.
20. CanBank Venture Capital Fund Ltd.
21. Chrysalis.
22. CISCO Systems.
23. Dar Capital Online.
24. Dawn Consulting.
25. Deloitte Haskins & Sells.
26. Frontline Venture Services Pvt. Ltd.
27. Gaja Capital Partners.
28. Gandhi & Associates.
29. General Atlantic.
30. Headway Capital.
31. HSBC Private Equity Management Mauritius Ltd.
32. ICICI Venture Funds Management.
33. IDFC Infrastructure Fund/IDFC Asset Management Co.
34. IFCI Venture Capital Funds Ltd.
35. IL&FS Venture Corporation Ltd.
36. Indian Angel Network.
37. International Finance Corporation.
38. Kotak Investment Advisors Limited.
39. KR Chawla & Co.
40. Kshitij Venture Capital Fund.
41. Meta Crossover Advisors Pvt. Ltd.
42. Paracor Capital Advisors Pvt. Ltd.
43. PE Consulting Invest into India (P) Ltd.
44. Pinkerton Consulting & Investigations (India) Pvt. Ltd.
45. Price Water House Coopers.
46. Punjab Venture Capital Ltd.
47. Resurgent India Limited.
48. SCFPL Siemens Venture Capital.
49. SIDBI Venture Capital Ltd.
50. Standard Chartered Private Equity.
51. Stern Fisher.
52. Trident Capital.
53. Unitus Advisors Pvt. Ltd.

54. UTI Venture Funds Management Company Pvt. Ltd.
55. Venture East Fund Advisors India Pvt. Ltd.
56. Walden India Advisors Pvt. Ltd.
57. Yes Bank Ltd.

4.8 Summing Up

This chapter portrayed the image of a blossoming but risky Indian Private Equity scene. The first part expounded, in brief, the history of venture capital in India, categories of VC providers, how funds investing in India are structured, the loopholes that advantaged foreign funds over domestic ones for years and the preference given to Mauritius as a foreign haven for low-taxed investments in the Indian private equity scene. The second part described the regulatory framework, objective and vision for VC in India and development of VC with current size of investments, their subdivision through various stages, the differences with their world averages, and their sectoral subdivisions. Furthermore, it continued by depicting the situation in competitor markets such as China. Thus, it is apparent that the Indian market is in an investment boom (at 0.61 percent of GDP Private Equity investment has about the same ratio as the U.S: or Sweden) and set to grow considerably in the coming years at a rate of about 60 percent. The later part deals in venture capital investment process and evaluation, appraisal procedure and practices, monitoring support and divestment mechanism. In the end a list of important private equity/venture capital funds in India is given for ready reference.

5

Research Methodology and Design

The choice of research methods is influenced by many factors including availability of the data, time and resources required to collect it, and the researcher's capabilities and preferences, but the most important determinants of the methodology must be the phenomena to be studied and the nature of the question.

5.1 Research Methodology

A longitudinal case study would provide an excellent approach to observe the relationship between contractual provision and performance. Historical case studies with careful documentation of the events and conditions at different stages of the development offer an alternative, but tend to lose much in translation as retrospective accounts may be prone to error, omission, or reinterpretation. The decision to use multiple case studies provides a unique opportunity to observe the effects of contracts on the performance at several different stages of development simultaneously. It further describes assumptions, propositions, boundaries, units of analysis and survey design and data collection.

It is assumed that Asymmetric information and conflicts of interests can lead to finance constraints and venture capital arrangements help reduce this asymmetry and help resolve these conflicts then venture backed companies are expected to be financially less constrained.

5.2 Research Questions

Based on the above discussion, there are reasons to expect that a major issue in the design of venture capital contracts is moral hazard and adverse selection. Venture capital structure attempts to reduce moral hazard and adverse selection problems by minimizing informational asymmetry and conflicts of interest between the venture capitalist and the entrepreneur. It is therefore expected that venture capital funds provide liquidity to recipient firms (entrepreneurs) even when their internal funds are low or even negative. Also, the presence of a venture capitalist on the board of a firm signals its potential profitability to other sources of capital. Thus venture-backed firms would be better able to signal their quality to outside investors and lenders. The research gaps and relevant questions that comes to our mind during the literature review can be listed as below:

- Whether VFs financial contract deal with adverse selection and moral hazard adequately and sufficiently?
- How these contracts affect the firm's performance (Principle Agent Problem)?
- What is its impact on Performance of firms funded by VC.

The three research questions probe complex relationship in which choice plays a central role. The first research question was to explore the existence of the relationships and to describe their dimensions. The second build a theory of the relationships generating testing hypotheses.

5.3 Hypotheses

On the basis of research gaps and questions, one can state the contractual arrangements with the following objectives:

Whether contract between the Venture Capitalist and Entrepreneur is complete?

Adverse Selection:

Statement 1: Venture capitalist's contract with Entrepreneurs include provisions to reduce screening costs

Statement 2: Venture capitalist's contracts with Entrepreneurs include provisions to promote self-selection of projects.

Moral Hazard:

Statement 3: Venture capitalist's contract with

Entrepreneurs include provisions to increase monitoring

Statement 4: Venture capitalist's contract with Entrepreneurs includes provisions to encourage performance by providing incentives (in the form of staged or additional investment) for management to perform diligently.

The hypotheses can be:

- H_{10}: Appraisal/screening and self-selection clauses improve the contractual performance (the repayment & firm's own performance).
- H_{20}: Equity contracts based on monitoring clauses improves the compliance with contractual performance.
- H_{30}: Equity contracts with incentivizing clauses improve the contractual performance.
- H_{40}: Equity contracts with self-selection clauses improve the contractual performance.
- H_{50}: Equity contracts with divesting clauses improve the contractual performance.
- H_{60}: Cases where returns are high, characteristics and clauses are high.

The performance in the above hypotheses can be measured in two ways: firstly, single firm over a period of time, if the case is monitored in successive years and secondly, cross sectional comparison of firm i.e when we move from a poorly monitored firm to a better monitored firm, it must have a corresponding impact from the poor to better contractual performance. In our study, we have adopted the cross-sectional comparison. Because of the nature of the venture capital structure, this is also a direct test of hypotheses that attribute capital market imperfections mainly to asymmetric information and agency costs. We are not applying any statistical test due to the limitations of case study approach. The present study involves observation of contents and its analysis. Thus, it is an attempt to test agency theory based on the structure of venture capital contracts. Venture-backed firms are expected to be financially less constrained. Finance constraints, if they exist, prevents firms from optimally accumulating capital stock and assets over time and their economic performance will be negatively affected.

5.4 Research Design

The information on Venture Capitalists include the contract/agreement between the VC and the Entrepreneur, date of establishment, Management team, nature of capital, paid–up capital, promoter, funds under management, investment details, investment philosophy, portfolio management style, investments made during the year, instruments of finance, stages of investment, investments by industry and investments by states.

Each case has been studied to test the assumptions, propositions, and preliminary findings that structured the grounded research [1], as well as the hypotheses of relationships between experience, contract and performance that will emerge from the case studies.

Experience in terms of "years of experience in the industry". Demographic data includes the entrepreneur's current role in the organization, time with the venture (tenure), education, industry and entrepreneurial experience, and history as well as information about the organization (size, age, current revenues and income, initial and subsequent investment, estimated growth rate and projections for the future).

Each case has been analyzed covering the following broad areas:

1. Business overview and chronology.
2. Entrepreneurs and VC background, experience, motivation
3. Contracts: Strategic opportunity, business concept, timing, resource specification and links to performance. Particular attention has been given to identifying the contract provisions dealing with limiting adverse selection and moral hazard.
4. Business performance: stage of life cycle, critical events, externally driven, internally determined, goals, measures,

and performance.

5. Challenges identified by respondents.
6. Appraisal by GVFL and other financial institutions.
7. Size of funds.
8. Method of structuring a deal or type of instrument (Equity, Hybrid, or Debt).
9. Number of years project took to flourish or had VC backing/assistance.
10. Revenue: Expected and Actual, Rate of return.
11. Exit-Divestment.

After collecting the above information from the cases we expect to get some of the following characteristics about the projects and entrepreneur:

- Characteristics of Entrepreneur and firm.
- Characteristics of Product.
- Characteristics of the Market.
- Financial Considerations.
- Investment Stage of Finance.

The data collected from the above sources has been used for analyzing the contracts of and contract provision with the performance.

5.5 Sample and Data

The above Hypotheses are tested by analyzing the contracts and concentrating on the projects that have been funded by a Venture Capital Company (VCC): Gujarat Venture Finance Limited (GVFL). The thirteen firms, funded and subsequently divested fully are analyzed.

GVFL was established on July 2, 1990 as a fore-runner management company promoted by Gujarat Industrial and Investment Corporation (GIIC) Ltd. with the assistance of World Bank. This fund was routed through the development financial institutions for creating venture capital funds. So four venture capital funds were set-up in 1990:

- GVFL set-up by Gujarat Industrial and Investment Corporation (GIIC)

- Andhra Pradesh Industrial Development Corporation (APIDC) Venture Capital set-up by APIDC.
- Canbank Venture Capital Fund set-up by Canara bank.
- Technology Development and Industrial Corporation of India (TDICI)

A venture capital firm enjoys tax exemption on income of dividends, interests and capital gains if the venture capital firm is registered with SEBI. All the funds of GVFL are formed under Indian Trust Act, 1852. Technocrats and eminent professionals are called for evaluation and guidance to entrepreneurs. Till year 2002, it has successfully raised and managed Rs. 1240 million in 4 funds invested in 56 companies across India. It focuses on early stage and start up technology intensive & innovative companies. It has been paying dividends since its inception to the investors of the fund. It has created a niche for itself in small and medium scale companies. Investment and monitoring such companies require considerable effort and involvement as compared to large projects. Over the last twelve years GVFL Ltd. has been developing an edge, dealing in such investments. Currently, GVFL Ltd. manages four funds:

- GVCF-1990
- GVCF-1995
- GVCF-1997
- Gujarat IT Fund

For the present study we are concentrating on the first fund of GVFL. First GVCF–1990, which is a broad based fund with investment from over 30 private and public sector corporate. The corpus of Rs. 240 million was used for investments in 26 projects. The nature of these investments was trust fund and close-ended with tenure of 15 years, date of maturity: Nov 2005. The Industrial Development Bank of India (IDBI) being the Settler and GVFL Trustee Company Ltd. was the Trustee.

The other investing institutions were: The World Bank, Commonwealth Development Corporation (U.K.), and Gujarat Industrial Investment Corporation. Its investment philosophy was to provide financial assistance and hands on management support to innovative and technology based projects and promising returns. The portfolio management style was to give active management advice.

Currently in its thirteenth year of operations, the fund is in its disinvestment phase, with 65 percent of the fund already redeemed to the investors. The different industries in which the investments has been made are related to Biotechnology, Computer Software & Services, Consumer related, Food & food processing, Industrial products & Machinery, Medical, Electronics, Telecom & Data Communications etc. Some of the key investments are: Permionics (India) Limited, Saraf Foods Limited, Systech Limited, Gujarat Lease Finance Ltd., Vikrant Dye Intermediate Ltd, Medisurg Surgical Ltd., Anjali BioTech (I) Limited, Colortek (India) Limited, H.K. AgroChem Limited, Shrechem Limited, Bals Ltd, Campco Industries Ltd, Madhulika Ceramic Industries Limited, etc. The different instruments of finance used in GVCF 1990 fund are Equity Shares, Convertible Preference Shares, Convertible Debentures, Income note loan and other (Temporary loan, Bridge loan). These investments are made in different regions of the country and at different stages (Seed, Star-up, Early and Later).

Only those investments have been analysed that have gone through the life cycle and have got divested which are thirteen in number. The investment in these projects range from Rs. 209.00 lakh to Rs. 15.60 lakh and the instrument used were equity contracts. For the academic purpose and to keep the confidentiality of the investee companies, fictitious names have been used in place of the real names of the companies/firms, promoters and other characters.

In these investments we are mainly concentrating on Contracts which are characterized by: Screening/appraisal, Self-selection, Monitoring, Incentivizing, IPO, Divestment, Legal remedies.

5.6 Assumptions, Propositions, and Boundaries

Even exploratory research has its theoretical foundations. Assumptions that underlie this investigation are:

- Entrepreneurs are rational.
- A contract implies some degree of control.
- Contracts are performance path-dependent.
- Entrepreneurs make intended rational choices in the course of funding.
- The relationships transcend industry and geography.

The exploratory investigation conducted is expected to have some constraints. They include:

- Entrepreneurs use a short-term time horizon within which to evaluate the consequences of their funding resource choices and they tend to ignore or underestimate the long-term effects.
- If entrepreneurs understood the significance of their funding resource choices for the overall health and well being of the new venture, they would change their decision-making priorities and methods.
- If entrepreneurs wanted to improve their decision-making models and methods, they would want to inform as to what specific actions they could take.

Because the focus of the research is on the contracts between the venture capitalists & entrepreneurs, no restrictions or boundaries (only fully divested cases) has been drawn like size, industry, geographical area etc. The scope has been kept wide.

The investigation can be made at two levels-contract between Investors & VC and contract between VC & Entrepreneurs. This study examines the contracts between VC and entrepreneurs. The three categories are the specification, the partnership selection, and the terms of agreement i.e. contract that centre the research.

The research consists of thirteen exploratory cases from GVCF-1990. The original thirteen cases are analyzed individually and aggregately hypotheses are tested from the data collected.

Notes

1. The grounded theory approach is a highly iterative process that uses cross-case comparisons to develop hypotheses. The hypotheses are then tested against each case. Hypotheses are then refined and new hypotheses developed on the basis of these tests and results from earlier published studies. The results are then examined (Glaser and Strauss 1967).

6

Case Studies on Venture Capital

6.1 Madhulika Ceramics Industries Limited

Madhulika Ceramics Industries Ltd. (MCIL) was set up as a subsidiary of Madhulika Industries Limited (MIL) by converting the ceramics division into a full-fledged company. It is an existing company engaged in the manufacture of ceramic walls glazed tiles. The plant of the company is located at Gajera Village, Jambusar Dist. The main advantages are availability of natural gas, proximity to raw material sources and major markets, exemption from sales tax and the infrastructural advantages of Gujarat. The company is promoted by MIL an existing, profit making, dividend paying company to manufacture 19250 MTA of ceramic wall glazed tiles by the double fast firing process. The company manufactured and marketed the sanitary wares and tiles under the well established and reputed brand name of "CERA".

GVFL has sanctioned Rs.209.25 lakh to the company in 15.5 lac equity shares at a premium of Rs. 3.5 per shares (GVCF-1990 Rs. 135 lakh and GVCF-1995 Rs. 74.25 lakh). In addition International Venture Capital Management (IVCM) had also invested in 34.5 lakh equity shares at a premium of Rs. 3.5 per share. MIL along with associates and some employees holds 67.74 percent of the equity.

MIL is a company managed by professional team having long and rich experience ranging from 14 years to 35 yrs. The promoters are Somany family members. The company has build up satisfactory organization set up for smooth management of the company.

GVFL Assistance: MCIL approached GVFL in 1990 for the financial assistance to meet the capital expenditure on expansion and diversification. After observing the salient features of the company: experienced promoters, sound financial position, use of gas-fired kiln technology and geographical advantage, GVFL agreed to finance the project.

Under GVCF-1990, it sanctioned Rs. 30 lakh on January 8, 1990 and subsequently Rs. 46.5 lakh by way of subscription to 30,000 Convertible Cumulative Preference Shares (CCPS) of Rs. 100 each at par to part finance working capital margin.

In January 17, 1995, GVFL sanctioned additional financial assistance from GVCF-1995 for by way of subscription to 16,500 CCPS of Rs. 100 each.

Capital Structure after conversion in post sanction period, the promoters accounted for 63.99 percent, GVFL 11.16 percent and other 24.85 percent of the paid-up equity.

The market for ceramic tiles of larger size was growing in the country from late 1993. CERA with the wide distribution network felt it could satisfy the latent demand of their dealers and entered into the ceramic tiles, which was a logical extension of complimenting the Sanitary-ware to the dealers and to become a bathroom company.

Cera Bicottura tiles commenced late commercial production in March 1997. The market was eagerly waiting for the production, expectation of the dealers was high and hype in the market: CERA designs and the tile quality would be the finest in the industry. The marketing of products started late. The marketing division went on to appoint the dealers selectively and sought fresh trade deposit to be eligible to deal in the products. Initially many dealers from major areas have shown inclination to deal with the product. In order to protect the dealer margins, marketing division thought of reducing the dealers in a particular area accordingly few of the dealer's deposits were returned. Advertising and promotional support was deficient. Due to delay in commercial productions, few of the dealers weaned away from CERA.

Product was launched with few designs, light, less gloss and were not appreciated by the dealers. In the beginning the printing quality and colour selection was not in tune with the market need.

On the external factors, the recession in economy, instability of central government, price reduction in housing sector intensified the competition in the tile market. Competitors were jostling for the shelf space of the dealers. Newer entrants in the larger size of tiles Orient and MPL were leveraging distribution due to their warehousing facilities. The fierce competition of the tiles market saw declining prices of tiles.

Dealers lost interest due to delay in launch of the products. In addition to delay when the company rejected the dealers, the concerned dealers thronged to competitors products with vengeance. When the product did not excite the market sentiments, and the gloss was not appropriate to the needs of competition, the existing dealers found it difficult to market the same. The quality of the product saw non-movement of product from the shelf. The complaints from dealers started mounting on the quality and the word spread about the perceived quality of tiles amongst the dealers. Consumer pull could not be created due to lesser advertisement and promotion amongst the dealers. Newer companies like Nitco was entering and getting into public relations exercise with the trade community to get a positive impression from them.

The external factors slowed down the demand. The increased credit allowed by the competition made CERA to abstain from pursuing the projects. The continuous drop in prices of tiles brought the sentiment among the dealers not to stock the materials. This also meant, amongst the dealers general inertia in becoming dealers for any company products directly.

The market conditions continued to be low. The election and the indifferent attitude of economy did not bring any cheers to the market. Added to which, the VDIS scheme had sucked the funds from the traders and project personnel. After October 1997, the company could not see cheer.

Taking clue from the above events, company started

introspecting the internal factors. The quality standards improved. The activities were towards the design improvement and gloss of the tiles. More marble designs and innovative geometric designs were introduced. The marketing department worked on the distribution strategy by instituting the Carry & Forward (C&F) agency in each market. Sample distribution was made in systematic way. Project follow up in major markets was pursued aggressively especially in Bombay and Delhi. Still the numbers of dealers were yet to increase up to the desired level. Exhibition participation and advertisement in trade journals facilitated in creating the awareness. During the FY 1998-99, operations and distribution was expected to strengthen. Good designs and excellent printing abilities were expected to attract new dealers.

MCIL did not succeed the way the promoters wanted, resulting in estimated loss of Rs. 55.3 m in FY-98. Madhulika group has though of reviewing and restructuring its entire group operations on core competency areas and exit from the others. As an outcome of this exercise, MCIL decided to exit from the tiles business on the consideration of market depression and substantial capital requirement.

M/s Initial Capital India Limited and MeghnaFinancial Services (India) Pvt. Ltd. were given a joint mandate for the sale of M/s Madhulika Ceramics Industries Limited (MCIL). The promoters and GVFL/CDC started identifying a buyer to take over the entire company. The promoters informed GVFL in February 1999 that a buyer has been identified who is willing to purchase promoters' holdings in MCIL. MCIL's promoters Shri Sumit Somany and his associates have entered into a negotiation with the promoters of Son Earth Ceramics Limited (SECL) for the sale of their stake i.e. 69.2 percent @ Rs. 4.55 per share.

GVFL and CDC hold 10.2 percent and 20.7 percent of the equity of MCIL. They have invested their stake at a premium of Rs. 3.4 per share as against the original promoters' entry price at par i.e. Rs. 10 per share. The proposed buyer of MCIL is reputed to be aggressive players in the industry and have grown through acquisitions. Thus further acquisitions cannot rule out. In such scenario, in case of future mergers, would further dilute GVFL's holdings in the merged entity.

6.2 Medisurg Surgical Limited

"The first of its kind plant in country for manufacture of import substitution products."

M/s Medisurg Surgical was incorporated in November 1989 as a public limited company in Mehsana district of Gujarat engaged in the manufacture of Health Care Products: sophisticated import substitute medical devices. It is promoted by a first generation entrepreneur Mr. Ganesh Talati, who had a diverse experience in setting up of projects and marketing of dye intermediaries, and had worked on the health care and medical products for about three years before embarking this project.

The company proposed to produce a variety of health care and medical devices under four different categories: 1. Urology: Haemodialysis, Peritoneal dialysis, General Urine Therapy. 2. Respiratory: Oxygen Therapy, Suction Therapy. 3. Gastro Enterology. 4. Transfusion Therapy: Solution Administration, Blood Administration Therapy.

The plant has been set up to manufacture a range of products at Village Dhanot, Taluka Kalol, and District Mehsana, Ahmedabad.

GVFL Assistance: GVFL had an experience of assisting 5 technology-based projects for innovative products. These products were manufactured for the first time in India, market price was quite attractive, labour intensive, cheap cost of manufacturing, favorable foreign exchange situation, growth in hospital beds was 2.5 percent p.a, market growth rate of 20 percent, price benefits being import substitute, international standards, GVFL accepted the project for providing the financial assistance. On November 1, 1991 GVFL sanctioned Rs. 134.30 lakh from GVCF-1990 in form of Equity participation. The cost of the project is Rs. 146.50 lakh for which Rs. 100.80 lakh (Rs. 95.00 Lakh +Rs. 20.377 Lakh: Bridge Loan against Subsidy) was disbursed by GVFL.

Before commercialization of the product the company faced initial in-house teething trouble, market acceptance as it required extensive and thoroughly trails by the doctors and medical institutions. However after a year and half the company could meet stringent quality standards in domestic and export market. Company started supplying to prestigious customers like defense sector in domestic market and also to developed international markets certifying that the company has internationally comparable products. But still due to above reasons the company could not regularize sales, incurred losses and resulted into erosion of Working Capital Margin. In order to solve the liquidity position, company started manufacturing low technology products like IV set, SV set, BT set etc. which have low value addition but high volume. Thus, the efforts started showing results and the order position of the company also started improving.

The most important part of the process was quality control tests at various stages starting from raw materials to finished goods. Quality set up included animal house for pyrogens and toxicity tests, microbiological testing lab, chemical testing and sterility testing as well as physical testing. The tests were carried out as per standards described in US Pharma Copia. In addition to this, physical tests for leakage as well as dimensional tests were also carried out.

Due to late commencement of the project, the production quality was not up to the mark. With some improvements in 1993, the company was approved by Institute of Kidney Research. The company had complaints of leakages and inconsistent dimensions of the product, deficient dealer network, and inefficient marketing strategy. GVFL introduced with many firms and organizations, informed about technology fairs in order to form dealer network in marketing.

The promoters were technocrats with sound product

knowledge but lacked marketing and financial know-how. The company was not following proper accounting policies, had below average products, improper functioning of quality control department, and dissatisfaction on the part of workers.

The company was not able to market the product successfully, facing liquidity crisis, increase in liability as a result there was increase in working capital margin In 1993 GVFL sanctioned another Rs.10.00 lakh in equity participation and later on it sanctioned Rs. 9.30 lakh in equity.

In 1992 GVFL sanctioned Rs. 19.30 lakh (Rs. 10.00 lakh in 1992 and Rs. 9.30 lakh in 1993) by way of equity participation. But still in 1993 the company was not able to market the product successfully and was facing liquidity crisis.

In 1995, GVFL sanctioned bridge loan of Rs. 24.53 lakh. There were many financial irregularities: improper financial statement, no provision for TDS, depreciation. Even after repeated notification by the internal auditors, the promoters did not pay attention and rectify the same. The promoters didn't inform GVFL about the cash accepted from Indian Overseas Bank. At the same time, company faced liquidity problems because the set up of the company was for low volume high margin product while products sold was high volume low margin product. As a result, it created working capital problem. In order to improve the situation, GVFL appointed finance executive at the company.

Medisurg Surgical Ltd. being financed by GVFL had to function according to the terms of the deal. Any decision to be taken was first supposed to be discussed with GVFL. There were many instances where the pre-determined norms of functioning were not followed:

1. Irregularities in maintaining of the balance sheet and cash vouchers were found about which company was informed repeatedly.
2. Large dealing in cash was done which was not allowed.
3. On December 20, 1994 Mr. Jignesh Bhatt of Easy Access informed about the monetary transaction between him and

Mr. Patel, which was not recorded properly in the cashbook.

4. Payments amounting to more than Rs. 10,000 were done in cash even though restricted.
5. On July 13, 1993 Medisurg Surgical Ltd. sold grinding machine for Rs. 13,000 about which GVFL was not previously informed.
6. Company was not able to achieve sales as forecasted.
7. Quality of the product produced was not up to the mark.
8. No installments of interest payment paid to GVFL even after rescheduling.
9. Investment of Rs. 60 lakh by LC Ltd. construction group even before agreement with GVFL about divestment. According to agreement Medisurg Surgical had to inform GVFL about external investor and investment in the company.

Surgical Ltd. was on lookout for and strategic alliance at that time. A NRI investor (brother-in-law) was interested in buying the stake only if GVFL divested. As GVFL was loosing interest, didn't want any association with Surgical Ltd and so agreed to divest at an IRR of 18 percent (with equity @ Rs. 12 per share).

But due to delay in transfer of funds, Surgical Ltd started looking for another source to bridge in gap. LC Ltd. approached Surgical Ltd at this time and offered to buyback shares and pay other dues of GVFL. (Actually NRI investor transferred funds in name of LC Ltd. and GVFL was not informed about this dealing. Also LC Ltd. had already invested Rs. 60 lakh in Surgical Ltd. before any agreement about settlement with GVFL). The shares worth Rs. 1 crore of LC Ltd. i.e. 250,000 @ 40 per share were pledge with GVFL.

After negotiations, Price of Rs. 12 per share and payment of other dues at the rate of 18 percent was agreed upon. This made total amount due to GVFL as Rs. 219.48 lakh. This amount was to be paid in 18 installments. Later on LC Ltd. decided to go for one time settlement and asked GVFL to reduce the amount to Rs. 200 lakh.

6.3 Bals Limited

M/s Bals Limited, an existing company, incorporated in 1984, engaged in manufacture of Computer Hardware and Distribution of Hardware and Software Products. The Company had a track record of introducing a number of innovative products in the market and had achieved Star Exporters status in 1989-90. The Company could foresee even at that time that margin in hardware manufacturing and distribution will be under pressure in coming decade. The company envisaged that 'value-addition' in domestic market was much higher in networking projects, systems study and providing custom made solutions in networking. Keeping this in view, the company decided to change its strategy and penetrate domestic market for Local Area Networking (LAN) and Wide Area Networking (WAN), the fastest growing sub sector of the industry. The Company was well equipped for entering this market in view of the fact that it was already manufacturing or marketing a large number of Local Area Networking products and had already entered into Distribution Agreements for WAN products like Bridges and Routers with ACC of USA. The Company had plans to manufacture Diskless Workstations and File Servers.

GVFL Assistance: During March 1992, due to the sharp decline in the export sales, government regulations in India, political instability in USSR and unfavorable changes in exchange rates, BALS approached Gujarat Venture Finance Limited (GVFL) for a major change in its strategy. At the time of financing by GVFL, the company was manufacturing/assembling many products from CKD stage. BALS operate through a network of dealers/distributors, almost in all the states of India. Upon receiving request for financial assistance from BALS, GVFL carried out a due diligence check. Satisfied with the result of due diligence check, GVFL apprised the company on its future potential, which looked bright.

GVFL invested Rs. 40.00 lakh in the form of Equity and Rs. 58.50 Lakh in the form of Secured Fully Convertible Debentures (SFCDs), in the first phase of the expansion programme through its GVCF 1990. After sanctioning financial assistance to BALS, GVFL had nominated directors on the board of BALS and the Chairman was also nominated by GVFL. Apart from nominating directors, GVFL had also set up a monitoring committee to look after the progress of the company and also to safeguard its own investment. The expected returns are in the form of 20 percent on SFCD, dividends and disinvestments on equity with P/E ratio of 8.

On July 10, 1992, GVFL disbursed the first installment of Rs. 18 lakh towards investment in SFCDs of BALS. BALS was later converted into a public limited company and GVFL was allotted 54,000—20 percent SFCDs of Rs. 100 each. Over the period of one year after the financing the company successfully implemented the overall strategy. The company added to its range of products a few more items which are important segments of LAN and WAN. The Company created substantial awareness in Local market for the Wide Area Networking products of ACC such as Bridges and Routers. The company also created a team of about 12 persons, who were qualified and trained in networking business, and had taken up about 20 networking projects. The company started Centers for Network Support (C-NS) to provide local supports to its networking clients and appointed 24 Value-Added Retailers/Business Associates, all over the country.

The cost of Phase II of the expansion project contained a sum of Rs. 50,000 lakh towards the land to be purchased for setting up manufacturing facilities at Gandhinagar, Gujarat. But under the directives of GVFL, BALS bought the land during Phase I of the project for Rs. 4.5 lakh thus taking the total cost of Phase I from Rs. 138 lakh to Rs. 142.5 lakh. GVFL approved the same by the way of investment in 4500—20 percent SFCDs of Rs.100 each, secured by first charge on the fixed assets of the company and pledge of shares held by Suresh, Deepak, and Panwar.

In the second phase of financing, GVFL invested Rs.30.00 lakh in the form of Equity and Rs.58.50 lakh in the form of Secured Fully Convertible Debentures (SFCDs). By September 1992 BALS started working on the proposed public issue of Rs. 300 lakh, and offered to make the public issue at par. BALS also suggested conversion of SFCDs worth Rs. 58.50 lakh at a premium of Rs. 5 per share after one year.

BALS had already started its expansion activities and by November 1992 had become Authorized System Integrator for AT&T's Premises Distribution System (PDS). The company had also started C-NS centres at Okhla, New Delhi, and Mumbai and also had orders worth Rs. 149 lakh for networking.

In April 1993, the Board of GVFL approved BALS for the conversion of SFCDs to equity shares at par. By May 1993, the total disbursements to BALS stood at Rs. 98.5 lakh, which were Rs. 4.5 lakh higher than the amount originally envisaged for phase I due to cost escalation on account of purchase of land stated for phase II of the expansion project.

Due to the long drawn repayment procedures of the government a lot of money was getting blocked up and the company expressed inability to pay interest on SFCD in time due to non-payment of dues by Government organizations.

Later on GVFL sanctioned additional Rs. 30 lakh of assistance, with a condition that the promoters would buy back the shares along with 25 percent interest on the value of shares, if they failed to make public issue by March 31, 1994. The investment was to be made only after the promoter had raised their stake to Rs. 72.11 lakh and the contribution would remain at that level during the currency of assistance from GVFL. But due to delay in public issue BALS sought to change the condition of conversion of SFCDs after 12 months to 36 months after the public issue. By December 1993, GVFL had disbursed Rs. 23.25 lakh of the additional Rs. 30 lakh of venture assistance. The company had again defaulted in interest payments on SFCDs for the quarter ended December 31, 1993, and GVFL had started expressing its concern over the poor performance of BALS.

In January BALS requested for an extension of six months for making the public issue and the name of the company was changed to Bals Limited. In April, GVFL made a further disbursement of Rs. 6.75 lakh and by the end of April 1994 the total disbursement stood at Rs. 128.5 lakh. BALS had also developed technology with Newgen Technology Pvt. Ltd. for Identity Cards System. It was a fully configured system consisting of hardware, software, camera, and printers (B&W or Color), which can be very conveniently installed for 'on the spot', photo identity cards. By June the payments to GVFL had stabilized, Company had closed its books with total sales of Rs. 680.85 lakh, PAT of Rs. 36.54 lakh, dividend of 0.85 per share on a share capital of 14.212 lakh shares.

In July, BALS approached GVFL with a request for release of second round of equity money to the tune of Rs. 30 lakh. BALS was asked by GVFL to increase the term loan component to the maximum possible from the present amount of Rs. 66.5 lakh, and BALS applied to Small Industries Development Bank of India (SIDBI) for a term loan to the extent of Rs. 120 lakh. Meanwhile Bank of India and Anagram Finance Ltd. were finalized as Lead Mangers to the proposed public issue. During this time BALS had received in-principle approval for term loan to the tune of Rs. 120 lakh from SIDBI.

In September, BALS came out with the public issue of Rs. 300 lakh, which was oversubscribed by 12.83 times. Out of the total amount of Rs. 300 lakh, Rs. 80 lakh were reserved for Mutual Funds and Financial Institutions on firm allotment basis. The remaining Rs. 220 lakh were offered to the public.

In October, the company received a large order for ID cards from Orissa Industrial Infrastructure Development Corporation (OIIDCO), and Govt. of Arunachal Pradesh. On December 15, 1994, the shares of the company were listed on the stock exchange and traded at Rs. 30 each.

In January 1995, the company received an order worth Rs. 380 lakh from Rajasthan Govt. for ID cards. Company had also completed orders to the tune of Rs. 410 lakh against orders from OIIDCO and Govt. of Arunachal Pradesh. There was also an increase in the total manpower. For the ID card projects, the company received financial assistance from Gujarat State Financial Services Ltd. (GSFS) by way of lease facility for Rs. 70 lakh, and bill discounting facility for Rs. 65 lakh. The lease facility called for a monthly rental of Rs. 1.69 lakh for 60 months.

Due to changes in government policies it was advisable to import the finished product rather than importing components and assembling them in India, as the whole operation would be adding costs in the form of interest burden, fixed manufacturing costs and overheads. Therefore the phase II of the expansion project could not be implemented. The company would get the LAN cards manufactured by jobbing as many manufacturers in Delhi, which were having idle capacities. The company had become a supplier to OEMs like HCL-HP, WIPRO, ICIM, ECIL, TATA-Unisys, and others. The company notched a turnover of Rs. 1401.99 lakh and PAT of Rs. 87.55 lakh. The company also declared a dividend of Rs. 0.72 per share on a share capital of 44.431 lakh shares.

During the year the company had bagged some prestigious orders from large public sector undertakings such as NTPC, BHEL, ONGC, GAIL etc., and from corporations like India Today, Silicon Graphics, L&T, MIDCO, RPG Sprint and many others. BALS also launched a workstation branded Relief, which received very good response from dealers and end-users.

Meanwhile the company had also placed ICDs with SNS Photo Company Ltd. and Abhinav Lease and Finance Ltd. at an interest rate of 23 percent and 27 percent p.a for a period of 120 days. As the Gandhinagar project was deferred, the funds flow position changed. An amount of Rs. 60 lakh, required for

Building for the SMT project would no longer be required and the total cost had come down to Rs. 538.72 lakh from Rs. 598.72 lakh. The company also proposed to reduce the term loan component to Rs.60 from the sanctioned Rs. 120 lakh. Total investment in equipment of Rs. 42.04 lakh originally planned for the SMT project would now be deployed in R&D hardware: Rs. 10 lakh, software: Rs. 14.97 lakh and development of C-NS Rs. 17.07 lakh.

The conversion of SFCDs into equity shares was done in two parts. In July 1995, SFCDs worth Rs. 54 lakh were converted to 540,000 equity shares of Rs. 10 each, and the remaining Rs. 4.5 worth of SFCDs were converted to 45,000 equity shares of Rs. 10 each in October 1995.

The block of Rs. 70 lakh were subject to lock-in for a period of five years, but the equity shares obtained from conversion of SFCDs could be sold readily. The lock-in period was up to June 2000.

The SFCDs were already converted to equity shares by June 1995, and as per the terms of the agreement GVFL had to offer the shares obtained out of conversion first to the promoters for buyback. Upon doing so, the promoters expressed inability to buyback and asked GVFL to sell the shares in the market, but requested GVFL to sell the shares to FIs/MFs to avoid any undue effects on the share price.

In the year 1995-96 Mr. Narendar S. Panwar- Director of the company resigned who was the only technocrat amongst the core promoters. The company had a turnover of Rs. 1752 lakh, PAT of Rs. 75.03 lakh debtors to the tune of Rs. 468.65 lakh, implying that though the company had shown profits, they were only book profits as the money invested in business was not generating any returns and instead they were locked up as Debtors. The company did not declare any dividend for the year.

In 1997, BALS became distributor for DELL computers in India. But BALS had to buy the computers first and then resell them in India. Moreover DELL computers were costlier than other international brands by almost 8 to 10 percent.

6.4 Suman Cables Limited

Suman Cables Limited was promoted as a Private Limited company at Cochin by Shri Joseph Disuza in 1980. Shri Joseph Disuza manufactured superfine wires for the first time in the country, – M/s. Southern Electromag Pvt. Ltd., and M/s. Deepthi Insulated Cables Pvt. Ltd. Both are profit-making companies and have good reputation among customers. Meanwhile promoters came across Ultra Fine Magnet Wires (UFMW), an import substitute. The promoters entered into the Memorandum of Understanding with M/s. Polydraht SA, Lugano, Switzerland in 1992, a company having the technology. M/s. Polydraht SA is a 100 percent subsidiary of the well-known Audemars Holding Group, Switzerland. Final collaboration agreement was entered into in July 1993. The agreement covered supply of major plant and machinery, installation and commissioning of plant in India and also training of Company's personnel. Later, the company decided to set up the plant in GIDC Electronics Estate, Gandhinagar as Gandhinagar Electronics Industrial Estate is well developed, having uninterrupted power supply and other infrastructures required for the project. It is near to Ahmedabad and moreover, electronic subsidy was available in Gandhinagar Electronics Industrial Estate.

GVFL Assistance: The company came to know about GVFL through GIIC. GVFL had determinant factors to help SCL in deciding funding project: Promoters' sound background, significant exposure and experience, assistance by GIIC, collaborator was pioneer in the field and had a history of successful technical innovations. The collaborator had agreed to invest in the equity of the project and also buy back a major portion of the production of the company. There was global demand and supply: the domestic demand for UFMW in the year 1992-93 was 1120 kgs, which was met entirely by imports. Conservative growth rate of 10 percent was assumed for the world demand of UFMWs for analogue quartz and telephones. The demand was assumed to grow for five years and then stabilize. Implementation of the project was in progress and the company expected to start commercial production in June 1994. The cost of the project was Rs 400.00 lakh.

GVFL decided to fund the project by the equity participation to the extent of 66.25 lakh, which works out to 34 percent of the total equity share capital of the company. The income to GVFL on equity investment of Rs. 66.25 lakh was expected in terms of dividend and capital gains.

The company was manufacturing the UFMWs for the first time in the country. So, it conservatively assumed P/E ratio of 8. IRR on GVFL's investment of Rs. 66.25 lakh worked out to 35.86 percent.

In December 1993, GVFL disburses Rs. 49.5 lakh to SCL and in March 1994 disbursed another Rs. 14.4 lakh. In July 1994, SCL commenced commercial production but the actual sales stared from October 1994. The Company suffered losses of Rs. 38.59 lakh mainly because of low sales than expected, actual realization had been Rs. 7,290 per kg as against the appraised figure of Rs. 8,970 per kg and electricity expenses.

In March 1995, the annual sales were short by 75 percent and price realization was down by 12 percent. Financial expenses as percentage of sales had been 94 percent, which were far more than 25 percent assumed during appraisal. In June, SCL received orders from the collaborator for worth Rs. 11.25 lakh. In August 1995, SCL made record sales of 222 kgs, amounting to Rs. 15.44 lakh during the month.

In 1996, with 355 kg order from Prestige and reduction in raw material SCL received orders from Prestige gross profit margin rose to 64.85 percent. There was a cash surplus of Rs.16.39 lakh for the month of April.

Production for the month of January 1998 was 2853 Kgs of wires in the range of 20 to 31 micron. The YTD sales realization per kg is Rs. 5161/- as compared to Rs. 8,500 approx in 96-97.The major liabilities: Interest to GIIC Rs. 3.58 lakh, Polydraht Rs. 29.15 lakh, Dividend Rs. 21.45 lakh, Southern Electromag Rs. 19.22 lakh, GIDC Rs. 5.38 lakh.

In the year 1996-97, company completed its long market acceptance cycle with a profit of 87.97 lakh. However this could not be sustained due to non-renewal of the long-term order from Prestige, resulting to fall in profits by 96.19 percent. Also, due to lack of promoter's attention and his poor health, the company could not develop other market segments such as telephone voice coils and miniature electronics and suffered in the year 1997-98.

On January 23, 1998 the promoters received an offer from Mr. Arunachalam of Hitech Investments to purchase their shares of SCL @ Rs.21 per share. But, as per the clause of Shareholders' Agreement entered into between SCL and GVFL, the promoters made an offer to GVFL to purchase their shares at the same price. However, this offer from Mr. Arunachalam raised several questions for GVFL such as whether the money used to buy shares is of Shri Joseph's or Mr. Arunachalam, interest and intent of Mr. Arunachalam and whether Mr. Arunachalam's money is a tactic to reduce share prices.

For a year GVFL was kept in dark on negotiation, but finally Mr. Abhishek (another associate of Hitech Investments, and Director of Viral Impex Ltd. and Gopal Textiles Pvt. Ltd.) wrote a letter to GVFL on February 4, 1998 detailing the current problems faced by the company, his intention of purchasing the shares and also quoted a price of Rs. 14 per share.

In the 37th board meeting of GVFL, the board keeping in view all the prevailing factors of SCL prepared a proposal of divestment of shares of SCL. As per share holders agreement executed between GVFL and promoters, on March 6, 1998 GVFL offered its 6.625 lakh equity shares in SCL to promoters @ Rs. 18 per share. The board meeting of SCL on March 21, 1998 brought an end to the negotiation process @

Rs. 18.25 per share. The meeting cleared all the legalities regarding transfer of shares, the pledge of the shares by the new investors and detailed payment schedule of the amount from the purchasers.

The company at present is managed/governed by the same management that bought the company in the year 1998 from the original promoters and the GVFL. The company still manufactures the same product having nearly the same product mix as before and the management has not tried to diversify the product range by introducing new-item. Polydraht—the collaborator is still with the company as a passive partner. The company operates at 100 percent capacity utilization and caters only international market having major client base in Hong-Kong and Switzerland. Corporation Bank is the present banker of the company. The company had 30 employees including skilled and unskilled manufacturing about 5000 kg of UFMW.

At present, the company's product is selling at an average price of US$ 95 per kg to US$ 100 per kg. The price of the product has seen sharp decline from US$ 240 per kg to recent price. Acc. to the president of the company, this trend can be attributed to the increased competition at the international level. When the company started, the company's plant was ranked 6th globally. Today, there are more than 60 plants of UFMW in the world, thus making market conditions more competitive and pushing the price downwards.

The company is active in the international market only. It has been successful in getting high profile quartz manufacturers in the global market who are in constant need for the high quality products of the company and not allowing the company run out of the orders. Thus, the company has achieved enough quality sufficiency to find out potent buyers and to retain them. Some of the company's buyers include watch manufacturers, telephone device manufacturers and also the manufacturers of micro relays. The market for this product has already entered in the saturation stage and further no growth is expected in the future.

During its course of association with the SCL, GVFL tried to rescue the company out of tough times. It helped to clear the statutory & legal compliances at the inception stage, pursued the collaborator Polydraht to invest into Equity, introduced with an international quartz watch firm Prestige, and facilitated the process of obtaining the electronic subsidy from the government. GVFL also helped the company in marketing tie-ups, granting Bridge loan, appointing auditors at its expenses from time to time for helping the company streamline its systems & procedures.

Promoters had started giving more importance to one of their other company, Southern Electromag (SEM). Due to this they became negligent towards SCL. GVFL had insisted several times that one of the sons of the promoter should look after the operations at SCL but even after several assurances from the Promoter this did not materialize. Had there been a good second line in the company, the situation may not have become worse in the absence of the promoters.

Also though the technicians had undergone training at the collaborators' plant, they were unable to maintain the desired quality of the product. During the time span of four years, out of the total production, on an average 45 percent turned out to be scrap. Due to this the sales turnover suffered severely. If the management had managed to minimize the amount of the scrap produced through better quality consciousness within the production department, it could have resulted in increased sales turnover along with reduction of the associated overheads.

The management was not able to keep the team in place. This is reflected by the resignation of its production technician, who was responsible for the day-to-day operations & supervision. GVFL tried to broad base the management and production team but since it was a minority stakeholder, it could not succeed in enforcing the same. If the management had seriously appreciated GVFL's attempts, the situation would have been handled in a better way.

The company was operating in 3 shifts with the limited order position, growing inventory levels and increasing liquidity crunch. The following factors could have been adopted by the management in this situation: 1. The company should have manufactured the required size of wires as and when it got confirmed orders. This could have reduced inventory built up. 2. Manufacturing overheads (electricity/power/fuel/wages) could be reduced if it had operated on a single/double shift basis depending on the order size.

The Buyback agreement with Polydraht did not have any mention about the quality parameters like acceptance of product within a certain amount of variation in quality. A more detailed buy-back agreement (with such specific criteria) with the collaborator could have helped reduce the rejection by the collaborators.

Even when GVFL helped the promoters in marketing its products in the South-East Asian markets; they did not put their serious efforts about exploring the other avenues to market their product. If the promoters had worked hard to find other avenues, they could have succeeded in procuring higher value orders (for finer wires) earning a better margin.

The Venture Capital Industry in India is not as developed as in the US. The reason for this fact probably lies in the mentality and attitude of the entrepreneurs towards the Venture capitalist. Normally, the promoters have the feeling of discomfort towards the VC firm just because the VC firm has a right to share the profit of the firm along with the risk and responsibility. To prevent sharing the profit with the VC firm, the promoters adopt wrong business practices and at times wrong ways to cheat the VC firm through mean business tricks. The case of SCL supports this prevalent attitude of the promoters.

6.5 Campco Industries Limited

In the year 1945, Mr. M.B. Thakur established India's first

Plastics raw materials manufacturing unit for Thermosetting Resins and Moulding compounds. In 1952, the firm was converted into a Private Ltd. company. In 1983, Campco was amalgamated with M.B. Thakur & Co. Pvt. Ltd. In the same year company had diversified and set a new plant at Valsad to manufacture various grades of filled and reinforced Thermoplastic material. In 1989, the company became a deemed public limited company. In 1992, as a corporate strategy, the company reorganized its structure and separated out the Thermoplastic and Thermoset Divisions with an object to give two separate identities to two different products namely: Thermoset Resins and Engineering Thermoplastics. Thermoset division was transferred to a new company, M/s Campco Polymers Pvt. Ltd. with effect from 1st October 1992. Name of the company was changed from B. M. Thakur & co. to Campco Industries Ltd.

Campco was engaged in the manufacturing of Engineering Thermoplastic (ETP) Compounds. The Company had a track record of innovations and new compounds such as Jute Reinforced Polypropylene etc. Campco had been an active partner in evolution of the Plastics Industry of India. CAMPCO introduced Filled Nylon Compounds based on technology from GE Plastics, UV Master batches based on technology from Constab Germany and Speciality Compounds for special application based on technology from Hoechst. The plant is located at Village: Masat, Dadra Nagar Haveli, Silvasa.

GVFL Assistance: Campco was a profit making and dividend paying company, promoters were capable and well qualified persons. It had a 50 years track record in the high priority plastics industry and was involved in diversified products and services catering to vital industries such as: Automobiles, Telecommunication, Power, ChemiBals, Appliances, Electronics, Packaging, Furniture, etc. It was a market leader, pioneer and one of the largest manufacturers of Engineered thermoplastic compounds (ETP), Blends and

Alloys.

Company had entered into an MOU with Polymer and B.V., the Netherlands, Europe, a wholly owned subsidiary of GE Plastics, BV Europe, also of the Netherlands to form a joint venture company, for the marketing, sales and distribution of Thermoplastic Compounds. The Cost of the Project: is Rs. 2366.00 lakh

On March 16, 1995, GVFL decided to fund the project by the equity participation to the extent of Rs.88.875 lakh by subscribing 1,18,500 shares of Rs. 10 each with the premium of Rs. 65 which works out to 2.18 percent of the total equity share capital of the company.

The company's cost-outlay had not been appraised by any financial institution/Bank. The other risk factors in the investment were: government policies on import and foreign exchange, recessionary trend in the end user industries, competition from existing and new units and adverse fluctuation in the raw material prices. GVFL invested 2.18 percent in the total equity of the Campco, so it was not having member in board seat of the company. As well as at the time of investment the company had not done any public issue, so GVFL was not having exit option for selling its stake to public. According to above-mentioned external forces of the company, GVFL might have to face the exit problems, if something goes wrong with the company due to above factors.

At the time of GVFL investment, Campco was a profit making company with good capacity utilization and dividend sharing ratio of 20 percent. GVFL entered into negotiation with a condition that public issue of Campco would provide exit route to GVFL.

The post-financial position of the company was very pathetic and was not able to survive in the competitive market. The auditors of the company in their audit report declared the Company as a Sick Industrial unit as per the provisions of the Sick Industrial Companies Act, 1985. Company has approached FIs and Banks for restructuring of their dues, as company had made consistence defaults in repayment of instalments and in payment of interest. Total outstanding amount towards secured and unsecured loans is Rs. 64.98 Crore. The total net current asset includes Sundry Debtors of Rs. 1632.08 lakh outs of which Rs. 1340.19 lakh is outstanding for more then 6 Months.

In the year 1994-95, Net profit came down by Rs. 78 lakh and EPS to Rs. 2.92. In November 1995, CAMPCO issued net dividend of Rs. 4399 to GVFL.

In November 2000, the company was receiving regular monthly orders from Finolex cables and Sterlite Industries for manufacture of cable compounds of about 200 MT. Company made a loss of Rs. 10.82 crore due to general downturn economy, increase in raw material prices, inability to increase selling price and liquidity constraints. Raw material/sales ratio was found to have increased from 49.8 percent to 62.4 percent. The current ratio of the company went down to 0.9 due to this company started facing liquidity problems. The company had a turnover ratio of 9.73 which decreased to 1.43 in 2001-02. The gross profit margin was 12.19 percent in 1994-95, which decreased tremendously. Net profit margin was also very low substantially, lower than industry average. Book value per share was higher at 69.75 in the year 1994-95 but after that it fell to 23.30, due to poor performance of the company. Interest coverage ratio of the company also decreased to (0.58) due to non-availability of funds. Debtors almost doubled from the year 1994-95 to 2000-01. On October 31, 2000, the tie-up with Polymerland and G E Plastics was terminated. The company was irregular in depositing PF Dues.

On January 9, 2003 the agreement was signed between GVFL & Campco to resolve long-standing problems between them. The financial performance of the company was continuously deteriorating and the main reason for that was under utilization of the plant. The company had never utilized the full installed capacity of both the plants. Sales after increasing in initial years had dropped in 2001-02. The company had never achieved economies of scale. The company never met the projected numbers. At the same time the administrative and selling expenses were constant irrespective of sales. The EPS of the company, which was 2.31 at the time of investment, decreased to (23.89) 2001-02, which shows poor performance of the company during the above period. At this juncture company had a carry forward loss of Rs. 24.23 crore.

In the initial stages there was proper flow of information about the happenings of Campco. But slowly information ceased to come from Campco. There was improper recording and auditing of accounts. And it was done on a periodic basis (at least once in three months). GVFL was not able to appoint directors in the board of Campco because it was having only 2.18 percent shareholding. But then also nominees from GVFL attended meetings and GVFL kept an eye on the proceedings of the company frequently. GVFL also helped Campco to take some of the vital strategic decisions, which were necessary for the growth of the company. GVFL had done its best to get proper information from Campco and also maintained the progress of the company through active participation in the affairs of the company through out the investment period.

6.6 Vikram Industries Limited

M/s Vikram Industries Limited was set up as a 100 percent EOU to manufacture Knitted Cotton Socks at Navsari, Gujarat. The company has proposed to import advanced computerized socks knitting and finishing equipments from reputed manufacturer M/s Lonati S.P.A., Italy and proposes to manufacture quality dress socks in wide design range like plain, jacquard, motifs, ribbed, high spliced, terry etc varieties for the export market. The company has retained M/s Gherzi Eastern Limited (GEL), a reputed engineering consultancy firm of Wadia Group for project formulation and overall technical assistance for project implementation and commissioning. The company intends to market socks mainly in the European Countries and has entered into Memorandum of Understanding with M/s Aryan International S.A., a trading company based in France for purchase of approx. 40 percent of its production capacity. The project is at an advanced stage of implementation. Orders for main equipments have been placed. Civil construction is in progress. Production is expected to start from April, 1995.

The project estimated to cost Rs. 766.00 lakh is proposed to be part financed by Equity of Rs. 429.00 lakh (including Public Issue of Rs. 215.00 lakh) and Foreign Currency Loan of Rs. 337.00 lakh. IDBI has appraised the project and sanctioned FC Loan of Rs. 337.00 lakh. The company intends to make Public Issue of Rs. 215.00 lakh in November/December, 1994.

GVFL Assistance: Vikram Industries approached GVFL in 1994 for Equity participation of Rs. 75.00 lakh (subscription to 7,50,000 shares of Rs 10 each at par) in firm allotment category with three years lock-in period.

In the month of August 1996, the company was expecting to take an order of 93,000 pairs and sales target of Rs. 134.54 lakh. But slow off-take of consumer goods in whole of Europe resulted in slow inflow of orders. Later, the company received poor quality of cotton yarn due to which an order was cancelled. It was therefore suggested to have alternate source of yarn supplier.

It was also observed that the management does not take care in the purchase of raw materials as to its quality and run ability. It was therefore suggested to conduct a reasonable quality tests on receipt of the raw material in factory and also request the suppliers to submit their quality report before dispatch There were many mechanical as well as electrical stoppages and breakdowns due to restarting of machine after their remaining idle for prolonged period. Workers were getting trained for regular and quality production. This caused acute shortage of Knitting Elements, with the result that the Knitting Elements procured through rush purchase or personally brought from Lonati got exhausted. The machines were worked for 3 shifts. Due to heavy workload of the machines and long working hours, the problem of absenteeism was also experienced which was further aggravated due to rains and disruption of transport means.

The sales of Rs 31 lakh is far below the target of Rs. 135 lakh. The fees paid to Gherzi were only for conducting and submitting a report on market survey. No fees for creating market have been paid to them nor was the market entry plan implemented.

Delay, over-run and initial cash affected the project viability. GVFL strongly suggests that viability study of the project should be carried out immediately.

A UK based Socks Manufacturer gave indication for long-term tie-up including equity participation which was too followed up seriously. Expenses towards salaries, wages and utilities were high. It was advised that the company should prepare a budget and monitor its cash flow. Because in case of failure to achieve the breakeven level, cash losses would further increase and promoters shall have to arrange for additional funds to make up for cash losses. It was decided to appoint an internal auditor.

For the period ended March 31, 1997 the company had projected sales of above Rs 110.00 lakh. However due to transportation strike, several consignments could not be dispatched and therefore company could achieve sales of only Rs. 93.00 lakh.

On account of Floods and subsequent Plague Outbreak in Surat, project suffered time and cost overrun and commercial production could be started only in April 1996 as against April 1995 as anticipated earlier. As product acceptance by overseas customers took several months due to long sampling time, Vikram incurred initial losses. After intensive efforts, company successfully established a respectable client base to which it supplies on a regular basis. Its clientele includes Flanders (UK), Ciro Citterio (Denmark), Next, Coats Viella, Magnificient, Benzer, Charles etc. Therefore for the expansion, Vikram requested and GVFL gave additional finance for expanding the capacity of the plant for manufacturing knitted cotton socks by way of Income notes of Rs 40 lakh.

With the constant efforts for market development, company has received encouraging response and active negotiations are in progress. The company has however, not received any major confirmed order. Most of the above customers have placed trial orders equivalent to about Rs. 50.00 lakh. The company expects to receive major orders by June/July for delivery in subsequent half year.

- In the domestic market the company also executed trial order.
- All the export orders were required to be placed approximately 6 months in advance, it was therefore impossible to get any order, which have to be delivered before June.

Vikram, in the long term will establish its own market brand. It also plans to enter in strategic marketing and production alliances with well-known companies for a wider and better market penetration. The overall objective of this assignment will be to identify potential importers, wholesalers of socks, who have at least 40 percent to 50 percent of the market cover in Germany and Britain and to finalise orders with them.

GVFL saw continuous fall in the financial position of the company and decided to divest. GVFL had provided the financial assistance of Rs. 75.00 lakh to Vikram Industries. Looking at a deteriorating condition GVFL divested the shares to a third party at a negotiable price.

6.7 Shrechem Limited

M/s Shrechem Ltd. (Shrechem) was set up in 1989, in Joint sector with Tamil Nadu Industrial Corporation (TIDCO) to manufacture 500 MTA of lactic Acid from Molasses. The project is located at Madhurantakam Taluk of Chengai MGR

District in Tamil Nadu. The project was to be registered as a 100 percent EOU and was planning to export 75 percent of its production to U.S.A. where it had already signed an MOU with M/s Roussel to market its Lactic Acid. The project was appraised and assisted by Canbank Venture Capital Fund (CVCF) by way of equity participation of Rs 40.00 lakh, Rs 15.00 lakh as State Subsidy and Rs. 198.00 lakh as Term loan by Canara Bank. Due to delay in the sanction of the term–loan from Canara bank, there was change in the location of the project to SIDCO Industrial Estate at Kakkalur Village, Tiruvallur Taluk, also in Chengai MGR District, Tamil Nadu. For strategic reasons the company decided subsequently not to register as an EOU. All these factors coupled with the reduction in sanction of term loan by Rs. 10.00 lakh resulted into an over-run in the cost of project by Rs. 69.50 lakh.

GVFL Assistance: The company proposes to manufacture I.P. grade Lactic Acid from Molasses, which is a cheaper raw material as compared to sugar and starch being used by some of the other manufacturers. There were three manufacturers of Lactic Acid in the country. There was domestic and international demand-supply. The worldwide demand was growing annually at the rate of 10 percent.

To overcome the problem of cost over-run, CVCF and TIDCO requested GVFL in 1991 for providing capital assistance to bridge the gap of Rs. 20.00 lakh in the means of finance. The project seemed to be very attractive with the project IRR of 29.57 percent, GVFL IRR of 36.34 percent based on book value and with a conservative P/E of 6. Therefore, on June 29, 1993, GVFL agreed and sanctioned venture capital assistance of Rs 25.00 lakh to the company by way of equity, based on the appraisal prepared by CVCF. The estimated cost of the project was Rs 357.50 lakh. It was also decided that CVCF would take a lead in monitoring of the project.

The plant started Commercial Production in February 1994. However, it was brought to the notice of GVFL, a cost over-run during implementation of Rs. 44.53 lakh, which was mainly on account of additional civil work, additional plant & machinery, preoperative cost because of delay in starting of Commercial Production. Looking at the progress the project has made, especially in stabilizing technology and good prospects identification on marketing front, the company was funded additional equity of Rs. 34.65 lakh from the existing shareholders (including Rs. 7.68 lakh from GVFL).

In its first year of operation the company established product quality with a number of customers and also developed process to make colorless, odorless, heat stable lactic acid. The company made a sale of Rs. 94.87 lakh in 1994-95 but there were cash losses due to lower turnover, lower production and sales and also loss of product due to leakages from corroded equipments, which eroded the working capital margin. The additional funds required for supplementing working capital margin were estimated at Rs. 40.36 lakh. Since TIDCO could not sanction any more equity, in order to fund the de-bottle-necking, promoters, GVFL and CVCF decided to split the project into two phases. The first phase shall cost Rs. 83.53 lakh and second phase can be taken up after the first phase becomes successful. The year ended with the untimely death of Mr. M.L.N. Srivastava on December 26, 1994. Mr. N.V.Gopalachary was appointed as a director in his place.

In order to bring the capacities up to 300 MTA, to replenish erosion in working capital margin due to cash losses and looking at the developing markets, the existing investors other than TIDCO invested Rs. 83.53 lakh by way of Preference Shares. On May 2, 1995 GVFL sanctioned additional investment of Rs. 19.50 lakh in form of RCCPS of Rs. 10 each. Thus, bringing the total exposure of GVFL to Rs. 52.18 lakh. The de-bottle-necking process for achieving capacities of 25 TPM (5300 TPA) was completed in October 1995. However the company was unable to achieve targeted levels of production in the balance portion of 1995-96 because of unexpected technical problems. The fludised bed boiler supplied by Thermax (only the second such boiler supplied by it) sprung leaks due to improper furnace design. In addition there was a problem of frequency falling refractory tiles in the graphite-lined hydrolyser. The company replaced the hydrolyser with a SS316 hydrolyser and was able to produce on an average only 16 tpm the last six months of this financial year. However, the company was able to stabilize the production process and achieve the desired level of efficiency in terms of recoveries and consumption norms. The product was also well accepted by all the customers.

The company produced 8.4 and 20.7 mt of lactic acid in April and May 1996, despite several shutdowns required due to boiler problems. Finally, in June 1996 the company prevailed upon Thermax to replace the boiler free of cost. However, due to this the company was able to produce only 3.15 mt of lactic acid in June 1996. The new boiler was commissioned on July 20, 1996 after which the company was able to produce 8.5 mt of lactic acid in July 1996. After replacement of boiler, the company was able to operate on an average at 23 mt per month (at break even levels) in August, September and October 1996. In the month of November 1996, Canara Bank started adjusting outstanding interest on term loan from the receipts in the current account. This resulted in a tremendous liquidity crunch. Due to working capital shortage the company was able to manufacture on an average 12.5 mts of lactic acid during the rest of 1996-97.

The company has been trying to raise funds since January 1997, initially for payment of bank dues, increasing capacities and supplementing erosion in margin for working capital. It was impossible for GVFL to fund the entire amount and meanwhile the company was declared a NPA and incurring losses since December 1996.

The financial performance for the year ending March 31, 1997 was reviewed: Sales increased from Rs. 128.71 lakh to Rs. 154.02 lakh, power & fuel cost increased by 34 percent, cash loss of Rs.43.23 lakh, Book value decreased from 5.83 to 3.46.

GVFL studied the viability of this proposition and informed the company that it would not be able to sustain payment to the bank, even after raising funds to pay off overdue amounts. Instead the company should ask the bank for a rescheduling and funding of interest. This proposal was not acceptable to CVCF, the other major investor. Despite repeated discussions with GVFL and promoters, CVCF sanctioned additional Rs 20 lakh by way of NCDs under a plan to pay Rs. 42 lakh of overdue interest to the bank. This along with the requirement to convince the bank to grant relief and concessions delayed the revival scheme for almost 8 months.

In September 1998, GVFL appraised the strengths and weakness of the company: The company has net loss cash for the period April to July 98. The accumulated loss is Rs. 264.28 lakh and the book value is Rs 1.11/share. The company is exploring export avenues and has contacted prospective buyers. The company is yet to make a major break through in the export market. The company has executed one export order of 3 tonnes. The future growth of the company depends on the export market. Alternatives for exit from the company are: through Sale of Technology to a prospective buyer in India or Abroad and the proceeds be utilized to buyback our shares.

In November 1998, there has been a positive development at the management level, which enhances the prospects of a turnaround in the immediate future. In the Shareholder-management of the Malladi group Prasanna has gained 75 percent control. The built-in synergy among the group companies could be efficiently exploited under a single management.

For the month of January 1999, company had achieved break-even sales but also made cash losses of Rs. 0.75 lakh, Working capital decreased due to increase in advance from customers.

After the commencement of the production the company

faced many serious operational problems. The process technology was reasonably well standardized. But there were difficulties in developing this technology. The unidentified impurities in molasses contributed to major problems in purification. The levels of impurities present were very high, requiring repeated purification steps. This was crippling the attainment of the rated production capacity. The process conditions were very corrosive which resulted in damage to plant & machinery, which came up for repair and replacement. This also resulted in loss of production and not attaining the rated capacity. Since the company was operating at low levels of capacity utilization, the financial costs were not covered. Thus total losses incurred by the company has large uncovered depreciation and unpaid interest dues. The pharmaceutical and the food industries normally require samples to be tested out for quality, which is very time consuming and involves gestation period. During its initial stage the product faced some difficulty in acceptance but later on the marketing problems were taken care of.

On account of the delay in quickly getting on to fast track performance the company has accumulated losses due to non-coverage of some fixed costs components. The implementation of the stabilization scheme was completed by October 1995 and there after normal production at 5 MT per month was achieved. In the meanwhile the fluidized bed boiler supplied by M/S Thermax limited failed due to faulty design. By the time the boiler was replaced and normal production was established the company ran into working capital problems due to the accumulated cash losses.

Thus the reason for the erosion in the net worth of the company was not due to any managerial or other problems but due to the circumstances beyond the control of Management.

In the months of June 1999, Mr. Prasanna one if the promoter of the company proposed to buyback the shares. But CVCF expressed to wait till March 31, 2001 for the exit from the company. They requested Mr. Prasanna to give a formal proposal-giving price at which the promoters will be ready to purchase shares. The performance of the company was reviewed for the month with the sales of Rs. 59.19 lakh, net profit of Rs. 7.63 lakh, increase in sales by 30 percent. For the month of August 1999, company registered sales of Rs 98.59 lakh and net profit of Rs 9.30 lakh.

For the month of November 1999, Shrechem showed improved performance in production by 82 percent, gross sales of Rs. 210.46 lakh (55 percent), PAT of Rs.18 lakh and Cash profit of Rs. 31 lakh. The company started concentrating on higher value added products and also made a break through by exporting 17 tonnes of Sodium Lactate to Japan. Company achieved monthly average sales of Rs. 32.34 lakh, gross profit margins increased from 15 percent to 21 percent net profit stands at Rs. 8.66 lakh during period ended March 31, 2000.

On January 4, 2001, Mr. Prasanna informed the Board, promoters' plans to offer to GVFL a proposal to buyout its stake for Rs 17 lakh before March 31, 2001, subject to GVFL's approval. The buyback proposal was casually discussed in the presence of Mr. Nagarjan, MD, CVCF, who felt that the consideration for buyback was too low and the investors may wait for some more time to fetch a better price. On March 8, 01GVFL gave the divestment proposal for buyback of 3,26,800 equity shares and 1,95,000 Preference Shares held by GVFL in Shrechem Ltd to Boston Education & Software Technologies Ltd for appraisal.

On March 30, 2001, Mr. Prasanna accepted the proposal to buyback of 3,26,800 equity shares and 1,95,000 Preference Shares held by GVFL in Shrechem Ltd. On September 12, 2001, GVFL received a one time settlement amount of Rs. 15,65,400 against 3,26,800 equity shares and 1,95,000 CRPS held by GVCF-1990 in Shrechem Ltd.

6.8 Abhinav Polyesters Limited

M/s Abhinav Polyester Limited (APL) was set up as a polyester yarn texturing plant in October 1986. GIIC had sanctioned financial assistance in March 1987 for the texturing unit. After successful commissioning of the plant, the company installed a two-for-one twisting machine. The company expanded its capacity by installing another texturing machine in March 1990 under financial assistance from GIIC. The company had made cash profits for all the four previous years and had also paid dividends. GIIC had appraised the proposed expansion project of the company to set up yarn sizing and warping facilities and estimated that it would cost Rs.766 lakh for the same. It had also sanctioned Rs.66 lakh under the Equipment Refinancing Scheme to the company.

The company was engaged in the manufacture of textured and twisted yarn at GIDC, Chhatral, Dist. Mehsana, Ahmedabad. The proposed diversification was to be made at Jalalpur, Taluka Dholka for sizing, warping and weaving of yarn.

GVFL Assistance: In 1991, Gujarat Venture Finance Limited had received a proposal from APL, an existing company, for equity participation in their proposed expansion project. The company was proposing to finance its expansion project by way of additional equity of Rs. 545 lakh. Being an existing profit making company, APL was eligible to offer equity shares at a premium. A premium of Rs. 7.5 per share was considered reasonable looking at the then net worth of the company and its proposed expansion plan. The cost of the project was Rs. 811.00 lakh.

On August 25, 1992 the Board of GVFL approved equity participation by way of subscription to 3,00,000 equity shares at a premium of Rs. 7.5 per share aggregating to Rs. 52.50 lakh. GVFL disbursed the amount in one single disbursement on November 20, 1992. The income to GVFL is expected in the form of dividends and sale of share and IRR of 25 percent on the basis of book value. APL was charged with the upfront fee of Rs. 7.5 lakh.

On September 16, 1992, IDBI gave an in-principle approval to grant term loan assistance of Rs.300 lakh under

ERS. A certificate of expenses incurred by APL towards project completion (Rs. 47.63 lakh), the authorised (Rs. 6.00 lakh) and paid-up equity share capital (Rs. 2.00 lakh) was obtained from Sanghvi & Associates, Chartered Accountants.

On November 20, 1992 SEBI acknowledged receipt of the draft prospectus for the public issue of APL. On November 25, 1992, Bank of Baroda enhanced working capital limits of the texturising and weaving divisions of APL as follows: Texturising division - CC (Rs. 60 lakh); BP/BD (Rs. 80 lakh); Inland L/c (Rs. 25 lakh); Deferred payment guarantee (Rs. 5.30 lakh); Weaving division (fresh limits) - Foreign L/c (Rs. 70 lakh); Specific guarantee (Rs. 25 lakh); Deferred payment guarantee (Rs. 275 lakh).

A visit by GVFL officers was made to the texturising unit at Chhatral and weaving unit at Dholka were made on April 8, 1993. The texturising unit had three machines and was completely commissioned. The weaving unit was not fully commissioned yet. It was likely to start commercial production by July/August 1993. APL had recruited senior professionals for Dholka project in the areas of Production, Administration and Finance. Sales for the first quarter constituted 35.7 percent of total sales of FY1992-93.

By the end of June 1993, APL successfully made the public issue of its shares priced at Rs. 17.50 per share. The issue was fully subscribed. APL achieved a capacity utilization of 89 percent for texturising and twisting for the year ended March 31, 1993. The company had imported 16-second handlooms from Belgium. The erection work was expected to start from July 1993. The company proposed to start commercial production for weaving from August 1993.

In the first half financial year of 1993-94, the sales increased by 48 percent and net profits by 61 percent. GVFL suggested APL to appoint part-time company secretary, marketing arrangements with companies like Mafatlal companies. The financial performance of the company was reviewed and it was observed that APL had a encouraging performance in the face of a general depressive phase in the textile industry with high excise levies in the Union Budget and rising cotton prices. It was also seen that the sales in the texturing divisions were affected due to transporter's strike in September 1993 and texturiser's strike in March 1994.

Considering the overall satisfactory performance of APL, the Directors recommended a dividend of 10 percent on the enhanced equity share capital of the company.

During the first half financial year of 1994, the turnover of the company increased by 53 percent, gross profit improved by 60.2 percent, Net profit increased by 75 percent, interest costs had risen due to availability of IDBI loan and increased working capital facilities. A detailed survey of the Denim market in India was carried out and following strategic steps were suggested: Quick assimilation of buyer requirements, concentrating on creating and developing a market for newer denims, etc. On December 14, 1994, GVFL received net dividend of Rs. 2.08 lakh.

The second half financial year of 1994-95 was considered the worst period for the textile industry particularly for texturising, cotton spinning and fabric sectors because of high cotton prices, stiff consumer resistance to price increase, imposition of excise duty in texturising, etc. The Board of GVFL felt to make up for the lost time and to pick up the opportunities that lie ahead. It was suggested that APL must gear-up and add balancing and additional equipments and install value-addition facilities. The Board discussed the need for increasing texturising capacity, developing value-addition facilities by putting yarn dyeing for dyeing polyester and cotton yarns and putting fabric processing facilities to process high quality fabrics. The Board approved the idea for this project with an outlay of Rs.10 crore. A proposal of sale and leaseback of the existing machine at texturising plant was discussed and the MD of APL was advised to put forward such a proposal for consideration if only felt desirable.

During the financial year 1995-96, sales increased by 41

percent, PBDIT increased by 102 percent, PAT increased by 56 percent. On October 19, 1995 GVFL asked for the profitability margins of texturising and weaving divisions of APL. It also asked APL to explain high level of loans and advances of Rs. 43 lakh at a time when the company was facing liquidity crisis and was forced to avail ICDs at a high cost. APL declared 10 percent dividend.

During January 1996 December 1996, the company proposes the expansion plan by installing 18 additional second-hand looms to increase weaving capacity to 56 lac metres p.a. at an estimated outlay of Rs. 2.25 crore. The company had already applied to GSFC for term loan of Rs. 2.00 crore. The total project cost was estimated to be Rs. 2.25 crore. The company expected to finance the remaining amount of Rs. 25 lakh through internal accruals. The company also proposed to set up a Woven Labels project with installed capacity of 263 lakh labels p.a. at an estimated cost of Rs. 2.90 crore. The project proposed to be financed by term loan of Rs. 2.50 crore from GIIC and Rs. 40 lakh from internal accruals.

The company had plans to promote a new company Abhinav Overseas Limited for implementing a yarn-dyeing unit. The project was estimated to cost Rs. 5.50 crore, which was proposed to be financed by term loan of Rs. 2.50 crore from GIIC, public issue of equity shares of Rs. 1.60 crore and promoters' contribution to equity of Rs. 1.40 crore.

On February 1, 1996, GVFL wrote a letter to APL reminding it of buying back GVFL's shareholding. The lock-in period of GVFL holding was due to expire in April 1996. GVFL also apprised APL that on the basis of the agreements executed earlier the repurchase price, based on interest formula, worked out to be Rs. 30-31 per share as against the then market price of Rs. 10-11 per share. APL was also requested to finalise modalities of repurchase at the earliest and insisted that the promoters should start repurchasing the shares at least for the amount equivalent to the dividend received by them.

Considering the then status of the texturising industry it was felt that performance of APL was not likely to improve substantially in the near future.

On April 6, 1996, GVFL communicated to APL the approval of the proposal for buy-back of its shares by the promoters, excepting the condition of sharing profits with the promoters if the shares were sold by GVFL in the market at a profit.

On November 20, 1996, GVFL handed over 1400 shares of APL to the promoters on receipt of Rs. 50000 from them and simultaneously released 1400 shares held in their name as collateral. This was as per the terms the terms and conditions of the divestment agreement.

On April 25, 1997 GVFL sent a letter to APL that the company was not performing well and that it was facing liquidity crisis. The letter also pointed out that a few parties had filed cases/sent legal notices u/s 138 (bouncing of cheques) against the company and its directors. GVFL requested APL to send the status of the various cases/notices against the company/directors and the actions proposed to be taken in the matter. It was also asked that APL send details of applications for rescheduling of loans made to institutions.

6.9 Anjali Biotech Limited

Anjali BioTech Laboratories Limited is an existing concern engaged in manufacture of Bio Fertilizer (Phosphate Solubilizing Micro-organisms) at Pune. The company has set up the plant with the installed capacity of 900 MTPA with the venture assistance of Rs. 46.00 lakh from IDBI under its VCF scheme in the year 1991 and went into production in Nov 1992.

The company has entered into marketing tie-up with M/s Zuari Agro Chemicals Ltd which markets Anjali's product under Brand name "BIOPHOS" in states of Maharashtra, Karnataka and Andhra Pradesh. With encouraging response, the installed capacity was proposed to be raised to 2400MT per annum (at the existing premises) at an estimated cost of Rs. 320 lakh- Funding proposed Rs 65 lakh from promoters including Rs 25 lakh by GVFL, Term Loan Rs. 75 lakh from IDBI and Public issue Rs 180 lakh (scheduled in February 1994). Neem based Biopesticides (6 lakh litres per annum) was also proposed for manufacture in 1994 based on the research work of Mr. Abhijit Pathak, the other main promoter.

GVFL Assistance: On October 6, 1994, GVFL accepted the proposal for setting up a plant to produce 2.50 litres p.a. of Neem based Bio-Pesticides based on the know-how developed by Shri Abhijit Pathak and granted financial assistance by way of subscription to 2,50,000 equity shares each of Rs 10 at par aggregating to Rs 25.00 lakh on firm allotment basis. The company had originally approached GVFL on 25 May 1993 for equity participation up to Rs. 30 lakh. It is not known whether GVFL could secure a copy of the originally appraised report along with the comments on dealings and creditworthiness of the main promoters in response to its letter dated 14 June'93 to IDBI. After the appraisal by IDBI the total investment has been curtailed from Rs. 320 lakh to Rs. 194 lakh.

The company approached GVFL on April 9, 1996 for financial assistance of Rs. 30 lakh by way of Fully Convertible Debentures at P/E of 4. The company stated on April 17, 1996 that IDBI agreed in principle to grant additional Venture Capital assistance for the amount of not exceeding Rs. 60 lakh as Convertible term loan to the company.

On May 18, 1996, 28th Board Meeting was held where ABIL proposed to expand manufacturing capacities of Bio fertilizers as well as Bioneem plant by addition of balancing equipment. The capacity of Bio-fertilizer was to be raised from 1500 MT p.a to 2400 MT p.a and for Bio Neem from 2.50 lakh to 6 lakh litres p.a. The expansion project cost was Rs. 115 with proposed financing by way of internal accruals Rs. 30 lakh, Convertible loan from IDBI Rs. 60 lakh and FCDs from GVFL Rs. 25 lakh carrying interest rate of 20 percent p.a.

GVFL's assistance was to be converted into equity share within 18 months of investments at P/E of 4 or Book value whichever is lower. Based on the profitability projections, the FCDs held by GVFL-1990 shall be converted into equity shares at a price of Rs. 19.18 per share.

Divestment of shares was proposed at the end of 4th & 5th year of investment at P/E ratio of 6. IRR on investment by GVFL was estimated at 35.14 percent based on the projected financial position. GVFL conveyed sanction for assistance of Rs. 25 lakh on May 29, 1996. Conversion to be effected at P/E of 4 or book value whichever is lower. Debentures carry an interest of 20 percent per annum payable half yearly. FCDs to be converted at the end of 17 months from the date of allotment based on the audited results of the year ended March 31, 1997. Company shall pay scrutiny fee of Rs. 25,000 to GVCF-90.

Supplemental shareholders agreement & Debenture Subscription Agreement were executed on August 10, 1996 and the amount of Rs. 25.00 lakh was disbursed on August 17, 1996. On December 4, 1996, maiden dividend of the company were declared in its Annual General Meeting representing 12.5 percent, an amount of Rs. 2,40,274 was paid on shares of Rs. 25 lakh. Interest on debentures was paid for the period 17.8.96 to 31.12.96.

The performance of the company was well during the year 1995 as sales increased by almost 100 percent. Company also started marketing Neem pesticide formulation using Neem oil and marketing through Zuari Agro Chemicals Ltd. The company's debtors as on 31.12.95 were very high due to the sale of Neem pesticides wherein as per the policy the payments were required to be made after 60 days. It was suggested to develop other markets where Zuari do not have representatives/network (e.g. in Gujarat) so as to reduce over dependence on single customer. The company had completed expansion of Biophos plant and the commercial production is expected to start by September 1995. Fifth annual report was published with the following details:

On March 29, 1996 performance of the company was reviewed: Total Sales for the year ended March 31, 1996 was Rs. 369 lakh, net profit of Rs. 36.52 lakh, EPS of 1.94 and Share Capital Rs. 188.85 lakh. The company has expanded its capacity of Biophos from 900 to 1160 MT and Bioneem production of 104 Kl. For the year 1996-97 company expects a sale of 1400 tonnes of Biophos and 170 Kl of Bioneem.

Provisional results for half year ending September 30, 1996 were reviewed by GVFL. The company has achieved sales of Rs. 178.31 lakh and PAT of Rs. 41.15 lakh. The company has maintained its performance in the current year and expects to improve in the second half. On March 10, 1997, ABIL proposed a new project on Photochemical for a project outlay of Rs. 725.45 lakh. The performance of the company for the year-end March 31, 1997 was reviewed with sales of Rs. 423 lakh and Net Profit of Rs. 61 lakh after Tax provision of Rs. 9 lakh. Company was facing competition for Bioneem as large manufactures like Godrej have entered the market. Budgeted sales for 1996-97 for Biophos was 1300 MT valuing Rs. 273 lakh and for Bioneem 125 KL valuing Rs. 150 lakh.

GVFL received Rs. 1,12,500 towards interest for the quarter ended March 31, 1997 and Rs. 1,10,651 towards payment of interest of fully convertible debentures on July 17, 1997. On July 29, 1997, a meeting was held with the GVFL officers regarding the proposal to diversify into Chemical Fungicides and Biocontrol Agents at the cost of Rs. 579 lakh.

However, a need was felt to access the present demand supply scenario of all proposed products and the marketing strategy planned by the company as it will have to directly or indirectly compete with some of the leading MNCs. In a Annual General Meeting held on September 23, 1997, the company proposed to make a bonus issue in proportion of one share for every three shares and dividend of 5 percent. The company also offered GVFL to opt for early conversion of FCDs into equity shares. On a visit to the company by the

GVFL officers, it was revealed that the promoters visit the factory once a month and therefore constant involvement in company's operation was suggested. Company had received a letter from IDBI for not clearing the interest of Rs. 9.1 lakh due to liquidity crisis.

On November 14, 1997, GVFL agreed for early conversion of FCDs and requested for the interest till date of conversion and share certificate. On January 31, 1998, GVFL received Rs. 1,01,096 towards interest on the FCDs for the period October 1, 1997 to December 21, 1997 calculated @ 20 percent, share certificate towards 2.5 lakh shares and Rs. 1,25,000 towards dividend for the year 1996-97. Cost study of the company was carried out. It was observed that the sales of both the products (Bioneem & Biophos) had dropped significantly due to poor off-take by Zuari Agro ChemiBals and irregular monsoon. Zuari markets the company's products in Maharashtra, Andhra Pradesh and Karnataka. The pick-up of Bioneem has been lower since Zuari has started sourcing part of its requirements from one more company. The pick-up of Bio phos is lower due to lower rains in areas growing Sugarcane and Cotton where it finds major application.

In order to increase sales of Bioneem, company has tied up with Chambal Fertilizers Limited for selling products in UP, Punjab, Harayana and Bihar and has also developed a new product "Neemayu" which will improve the effectiveness of urea when applied along with it. For the year 1997-98 the production of Bioneem was 56 kl and Biophos 840 Tpa. The employees expenses have increased marginally from Rs. 34.9 lakh to Rs. 36.00 lakh, Selling, distribution and administration expenses as percentage of sales increased from 6.5 percent to 8.6 percent due to lower sales, operating Profit Margin decreased from 29.92 percent to 27.46 percent, interest has gone up sharply from 12.08 percent to 17.11 percent, depreciation increased from Rs. 17.3 lakh to Rs. 20.5 lakh due to addition of automatic mixing and packaging plant and Net profit has come down from Rs. 55.37 lakh to Rs. 8.98 lakh.

Equity has increased from Rs. 188.84 lakh to Rs. 326.10lakh due to conversion of debentures held by GVFL and Promoters into equity and subsequent bonus issue. Net worth has increased from Rs. 287.11 lakh to Rs. 356.68 lakh due to issue of bonus shares, and reserves has gone down from Rs. 98 lakh to Rs. 30.5 lakh resulting in a reduction in Book Value from Rs. 15.20 to Rs. 10.98 per share. Debt-equity ratio has improved from 0.72 to 0.61 as IDBI has converted a part of loan into equity.

On February 18, 2000, a letter was sent by ABIL to GVFL regarding offering of shares to some buyer at a discount and also proposed selling shares at Rs. 4 per share to GVFL. With respect to the above letter on March 4, 2000, a divestment note of Anjali BioTech Ltd was prepared and placed before the divestment committee of GVFL.

Due to deterioration in performance and poor liquidity position, the company is unable to pay and dues to IDBI since March 1999 and has over-dues of Rs. 57.81 lakh. The company is not in a position to clear even the current dues and has made an application for rescheduling.

As a desperate measure, the company has offered its neem plant on job working basis for a nominal charge, which might reduce the cash losses to some extent. However, on the whole, the performance is unlikely to show major improvement over the next 2-3 years. It may also be mentioned that even though the promoters are technically sound they lack focus and have been trying to introduce new products before consolidating earlier projects, which has affected the performance and led to serious differences in the past.

On March 11, 2000, a meeting was held by the divestment committee of GVFL and approved the divestment of 6.5 lakh shares of Anjali BioTech (India) Limited at Rs. 4 per share or a negotiation price above Rs 4 per share. On March 14, 2000, ABIL also agreed in principle to accept the offer for acquiring holding of 6.5 lakh shares in Anjali BioTech for a total consideration of Rs. 26 lakh (at Rs 4 per share), which was valid for a period of 45 days from the date of the letter. Finally on March 16, 2000, GVFL sent the confirmation to accept the offer to buyback the shares of Anjali BioTech.

6.10 Microtech Private Limited

Microtech Private Limited, an existing Pune based Company started in the year 1980, engaged in manufacture of Special Digital Systems and other high technology electronics items for wide range of industrial applications. Since its inception, there has been steady growth in Company's operations. The Company has created necessary infrastructure and also built up a professional team. The Company had a turnover of Rs. 49.00 lakh, Paid up capital of Rs. 7.56 lakh and nominal loss of Rs. 5.25 lakh for the year-end March 1992. The company after having its operations stabilized at profitable level is now on the threshold of substantially increasing its turnover and profitability by entering into high technology Defense Electronics and sophisticated Consumer Electronics segment.

As a result of Company's own continuous research and development efforts Microtech has successfully developed Flight Data Acquisition & Analysis System (FDAAS) for Defense Aviation for the first time in the country. Microtech has already supplied eight such systems for MIG 27 and MIG 29 aircrafts valued approx. at Rs. 80 lakh. Such systems were so far being imported by Defense. FDAAS, which are very important for Air safety, are currently being imported. Such imported systems cost around Rs. 70.00 lakh to Rs. 80.00 lakh, whereas the cost of systems supplied by Microtech is substantially lower as compared to imported ones (approx. $1/6^{th}$ of imported price). Even at the lower price, profit margins are attractive.

The company after having developed FDAAS for MIG 27 and MIG 29 Aircrafts is now trying to develop FDAAS for other types of Aircrafts. This would not only increase its market share but also open up the lucrative export market. The

Company has also indigenously developed Car Remote Controller (CRC) for the export market. This product has also received encouraging enquiries from overseas customers and also offers an attractive margin.

GVFL Assistance: Microtech has already developed FDAAS System for Russian Standard Fighter Aircraft (MIG 27 & MIG 29) and has successfully supplied eight systems (order value Rs. 80.00 lakh approx.) to Indian Air Force (IAF). Further developments to make system compatible for other types of Defense Aircrafts as also for other segments like Civil Aviation, Export etc. is proposed to be undertaken, for which they have approached GVFL for assistance.

The project cost estimated at Rs. 49.50 lakh is proposed to be financed by way of Additional Equity of Rs. 8.5 lakh by promoters, equity of Rs. 25.00 lakh and Redeemable Cumulative Preference Shares of Rs. 16.00 Lakh from Gujarat Venture Capital Fund-1990 (GVCF-1990). Income to GVFL is expected in the form of dividends of equity and preference shares and sale of equity shares with an expected IRR of 39.72 percent.

It was proposed to form a monitoring committee consisting of officers: Shri Vishnu Varshney and Shri Vipul Mankad. All major decisions were taken by the committee members and feedback on periodic reports, status of product development, marketing plan, recruitment, traveling plan etc were required to be submitted by the company. The decisions were carefully taken at the policy level so that the monitoring by GVFL could act complementary to the efforts of promoters.

On May 16, 1992, GVFL accepted the proposal of Microtech and in principle granted venture capital assistance of Rs. 41.00 lakh comprising of direct subscription to equity of Rs. 25.00 lakh at par and CRPS of Rs. 16.00 lakh. On June 18, 1992, GVFL disbursed Rs. 16,50,000 against Equity subscription, venture capital assistance to MPL and on July 15, 1992, Rs. 8.55 lakh were disbursed for a shareholding of 49.94 percent. GVFL appraised the status of the company. There was increase in the range of the Car Remote Controller and was also introduced to a USA based supplier of CRC. On August 20, 1992, the Company was converted into Public Limited: Microtech Limited (ML) and was advised to take effective steps for increasing its working capital limits from the Bank. ML also participated in Moscow Air show

During the first half year ended September 31, 1992, company suffered loss of Rs. 9.24 lakh which was mainly due to interest burden, sales was (Rs. 11.53 lakh) below break-even, increase in term loan from Rs. 15.94 lakh to Rs. 18.15 lakh, unsecured deposits/loans of Rs.1.66 lakh were repaid. Low turnover of Rs. 42.00 lakh due to lack of orders that were expected to be received from the Defense Aviation and Russia. The company was also expecting order from Indian Air Force. The technical development of CRC was completed but had some finishing problem. It was suggested to place order for moulds with reputed supplier like Philips for making an export quality goods.

After great efforts on August 25, 1993, Microtech received Defence order for FDA which was delivered for worth Rs 18 lakh, supplied two Response Measurement Systems' for IMRB on trial basis and 15 encoders within 6 months. The company has received development orders for "Picture Data Inscription and Transmission device" from Defense for its project VICON, for "Micro Processor based Test Rigs" from M/s Bajaj Auto Ltd for Speedometers. Company has received good response for its People Meter from IMRB and expects to receive repeat orders for 200 units. With all the above efforts and enquiries from Customers, the turnover was expected to reach Rs. 80-10 lakh.

The company achieved turnover of approx. Rs. 123.00 lakh by the end of December 1995 through sale of standard products, Peole Meter and FDA. It was further expected to increase to Rs. 220 lakh to Rs. 230 lakh by the end of financial year. Dr. Narsimha informed that they have dispatched 2 FDAs to Malaysia. Company has cleared all the outstanding term loans with Bank of Baroda and has availed working facilities to the tune of Rs. 15 to 17 lakh. It was also informed that M/s Crown Corporation Ltd is not responding to the efforts for settling outstanding dues of Rs. 9.00 lakh. A legal action was taken and in response to the notice, MOU was signed with Microtech wherein Crown Corporation would pay Rs. 3.00 lakh upfront and the balance Rs. 5 lakh on successful installation of FDA. In order to strengthen its existing infrastructure, company is in the process of recruiting personnel for the post of General Manager, Finance Manager & Company Secretary and R&D Engineer.

On September 10, 1996, Microtech Limited proposed for financial assistance for expansion and diversification which was accepted in principle and GVCF-1990 granted financial assistance by way of subscription to 50,000,20 Unsecured Redeemable Partly Convertible Debentures of Rs. 100 each aggregating to Rs. 50 lakh on firm allotment basis but as per the condition Microtech is required to obtain satisfactory order from IMRB prior to seeking the disbursement.

On September 27, 1997, GVFL meeting with the Microtech Ltd was held with the purpose to know about the proposed buyer. Dr. Narsimha indicated that a Mumbai based investor (Mr. Ramesh Nair), who is interested in Microtech Ltd in software business and may want Microtech to get into Software.

It was observed that apart from the financial performance the staff strength also reduced from 40 to 20. The company is expecting sales for the year 1997-98 of Rs 30-40 lakh and a loss for the period of Rs 15-20 lakh as the company has executed orders of Rs. 13.22 lakh till date and pending orders are of Rs. 13.86 lakh for the year. The company has not paid salary since April 1997 and PF, ESIC dues amounting to Rs. 3.5 lakh since January 1997 as the company is facing liquidity problems. Dr. Narsimha is exploring new business avenues like: The company is negotiating with TCS for providing manpower for providing Y2K solutions, pursing with Birla Exports for FDAAS order.

Looking at the above position, GVFL requested Microtech to settle the statutory dues and the interest dues of Bank of India to the tune of Rs. 1.66 lakh for the period ended Sep 1997 in order to avoid getting classified as NPA.

In 1998-99, a visit was paid by the GVFL officers and observed that the company is expected turnover of about Rs. 24 lakh, net loss of Rs. 30 lakh wiping out its complete net worth, high debtors, inventory of Rs. 46.34 lakh fixed salary expenses of Rs. 2 lakh per month, wage bill reduced to Rs. 70,000 and with a skeletal staff of 16 persons. The company had statutory outstanding of about Rs. 4 lakh of PF, and Rs. 37,000 of TDS. Due to the under performance of the company, unsecured loans from promoters were exceeding 10 percent of the paid up capital and free reserves and other unsecured loans exceeding 25 percent of the paid up capital and free reserves. These deposits from public and shareholders were above the limit prescribed by the company's act. As Microtech has failed to pay the interest dues for the last 3 quarters, it has been declared as NPA.

On December 28, 1999, Board meeting was held with respect to the proposal for Divestment of Microtech Ltd and approved divestment of entire stake of GVCF-1990 in M/s Microtech Ltd in favor of M/s Natasha Consultants, Pune for a consideration of Rs. 7 lakh. On February 18, 2000, an agreement was signed between GVFL, Microtech and M/s Natasha Consultants

6.11 Hartec Seamless Limited

The company traces its origin to Hartec Engineers Pvt. Ltd., a Private Limited Company incorporated in 1980 at Ahmedabad, with the immediate object of manufacturing Steel Tubes and Pipes. The Unit was established at a cost of Rs. 12 lakh at the GIDC (Gujarat Industrial Development Corporation) Industrial Estate in Naroda, Ahmedabad. Production of Carbon Steel Seamless Tubes started in March

1982 and the company posted net profits in the very first year of its operations. The Company has grown steadily thereafter and has registered Sales of Rs. 213.71 lakh and Net profits of Rs. 21.27 lakh for the year ended March 31, 1992. The Company was changed into a Public Limited Company, Hartec Seamless Limited (HSL) and a fresh Certificate of Incorporation was obtained on May 28, 1992.

GVFL Assistance: On the August 11, 1992 Gujarat Venture Finance Limited (GVFL) received an invitation from PROMOTER on behalf of HSL for equity participation of Rs. 25 lakh to meet the long-term working capital requirements and to enlist the shares of the company on the Stock Exchanges.

From the appraisal report it is clear that company has a potential to raise its capacity utilization and turnover substantially with the availability of working capital funds. It is an existing, profit-making company, under an able management, is seeking to expand rapidly by taking advantage of its reputation and good scope in the market. The entrepreneurs have a strong technical background that is a major advantage. The promoters have issued bonus shares in the ratio of 1:1 and thereby increased the equity base of the promoters to Rs.49.6 lakh. The total promoter's contribution is envisaged at Rs. 140 lakh i.e. 32.94 percent of the enhanced equity of Rs. 425 Lakh.

Though the investment proposal was attractive but GVFL did not agree at the first approach, as GVFL was more interested in investing in company that can go for some innovation and as they were asking money for their filling up of the working capital gap it was not possible for GVFL to make the investment in such a situation. On the next approach HSL came up with the innovative project of manufacture of Stainless Steel Welded tubes with on line annealing process. Actually this project consisted of two phases: On line annealing in Phase I and on-line Eddy Current Testing in Phase-II.

Though the first proposal was first of 25 lakh but as the company was planning for a IPO within a year hence according to SEBI guideline HSL could not offer GVFL at discount. Hence GVCF-1990 proposes to invest Rs. 37.5 Lakh in the equity share capital of the company in 2,50,000 shares @ Rs.10 per share and a premium of 5 Rs. The present book value of the share was Rs. 14.43. The returns to GVCF-1990 were expected in the form of dividend and appreciation at the time of disinvestment of the equity. The yield formula gives a return of 33.33 percent. It was noticed that return to GVFL will be more than 25 percent in any case. Hence it was supposed to be a profitable investment for the fund.

GVFL appointed M/s Chowksi & Co. Chartered Accountant as the Concurrent Auditors. Still HSL did not provide with enough details as and when required by the appointed auditors. As a matter of fact GVFL appointed the said auditors as early as May 22, 1995. In spite of valiant effort from GVFL's side HSL did not produce the required document saying that the documents are present in the factory premises, which has been confiscated by GIIC.

Though many a time HSL consistently requested for not presenting the cheques that were given to GVFL as a part of buy-back agreement. But GVFL did not agree to those as HSL as per the Buy-back Agreement were liable to pay the due as can be understood from the letters to HSL.

In this regard both the promoters were arrested on the basis of the cases listed above. They were arrested on September 12, 1996 for bouncing of the cheque of value 17.5 lakh to GVFL.

HSL proposed to buy-back all the remaining shares at the price of Rs. 2 per share and sent a cheque of Rs. 60,000 as an advance. GVFL did not accept that offer as the price offered by them was far below the expected value.

Around this time GVFL also complained about HSL to GIIC and Canara Bank about the non-payment of dues. GIIC threatened to act as under State Finance Corporation Act under section 29. They clearly state the following: "...how HSL entered into an agreement of buying back the equity when HSL have not fulfilled the obligation to clear the interest and installment due with GIIC."

On September 1995 GIIC threatens again to take action against HSL under section 29 of State Finance Corporation Act and finally on January 2, 1996 GIIC sealed the factory of HSL. Interestingly this incident was used by HSL as an excuse of not producing the required documents asked for the concurrent auditing as ordered by the High Court.

Later on February 13, 1996 High court of Gujarat proposed to sell off the surplus assets of the HSL, and to use proceeds of such sales to pay and completely liquidate loan availed by GIIC for the purpose.

GVFL also warned GSFC about HSL. HSL approached GSFC for availing 'Bill Discounting Facilities'. At that point HSL was doing business of EPBAX under another name from the same office of HSL.

From the documents, one of the cheques has been honored by one of the promoter and hence the total inflow from this investment comes out to be around Rs. 13 lakh for GVFL. GVFL went for out of the court settlement with one of the promoter and has withdrawn the cases against him. The other case against the other promoter is still pending. The other promoter is right now absconding from the country.

It was expressly understood between GVFL, the promoters and HSL that the funds raised from GVFL against its investment in HSL as shall be utilized by HSL for the purpose of procurement of on-line induction heating and forced water quenching equipment. This was also stated in the Prospectus of HSL issued for raising the capital. HSL could not acquire the said equipment in spite of its various efforts at the relevant time and subsequently the proposal for the said acquisition had to be abandoned.

There was a continuous increase in amount of Sundry Debtors more interestingly HSL in spite of not making expected turnovers was continuously writing off those debtors as bad debt. This was also brought into the notice of HSL by GVFL in several letters. Promoters were siphoning off the money from the company's account for themselves. When GVFL asked for the list of debtors most of the companies were located in or around Punjab and many of the companies may also be fictitious as suspected by GVFL.

Suspecting the above manipulation GVFL asked for concurrent auditors. In the year 1995 that on a turnover of Rs.109.94 lakh, company has incurred gross loss of Rs. 222.97 lakh, company incurred gross loss of Rs. 222.97 lakh. Besides, an amount of Rs. 187.94 lakh (as against 12.8 lakh in the previous year) has been shown as write off as Bad Debts. In the year 1996, HSL proposed to write off bad debts in the tune of 180 lakh. GVFL vehemently opposed this move asked the promoter to take strong steps to recover the debts written off. Other irregularities were also shown by the company like they did not held the board meeting between September 1996 and July 1997 which was gross violation of Companies Act 1956.

GVFL also complained to the Registrar of the Companies about these irregularities. GVFL even inspected Company's Record from Roc's office. It was observed that management has defaulted in filling the annual Returns and Balance Sheets, for the respective years within stipulated time. Not only that they also did not filed the Annual Returns ending June 30, 1995 till October 1996. GVFL also proposed to Roc to prosecute the promoters of HSL under section 162, 168, 210(5) and 220(3) of the Companies Act, 1956.

On the issue of concurrent auditors GVFL filed a case in High Court. In the defense HSL argued that the Shareholders agreement was done before the public issue and was not verified by the shareholders later on hence it was void. GVFL made a strong reply to this defense.

6. 12 Beautiful Dekor Limited

M/s Beautiful Dekor Limited engaged in the manufacture

Specialty grade decorative laminates. These laminates were proposed to be introduced for the first time in the country. The company planned to give major thrust to exports and expected export income to contribute to around 50 percent-60 percent of the turnover. While the company would initially export Specialty grade laminates, these products would also be gradually introduced in the domestic market with increase in awareness and applicability.

GVFL Assistance: In 1993, M/s Beautiful Dekor Limited had approached GVFL for equity participation to part finance its project to manufacture Specialty grade decorative laminates. As part of its pre-disbursement due- diligence, GVFL sought a creditworthiness report and repute of Dr. Sujal Gokhle and his associate concern M/s Sundek India Limited from Bank of Baroda, Usmanpura Branch in Ahmedabad. The bank's reply was positive as far as dealings in the cash credit account maintained with the bank was concerned and it assigned a health code of 1 (one) to M/s Sundek India Limited. Continuing with fulfilling of pre-disbursement conditions, GVFL instructed BDL to make certain changes in the draft prospectus filed with SEBI for public issue of equity shares to the tune of Rs. 236.50 lakh.

GVFL's disbursement of Rs. 32.50 lakh was made in one shot on August 23, 1993. Equity shares (of Rs. 10 each at par) were finally allotted in GVFL's favor on October 13, 1993. Returns to GVFL–1990 were expected in the form of dividend and appreciation realized at the time of disinvestment of the equity shares. There is only one listed company M/s Bakelite Hylam, which primarily manufactures industrial laminates. Market price of its share is Rs. 47.50 with P/E ratio of 28. The project cost was estimated at Rs. 430 lakh.

On December 2, 1993, a news report appeared in The Economic Times that the city civil court of Morvi had directed BDL to maintain status quo on the allotment of shares alleging irregularities. GVFL asked BDL to immediately take corrective actions and provide the following information: basis of allotment of shares and approval of concerned stock exchanges; date of allotment of shares floated in Public Issue along with certified true copy of the resolutions and also copy of Form no.2 filed with ROC along with copy of receipt issued by ROC. BDL provided the above details after a reminder from GVFL.

BDL clarified through a detailed communiqué dated January 4, 1994 that disgruntled people filed various civil suits at various places and were able to get ex-parte ad-interim orders against allotment, dispatch, transfer of share certificates, listing on stock exchanges and utilization of public issue funds. However, BDL was able to get the couple of ex-parte orders vacated by the High Court of Gujarat. In addition to that, Ahmedabad and Bombay Stock Exchanges had already given BDL permission to list the equity shares within a specified time frame.

On January 5, 1994, a telephonic request was made by BDL for immediate requirement of Board resolution for opening of L/C for imported equipments. It was communicated by GVFL that its nominees could not attend Board Meetings at such short notices and advised BDL to plan Board Meeting and circulate the agenda in advance. GVFL also dissented in passing the circular resolution for the above because of non-confirmation of compliance with provisions of sections 289 and 292 of Companies Act, 1956.

Beautiful Dekor submitted to GVFL on January 13, 1994, a 90-day final report of the lead manager (from the closure of the public issue), copy of letter from Ahmedabad Stock Exchange permitting trading in its equity shares from 10th January 1994. It also clarified that none of the ad-interim orders effective against the company were on utilization of funds raised through public issue. Dr. Sujal Gokhle later on in a meeting with GVFL officials clarified that a group of speculators have contributed to the controversy of irregularity in share allotment with the ulterior motive of delaying the delivery of shares in the market so that their commitment of honoring their transactions could be delayed or avoided. On January 22, 1994 BDL informed GVFL that the Supreme Court of India had stayed the operation of the interlocutory orders made by various civil courts and had also stayed further proceedings in these suits until further orders. Hence, there was no operative injunction against BDL.

Mr. K.S. Varma relinquished the post of Director of BDL on May 5, 1994 and Mr. Vipul Mankad, Chief Manager (P&O), GVFL, was appointed as a nominee director on the Board of BDL. A Board Meeting of Beautiful Dekor Limited was held on June 28, 1994 to discuss the financial performance: the cost overrun in completion of the project was shown to be Rs. 70 lakh on that date (Rs. 410 lakh against Rs. 340 lakh (appraised)); that BDL proposed to approach its banker, Union Bank of India for bridge loan against subsidy after the sanction of its working capital limit (likely to be Rs. 200 lakh); that BDL would also undertake a detailed exercise for estimation of overrun and assessment of fund requirement for project completion and working capital margins; the Board also approved issuing of forfeiture notice for non-payment of outstanding call money on equity shares.

On September 1, 1994 GVFL asked for the justification of placing inter-corporate deposit of Rs. 30 lakh in favor of two public limited companies, which were defaulting in payment of principal and interest. GVFL also wanted to know the steps being taken by BDL for recovery of the amount. GVFL conveyed that its objection in the above matter be recorded in the minutes of the Board meeting on August 31, 1994, convened to approve accounts for FY 1993-94. Beautiful Dekor provided a justification saying that it wanted to recover part of interest costs on Rs. 100 lac bridge loan from IDBI and for that it had placed Rs. 30 lakh as inter-corporate deposit.

In a meeting with GVFL on January 8, 1996, Dr. Sujal Gokhle informed that BDL had already forwarded a list of forfeited shares to the concerned stock exchanges and therefore any such forfeited share given as delivery would be regarded as a bad delivery. He also informed that BDL had received a proposal for a Bombay based investor for taking up the forfeited shares at a premium, which was under negotiation. He also said that BDL was facing problems of availability of furnace oil and therefore proposed to increase the storage capacity after obtaining requisite permissions. Possibility of buy-back of GVFL shares by the promoters were also discussed in the meeting. Dr. Gokhle indicated that BDL was willing to consider the proposal.

On January 29, 1996, GVFL informed BDL about the necessity of conducting secretarial audit of transfer of shares and also of appointment of internal auditor. On February 5, 1996, GVFL wrote to advocate, Shri Ashok Gandhi about the non-cooperation from BDL for enabling secretarial audit of transfer of shares. GVFL indicated that it may have to take unpleasant action in this regard.

GVFL obtained the detailed list of forfeited shares of BDL submitted to Ahmedabad and Mumbai Stock Exchanges along with the advertisement released in a leading newspaper (Indian Express) and also the copies of the letters sent to Ahmedabad and Mumbai Stock Exchanges for forfeiture of shares.

A certificate was obtained from M/s Myraj Consultancy Pvt. Ltd, registrars and share transfer agents of BDL, about the summary of share transfer requests received during September-December 1995. It was indicated that only one share certificate was received for transfer during the quarter, which had earlier been forfeited by BDL.

On October 18, 1996, GVFL wrote a letter to Union Bank of India, Relief Road Branch, Ahmedabad, asking the latter to send a statement of accounts of BDL for the months of September and October 1993. This period was just after disbursement from GVFL was made.

GVFL wrote a letter to BDL on October 25, 1996, reminding the latter of delay in finalizing the annual accounts for FY 1995-96. BDL was asked to inform about completion of audit and scheduling of board meeting.

On November 6, 1996, a request was sent by GVFL to Union Bank of India, Relief Road Branch, Ahmedabad, to send a statement of BDL's account operations since opening of the account. On this date GVFL wanted to know about the status of the lawsuit filed against M/s Ambic Proteins Ltd, with whom Rs. 30 lakh ICD (Inter-Corporate Deposits) was placed three years ago and which was then defaulting on repayments. GVFL wanted to know about the details of transfers of shares in the name of Dr. Sujal Gokhle/Rupal Gokhle. Finally, GVFL wanted an update of the legal cases filed against BDL.

On November 28, 1996, GVFL sent a letter to BDL saying that annual accounts and details thereof were given during the board meeting on November 27. This was pointed out to be an insufficient notice. Further, there was a large variation in the net loss (it had increased by more than Rs. 60 lakh from the provisional figure of Rs. 121 lakh to the final reported figure of Rs. 183 lakh), which, it was pointed out, constituted violation of listing agreements of stock exchanges. Further, auditors had qualified the accounts with serious remarks about recording of fixed assets, valuation of stocks, need to strengthen internal control system, recovery of deposits, etc. GVFL communicated its dissent on the agenda item for passing of annual accounts for the FY 1995-96. Further on November 30, 1996, GVFL wrote to BDL seeking clarification on the following: variation in provisional and audited results, auditor's remarks, valuation of finished goods, fixed assets register being incomplete, granting of interest-free unsecured loan to a firm in which director of the company was interested, ICD of Rs. 30 lakh placed with M/s Ambic Proteins Limited and legal suit filed thereof and various other operational details.

A formal request was received from BDL on December 30, 1996 for issuing no-objection certificate for sending back defective moulds to Germany for examination. This was in the case filed against Hindrichs-Auffarmann, the German manufacturer of the moulds. GVFL replied that it could issue a no-objection certificate if BDL could obtain approval of SBI and GSFC for reshipment of the plates to Germany, all necessary approvals/clearances for sending those plates, necessary permission for payment of lawyer's fees/expenses and adequate measures of security of the said plates in Germany. GSFC via its letter dated January 7, 1997 declined to issue a NOC.

6.13 Esha Cubidor Containers Limited

The company incorporated on 14.6.1988 as Esha Cubidor Containers limited on June 24, 1991. An existing Company engaged in manufacturing and marketing of Rigid Foldable Containers. The Company proposes to expand its capacity, which is proposed to be financial by Public issue. The main objects of the company is to carry on the business of manufactures, processors, designers, buyers, sellers, importers and exporters of plastics rigid and folding containers and its corrugated outer cartons

GVFL Assistance: The company has successfully implemented the first phase of project by installing the Blow Moulding Machines with the financial assistance of GIIC and GSFC (Gujarat State Financial Corporation). The Company has commenced commercial production since April 1992. Esha Cubidor container was a unique product and a unique process technology. The company was a start up and the company was closely held by the technology only. The product of the company has found good acceptance in the market. It is in its Public issues. Company's Merchant Bankers M/s India Securities Limited has appraised the expansion project. The project is prima-facie attractive and offers good opportunity for investment. The company has planned to expand its capacity from 10.56 lakh containers to 37.54 lakh containers by installing four blow molding lines from M/s Klockner. The company has approached GVFL for equity participation of Rs. 25 lakh @ Rs. 10 per share, as a co-promoter on firm–

allotment basis. The cost of the project was estimated to Rs. 574.74 lakh. Incomes to GVFL are expected in the form of sales of equity shares. P/E ratio of the listed companies of the plastic packaging industry was in the range of 15.25 but taking a conservative approach, P/E ratio was assumed to be 8, IRR of 16 percent. Most importantly, GVFL had an exit option available as the company was planning to go in for an IPO in near future.

GVFL did close monitoring which included regular visits to the company, attending the board meeting, asking for the balance sheet and P&L accounts looking in to the debtors list and age cycle analysis. GVFL was also asking for the periodical reporting of cash flow, P&L and Financial positions, checked for the order position with quantity, amounts, payment terms and delivery schedule.

In 1993, the promoters of the company informed that expected expenditure of the Public issue to be approx Rs. 45.00 lakh. Public Issue of 27,20,000 equity shares issued by the company was fully subscribed and the allotment was made in consultation with the Stock Exchange, Ahmedabad. Appointments of shares transfer Committee to facilitate quick, shares transfer agent and a Registrar to look after the work of transfer, transmission, split etc. A meeting was conducted to discuss the order book position, statistical information and to finalize the market strategy of the company's product.

On GVFL visit it was observed that due to lack of orders, capacity utilization is low and daily production averages around 500-700 cubipacks, no problem with quality of product and availability of raw material. Main raw material LLDPE is freely available from the market, power failure was frequent, and the factory staff comprises of approximately 14 people.

On February 15, 1997, the overall performance of Esha was observed for buyback of the GVFL shares. The company was facing problems of very slow product acceptance and has been making cash losses since beginning. Accumulated losses as on March 31, 1996 were Rs. 98.06 lakh and estimated to increase to Rs. 125.00 lakh at the end of March 1997. At the time public issue the actual performance of the company was compared with the projected and was observed to be much below the projections, which was mainly due to very low product acceptance and resultant low capacity utilization. The company's diversification plan into the other packaging products likes caps and closures, PVC packaging (transparent packaging), did not materialized. The promoter was also not interested in the business. One of the promoters applied for loan from GIIC for a new business. It is also observed that the relation between the two promoter viz. Mr. Chimanlal Kapoor and Mr. Bakul Sharma strained over a period. Considering the above-mentioned points, it was felt that the performance of the company will not improve significantly in near future. Even if the company turns around, it would take long time before it can wipe out its accumulated losses.

The scrip was trading at an average of Rs. 1.75, the historical low price for the company and the volume was also low. Between October 1, 1996 and December 1, 1996, the peak volume was 2000 share and price was Rs. 2.00 per share. Holding the equity for more time may further lead to reduction in the share price and thus in the investment. On March 1997, the 52-week highest was Rs. 4 and lowest was Rs. 1.00. The possibility of the strategic tie up or sell was negligible, as the company was not offering synergy to the other existing packaging firm.

Looking at all these factors GVFL decided to divest from the company. At this moment, GVFL had two options. Either divests through stock exchange or through negotiation deal with the promoter. It was observed that the SEBI takeover code would not be applicable. The buyback can be made on the basis of inter se transfer between the core-promoters and GVFL. On February 28, 1997 GVFL asked Esha Cubidor's promoters to buy back 2.5 lack equity shares from GVFL.

After considerable persuasion, on March 12, 1997, Esha Cubidor agreed to buyback the share at Rs. 4.10 per share as against the market price of around Rs. 1 or 2 per share. If the scrip were sold at a market price of Rs. 2.00 per share, GVFL would have made a loss of 20 lakh. So after evaluating company's performance, stock market condition and the market price of the scrip, GVFL fetched a good price of Rs. 4.10 per share.

During the negotiations, promoters of the Esha Cubidor have requested to allow purchase in four installments over four months viz. April 1997, May 1997, June 1997 and July 1997 which GVFL had accepted, GVFL received payments aggregating to Rs. 10,24,500 (instead of Rs. 10,25,000)

The performance of the Esha Cubidor never matched with the projected one. The major reason for under performance was the inadequate utilization of the capacity. The product was not accepted in the market. Being a new product, the marketing efforts done by promoters were not adequate. So the failure of the company can be attributed to two major reason and that are: product failure and poor marketing & advertising efforts. Esha Cubidor failed on managing regular orders from any major clients. The company had never developed any client specific packaging and the technology was also not able to support customization. The company got few orders from the Hindustan Lever and IBP but later on it failed to generate repeat and big orders from these clients. The marketing team of the Esha Cubidor was not able to get repeat orders from clients like Pidilite Ltd. as they felt that the containers were not suitable for its products. Esha Cubidor was concentrating on Chemical exporters, FMCG and food companies. The marketing staff was also visiting industrial areas. So instead of giving advertisements in the business newspaper, magazines and trade magazines, the company gave advertisements in the local daily and English dailies.

This shows that the company had not prepared their marketing strategy properly and was lacking a business vision. Private companies and government organizations were the big clients of Esha, but it never tried to approach these government agencies and organizations. Middle East and African countries were looking for alternative packaging material but Esha failed to explore these potential markets. The promoters were experienced in a plastic manufacturing but they were lacking on a marketing front. Later on one of the promoters applied to GIIC for the loan for new business which showed that their interest in the product and company had reduced.

7

Characteristics and Contractual Performance of Firms Funded by GVFL

7.1 Characteristics/Profile of Entrepreneurs

The characteristics of the following firms and entrepreneurs have been studied by analyzing the profile of entrepreneur, date of incorporation, project location and various other factors:

1. Madhulika Ceramics India Limited.
2. Medisurg Surgico Limited.
3. Bals Limited.
4. Suman Cables Limited.
5. Campco Industries Limited.
6. Vikram Industries Limited.
7. Shrechem Limited.
8. Abhinav Polyester Limited.
9. Anjali Bio Tech Limited.
10. Microtech Limited.
11. Hartec Seamless Limited.
12. Beautiful Dekor Limited.
13. Esha Cubidor Containers Limited.

These indicators of characteristics help in analyzing the contractual performance of the firm.

Most of the companies approached GVFL between 1990-94. On an average every year GVFL received and disbursed two projects.

Most of the proposals received the financial assistance in the same year when they approached GVFL. Appraisal of the project and other market research took five-six months, sometimes it might have taken more time depending on the type and stage of investment.

7.1.1 Age of the Company: The companies in our sample can be divided into age groups: Infant, young and mature. Infant companies having the age from 0-5 yrs, young having age in the range of 6-20 years and mature companies of age 21 and above. In our sample, there were seven infant companies: Beautiful Dekor (0 yr), Vikram Industries (1 yr), Medisurg Surgical Ltd & Shrechem Ltd (2 yrs), Anjali Bio Tech (3 yrs) and Abhinav Polyester & Esha Cubidor (4 yrs). Four companies were young: Suman Cables (13yrs), Hartec Seamless Ltd (12 yrs), Microtech (12 yrs), Bals (8 yrs). Finally two were very old and mature companies: Campco (49 years) and Madhulika Industries Ltd (45 years).

7.1.2 Location: While considering many proposals during the course of the business, venture capital funds screen proposals on a broad basis to weed out unpromising ventures at the initial stages only. Various components become a part of such initial screening criteria. One of such components is 'Location'. As most of the studies indicate that location is a less important but considerable factor in screening, none of investors can afford not to think about location of their investment. Many of the investors have the location preferences in a country. It may be because of the benefits that a state is offering particularly for a venture in which venture capitalist is intending to invest. As the study of Pandey IM and Jang A. (1996) states that investors are very particular while choosing the location and they have regional preference also. They may want to establish himself or herself near the market where the product is to be sold or where the raw material is easily available. They are interested in setting up their industry in safe areas. The location choice may also get affected by availability of the much-desired skilled human capital in case of knowledge-based ideas.

Most of the companies located their plant in Gujarat. There were eight companies located in Gujarat and rest five in other parts of India: New Delhi, Dadra Nagar, Tamil-Nadu, and Pune.

Most of the companies were engaged in Consumer Related (4), Industrial Products (3) and one or two each in others.

7.1.3 Amount Sanctioned and Disbursed: In all the cases, the amount sanctioned by GVFL for financial assistance at the time of agreement was fully disbursed. From the above data, the amount can be grouped into three: Rs. 0-50 lakh, Rs. 51-100 lakh and Rs. 100 lakh & above. Madhulika, Ceramics (I) Ltd has received the largest amount of Rs. 244.75 lakh and Esha Cubidor Containers Ltd has received the smallest amount in our sample of Rs. 25.00 lakh. In the category of Rs. 0-50 lakh, there were five companies: Esha Cubidor, Beautiful Dekor, Hartec Ltd, Microtech Ltd and Anjali Biotech Ltd. In the category of Rs. 51-100 lakh, there were again five companies i.e. Abhinav Polyester Ltd., Shrechem Ltd, Vikram, Campco Ltd and Suman Cables Ltd. Lastly in the category of Rs. 100 lakh and above there were three companies namely: Bals Ltd, Medisurg Surgical and Madhulika Ceramics Ltd.

7.1.4 Management Fees: It is also referred as scrutiny fee or upfront end charges. It is the fee paid by the promoter(s) to GVFL for appraisal, R&D, monitoring etc.. Normally it was 1 percent of the total investment/amount disbursed by GVFL and sometimes it was lump-sum amount or fixed amount in addition to 1 percent. In our sample eight cases had paid the scrutiny fee of 1 percent of total disbursed amount. Others were charged @ 2.6 percent, 5 percent, 50 percent, 1 percent + 1.25 lakh, Rs. 7.5 lakh.

7.1.5 Stage of investment: Another important aspect of venture capital management is the stage of financing. Various studies conducted by different authors like McMillan (1985), Ray and Tupin (1993) and Pandey IM and Jang A. (1996) show that the stage of financing any venture is a major factor. The studies conclude that development and growth stages occupy the major investment in the world. Start up or seed money financing is comparatively less important. The venture capitalists think that the most important thing for them is survival and that by investing more at later stages they can survive longer. It is, however revealed in the study that the venture capitalist invests at every stage of the venture.

In our sample, seven of the thirteen cases were in the later stage of investment, having medium risk and involves expansion and diversification of the existing set –up. Next common stage is the start-up (3 cases) and seed stage (2 cases) i.e. early stage having extreme or very high risk. The purpose/objective of financing is to conceptualize product, planning, and operations/production through R&D.

Various instruments such as equity, debt, convertible instruments bearing characteristics of both debt and equity have been introduced in the venture capital industry so as to provide financial assistance to the investee companies.

In all the thirteen cases, instrument used for providing financial assistance was by way of equity participations. However, other supporting or additional instruments were Income Notes, Bridge loan, Secured Fully Convertible Debentures (SFCDs), Fully Convertible Debentures (FCDs), Cumulative Convertible Preference Shares (CCPS), Redeemable Cumulative Convertible Preference Shares (RCCPS), Optionally Cumulative Convertible Preference Shares (OCCPS).

Financial assistance provided by GVFL was recovered mainly by the scrutiny fee /management fee (13 cases) and the sale of equity shares (12 cases). Other instruments of recovery were: Interest on FCD or funded (6 cases), Dividends (5 cases), Repayment of OCCPS (3 cases), Interest on Bridge Loan (2 cases). Income Notes, Royalty, Repayment of Bridge loan, Interest on Debentures were other instruments of recovery.

7.1.6 Number of Promoters/Entrepreneurs: Out of 13 companies eight companies were family enterprise i.e. either single or more than one family member was engaged in the project (Suman cables, Shrechem Ltd, Campco (I) Ltd, Abhinav Polyester Ltd, Vikram (I) Ltd, Hartec, Beautiful Dekor and Esha Cubidor Containers. Other five were independent businesses where the promoter was the whole and sole person engaged in developing the business.

The graduation was common qualification of all the promoters i.e. B.E, B.Sc, Commerce mostly in their related area/industry. In most of the cases the promoters found to be Post–Graduate (Technical or Management). Only two promoters had doctorate degree.

Work experience of the promoters can be grouped into two (a) 1-20 yrs: experience of one generation and (b) 21-40 yrs: experience of two generations which is very beneficial for the business. In our sample, in seven companies promoters had the average experience of one generation (Medisurg Surgical Ltd, Bals, Suman Cables, Abhinav Polyester, Anjali Biotech, Microtech and Beautiful Dekor). Other six had the average experience of two generations: Madhulika Ltd, Campco, Vikram, Shrechem, Hartec and Esha.

Age of the promoters & Generation: Most of the entrepreneurs were in the young age of 40s & 30s.

In our sample, only four entrepreneurs belong to first generation that didn't have any business experience. They started or set-up the plant/project on their own on the basis of their core product knowledge without any business base or managerial background. Remaining nine promoters were of second generation. In our study, Second generation means that the promoters already had a business set up by their parents or were engaged in the family business or they had a experience of two generations.

7.1.7 Disbursement by GVFL: Madhulika Ceramics received the largest disbursement (Rs. 244.75 lakh) followed by Medisurg Surgical (Rs. 158.50 lakh) and Bals Ltd (Rs. 133.50 lakh). In the remaining cases the disbursement varied from the minimum of Rs. 25.00 lakh (Esha) to Rs. 91.25 lakh (Suman).

7.1.8 GVFL Shareholding: GVFL shareholding in Medisurg Surgical was approximately 88 percent of the total equity. It was followed by Microtech Ltd and Suman Cables with 49.89 percent and 34 percent respectively. GVFL's shareholding in six cases was in the range of 0-10 percent and in remaining four cases it was in the range of 11-25 percent.

In our sample of 13 cases, for three GVFL's recovery was more than the disbursement namely: Medisurg Surgical Ltd, Bals Ltd and Suman Cables Ltd. In remaining ten, the recovery was smaller than disbursement- varying from Rs. 1.13 lakh (out of Rs. 88.87 lakh disbursed to Campco Industries Ltd) to Rs. 165.28 lakh (out of Rs. 244.75 lakh disbursed to Madhulika Ceramics Ltd.). Thus, for the three cases net profit was positive whereas in others it was negative. However, overall Rs. 1092.55 lakh were disbursed by GVFL and the total recovery was Rs. 881.79 lakh resulting into aggregate loss of Rs. 210.76 lakh.

The aggregate returns available from the successful recovery of three cases were 77 percent in Suman Cables, 50 percent in Medisurg Surgical and 11 percent in Bals. In remaining the return was negative varying from the lowest negative of 23.98 percent to highest negative of 99 percent.

Returns on Investment for GVFL can be calculated in two ways: ROI for GVFL = [(Receipts minus amt given) / amt given by GVFL]. The values obtained to be divided by no of years in tenure (for per annum) and multiply by 100 (for percent) Or ROI for GVFL = [(Receipts/Investment)-1] /no of yrs of tenure (for per annum) multiply by 100 (percent). Using both the methods will give same values. We have used the first method to calculate the ROI for GVFL. Out of thirteen cases, ROI for GVFL is positive for three cases namely: Suman Cables, Medisurg Surgico and Bals Ltd having ROI of 15.4 percent, 9.90 percent and 2.10 percent respectively. In the rest ten cases, the ROI is negative. Madhulika Ceramics Ltd having the lowest negative ROI of –2.71 percent followed by Anjali BioTech (–4 percent) and Shrechem Ltd. (–6.57 percent) and Campco Ltd. having the highest negative ROI of –12.3 percent.

Overall, there was a negative return of 19.29 percent on

the total disbursement and a negative return on investment from the to thirteen cases.

Of thirteen cases, for four there were no data available either on expected sales (Bals Ltd and Shrechem Ltd.) or actual sales (Madhulika Ceramics and Gujarat Surgico). However, two of the four cases were the successful ones giving positive rate of return to GVFL. Even in other cases, data were reported for few years. In these cases, the actual sales volume was far below the expected volume – as high as 80 percent and above in many years. It appears that the shortfall in the cash flow contributed significantly to the liquidity constraints of the firm.

Of the thirteen cases, six did not report either the actual or the expected net profit figures. Others reported the figures, though incomplete, suggesting significant deviation of actual net profit from the expected net profit during post disbursement years.

The shortfall varied from minimum negative 19 percent in Anjali Biotech Ltd to the highest negative of 246 percent in Beautiful Dekor Ltd.

However, cases wise the shortfall was 194 percent in Suman Cables Ltd, 36 percent to 150 percent in Vikram Industries, 65 percent to 90 percent in Abhinav polyester Ltd, 45 percent to 246 percent in Beautiful Dekor Ltd, 73 percent in Hartec Ltd, 293 percent in Esha, 19 percent to 212 percent in Anjali Biotech Ltd.

It seems that negative net profit indicated in most of the years of all cases suggest the effect of the shortfall between expected sales and actual ones. This perhaps led to affect the recovery of the GVFL's disbursed amount.

The disbursement year was 1990 for one case (Madhulika Ceramics), 1991 for one (Gujarat Surgico), 1992 for four cases, 1993 for three cases, 1994 for one case and 1995 for two cases. Tenure of the company with GVFL has been estimated as difference between disbursement and the divestment year. Majority of the promoters/cases have tenure of 5-8 yrs with

GVFL, which indicates a good relationship and a proper blending of co-operation and understanding. Maximum time spend was with Madhulika Ceramics (I) Ltd and minimum time is with Beautiful Dekor Ltd.

The essence of venture capital investment philosophy is very much the realization of future liquidity and capital gains. The commonly used exit vehicle for venture capital fund is 'going to the public' or 'initial public offering'. But it is very difficult for high technology company to go to public because of minimum capital and profitability requirements. The other exit routes like 'selling the shares to a third party' or 'repurchase of share by the investee company' are also worth consideration up to a great extent. Liquidation is another important method of disinvestment mechanism. This is used by many of the companies in India.

Out of the various options available to GVFL to withdraw from the investee company, the most preferred exit policy was repurchase of shares by the investee company. In our sample of thirteen cases, eight cases were divested through the repurchase of shares by the investee company. In remaining five cases, the equity shares of the company were sold to the third party in order to exit from the case.

One major aspect of exit policy is the time frame within which the venture capitalist exits from the venture. Venture capital is capital invested or available for investment in new projects. Once the venture has succeeded in introducing new products and earning revenues, it will make its initial public offer of stock. At this point of time, the venture capital firms are in a position to reap their rewards. It basically speaks of time horizon of exit policy.

Hurry and Miller (1991), in their study comment that a project advocating direct gains includes a clear perception of a time horizon in which the project must earn profits. On the other hand, it is not so in case of an option strategy where the opportunity of 'entering new technology' may become realizable at some currently unforeseeable point of time.

GVFL favoured exiting out of the venture within '1-5 years' with short-term direct gains. In our sample out of thirteen cases, seven cases had the time horizon of 1-5 years. The present finding is in conformity with the strategic choices of the US firms as against Japanese firms. Time horizon of '5-7 years' and '7-10 years' have also been given due important showing a tendency to opt for medium/long term gains. Anjali Bio Tech had a time horizon of 5-7 years, four cases had a time horizon of 7-10 years: Campco Ltd, Vikram Industries, Shrechem Ltd and Microtech Ltd. Preference to long-term indirect strategic gains resulting from long term investments (10 years and above) was given only to Madhulika Ceramics. Thus, it is evident that in view of short-term direct gains that are within a period of 1-5 years, GVFL opt for going public.

The annual net profit earned during post disbursement period has been calculated by dividing the total net profit by the tenure of GVFL with the company i.e. the time during which both the VC and the entrepreneur stayed together in the project. Of the thirteen cases, five cases had negative annual net profit. Campco Industries Ltd. having the highest negative annual net profit of Rs. 263.37 lakh and Madhulika Ceramics Ltd. having Rs. 5.57 lakh. Other seven cases had positive annual net profit, Abhinav Polyester Ltd. having net profit of Rs. 74.60 lakh followed by Suman Cables Ltd with 59.67 and Shrechem Ltd having the lowest annual net profit of Rs. 0.03 lakh.

As regards total receipts through different recovery instruments, the most common instrument is by way of disinvestment/sale of equity shares and scrutiny fee. Other recovery instruments vary according to the agreed provisions in the contract between GVFL and the entrepreneur.

The expected IRR at the time of appraisal were minimum in case of Shrechem Ltd (13.90 percent) and maximum in case of Vikram (45.52 percent). For most of the others, the expected IRR was 30 percent and more. The expected IRR at the time of divestment was available for five cases. Against these expected values of internal return at the time of appraisal and divestments, the actual rate of return was negative for ten cases and positive for three cases only.

The expected Earnings per share at the time of appraisal were available for ten firms with minimum of less than Re.1 and maximum of Rs. 8.00 per share. At the time of divestment its expected value was available for eight firms with a minimum of less than Re 1 and a maximum of Rs. 18.25 per share. The expected book value at the time of appraisal was available only for few cases. These factors can be broadly classified into Professional teams, financial constraints, financial control system, transparency in financial decisions and legal compliance.

Professional team consists of the financial personnel (with professional qualification and relevant experience) looking after the financial function and operations of the firm. Out of thirteen cases, seven cases did not have an effective professional finance team. In three cases (Anjali Biotech, Microtech, Hartec) poor performance of the professional team was observed, in Madhulika Ceramics finance executive was appointed, in Suman Cables there was lack of attention paid by the promoters, in Vikram Industries promoters didn't take care of purchase of raw material and in Beautiful Dekor promoters were dishonest and non co-operative.

Financial constraints of the firm can be severe or modest due to cost over-run, liquidity crisis, siphoning off money, overhead cost, working capital limits/margins, delayed realization of sales, high interest cost due to cost of funds and mis-utilization of funds. All the cases irrespective of their performance were affected by this factor. Out of thirteen cases, eight cases (MIL, Gujarat, Campco, Vikram, Shrechem, Abhinav, Beautiful, Esha) faced the problem of cost over-run in implementing the projects. Five cases (Gujarat Surgico, Campco, Abhinav, Anjali Biotech, Microtech) had a problem of liquidity crunch or liquidity crisis. In three cases (Suman cables, Hartec and Beautiful Dekor) siphoning off money from the company's account for personal needs was also recorded. In another three (Shrechem, Anjali and Beautiful) there was problem of working capital limits/margins. In addition to these there were some case specific problem such as Anjali Biotech suffered from the delayed realization of sales, Microtech from high interest cost, Hartech from mis-utilization of funds and Vikram from increased overhead cost.

7.1.9 Financial Control System: The poor and inadequate financial control system affected only three cases namely; Anjali Biotech, Microtech (anomalies in books of accounts) and Beautiful Dekor (no proper maintenance of records and internal audit). Remaining cases were maintaining the records as desired.

There was very poor transparency of financial system in three cases. In Bals Ltd, the promoters were not showing true and fair picture of the company. In Anjali Biotech, the promoters undertook diversification of project in violation of provisions of contract- improper planning and not informing GVFL. The promoters of Beautiful Dekor had absence of transparency in their financial system and records.

Of thirteen cases, six had violated the provisions of legal compliance, which were of statutory nature. Suman Cables, a successful company was proposing the sale of company without informing GVFL. Shrechem had poor maintenance of statutory records. Microtech Ltd had a liability of Non-payment of Gratuity, PF, ESI, Stock options, professional tax and TDS. Hartec Ltd had financial irregularities: names of fictitious companies as debtors, Violation of Companies Act- Board meetings were not held timely and non-compliance with the Registrar of Companies. In Beautiful Dekor there were irregularities in issuing equity to public (Shares), allotment of shares, dispatch, transfer of shares, listing on stock exchange, non-confirmation of compliance, forfeiture of shares/call money, violation of takeover code of SEBI, violation of listing agreements and issue of fictitious shares.

In sum, all cases had one or the other type of financial

problem. However, three cases namely: Beautiful Dekor, Anjali Biotech, and Microtech had four/five factors affecting the performance.

Professional marketing team consists of the marketing personnel (with professional qualification and relevant experience) looking after the marketing of products for the firm. Of thirteen cases, five did not have effective marketing professional team. Madhulika Ceramics had inadequate professionalism in its team. Poor marketing management team was observed in Gujarat Surgico, Suman Cables and Esha. Beautiful had dishonest marketing personnel with inefficient marketing team.

Wholesalers and retailers. Of thirteen cases, seven had poor distribution network either at a wholesale or retail level. Madhulika Ceramics, Campco, Vikram and Medisurg Surgical had poor dealer's management. Madhulika had an additional problem of reduced dealer. Like wise Anjali Biotech had inefficient representatives. Microtech Ltd had no distribution network and depended solely on defence purchases. Esha had lack of business vision and poor marketing strategy.

Five cases had deficient marketing support in terms of weak promotional activities and advertising. These cases are: Madhulika, Abhinav Polyester, Esha, Anjali Biotech and Gujarat Surgico. In addition to this, Abhinav Polyester and Esha suffered from poor market development and Anjali Biotech lacked concept selling to farmers.

Seven cases suffered due to poor quality of either product or raw materials. Madhulika and Medisurg Surgical faced problems on account of delayed launch and limited range of products. Low quality products were observed in Esha and Gujarat Surgico. Vikram had poor quality of raw material. Anjali Biotech had low shelf life of its products. Beautiful Dekor had complaints from customers regarding defective moulds and products. Lastly Esha had absence of repeat /regular orders.

There were also other marketing factors affecting the

performance of the firm. Madhulika was facing problems due to decline in prices. Vikram had to change the product mix and lost its advantage of availability of good quality cotton yarn at competitive price. Esha had problems due to increase in marketing cost.

In sum, all cases had one or the other type of marketing problem. However, five cases namely: Madhulika Ceramics, Gujarat Surgico, Vikram, Anjali Biotech and Esha had three/four factors affecting the performance.

7.1.10 Market Conditions: Of thirteen cases, nine had suffered due to change in market conditions. Domestic recession affected four firms: MIL, Campco, Abhinav and Esha. Increase in competition due to new entrants was observed in MIL and Campco. Medisurg Surgical had normal market conditions but products being export oriented & Import substitute faced problems. Bals suffered due to disintegration of export market (Russia). Shrechem suffered decline in sales. Abhinav Polyester suffered due to depressive phase in textile industry, increase in raw material (cotton) price and texturing operations were highly competitive. Anjali Biotech had increased competition, drop in sales and unable to create export market. Microtech Ltd had segmented market (Defence purchase only) and fall in sales order. Esha suffered due to recession in the economy and inadequate utilization of capacity.

Four cases faced problems due to change in policy regulations. MIL suffered due to instability of central government and Bals faced changes in policies. Abhinav Polyester had run into trouble because of imposition of high excise duty and Anjali due to imposition of sales tax.

Three firms had problems due to technological changes namely: Bals-no specific technological edge, Shrechem– unable to support operational technical problems, Esha- unable to support customized products.

Six firms had other environmental problems: Voluntary Disclosure of Income Scheme in Madhulika, statutorily declared Sickness in Campco, Exchange rate fluctuation and absenteeism of workers in Vikram, Transporter's strike in Abhinav Polyester, NPA and Debt trap in Microtech Ltd, unable to trap the market potential in government sector and exports in Esha.

In sum, all cases had one or the other type of environmental problem. However, four cases namely: Madhulika Ceramics, Bals, Abhinav Polyester and Esha had three factors affecting the performance. Overall, in the characteristics of the firm and entrepreneurs, we have eight companies set-up in 80's and Pre 90's. On an average every year GVFL received and disbursed two projects. Most of the proposals received financial assistance in the same year when they approached GVFL after the appraisal of project. There were seven infant companies having age in the range of 0-5 years, four young companies having age of 6-20 years and two very old and mature companies having age of 21 and above. Eight companies were located in Gujarat and rest five in other parts of India: New Delhi, Dadara Nagar, Tamil Nadu and Pune. Most of the companies were engaged in Consumer Related and Industrial products.

In our sample, nine companies belong to family enterprise and the rest four were first generation entrepreneur having independent business where the promoter is the whole and sole person engaged in developing business. Most of the entrepreneurs were young (age of 30s and 40s) and Post-Graduates in their related area/industry with an experience of one generation (1-2 yrs). Tenure of the company with GVFL has been estimates as the difference between disbursement and divestment year. Majority of the promoters had tenure of 5-8 years indicating a good relationship and a proper blending of co-operation and understanding.

7.2 Financial Contract and Performance

7.2.1 Appraisal: The provisions include the activities related to direct participation in management by VC, Staged investment, Management fees, Project & location of plant and financial plan.

Appraisal clauses include the provisions/activities that are required at the time of appraising the project, which has approached the VC for financial assistance. In the equity contract framed by GVFL, the maximum numbers of appraisal clauses are five. These Clauses included primary information relating to the following:

- Project in which the company is presently engaged/desires to start or the proposed expansion or diversification and the location of the proposed plant.
- Financial plan includes the cost of the venture and its means of financing.
- Staged investment is the progressive release of equity or re-investment in successive steps.
- Management fee is the scrutiny or upfront end charges that the company has to pay to GVCF-1990. It is generally @ 1 percent of the total investment prior to disbursement by GVCF-1990. Sometimes, The Company also has to pay in addition, fee for appraisal and assistance for Public issue of the company.
- Lastly, but the most important, direct participation in management by VC.

Medisurg Surgical had the lowest clauses at three. Bals and Campco each had four core clauses. Most of the cases were subjected to all the core clauses relating to appraisal in their contracts.

7.2.2 Self-Selection: The provisions include profit participation, Compensation vs. option, subscription by GVFL, progressive release of equity funds, Equity contribution by entrepreneur, Capital structure, Size of board etc.

Self-selection clauses along with the Appraisal clauses help in mitigating the problems caused by the adverse selection due to asymmetric information. Some of these core clauses are:

- GVCF-1990 will have profit participation in the company.

In case of losses, GVFL will share the compensation against the options.

- Subscription by GVFL to the share capital of the company. For the implementation of the project, GVFL GVCF-1990 agrees to subscribe to share capital and the company agrees to allot the same in the name of GVFL trustee/manager GVCF-1990.
- The promoters agrees to bring in additional funds in a form and on terms acceptable to GVFL to meet any shortfall that may arise in financing the project & working capital requirements.
- Size of board and membership to the board: GVFL shall have the right to appoint and remove from time to time the Directors(s) on the Board of Directors of the company in proportion to the equity held by GVFL and Promoters excluding public offering in the ensuing public issue of the company. Maximum size of the board can be 12.

There are also some special clauses varying between 1-4 that are particular to cases. Disbursement by GVCF-1990 shall be made to the company not earlier than ten days before the opening of its public issue.

Maximum number of self-selection clauses was eleven and none of the cases recorded the highest one. One case (Microtech Ltd) agreed with 10 clauses, three cases (Madhulika Ceramics, Suman Cables, Beautiful Dekor) 9 clauses, another three (Bals, Vikram Industries and Anjali BioTec) 8 clauses, five cases (Campco, Shrechem, Abhinav, Hartech and Esha) with 7clauses.

Most of the cases contain all the core clauses in their contract with one exception. This exception was Medisurg Surgical Ltd., with one core clause of Equity subscription from GVFL. Microtech Ltd and Campco had 6 and 5 core clauses respectively.

The maximum special clauses were four that were observed in Microtech Ltd only. Others had two or less special clauses each.

With regard to self-selection clauses, GVFL's contract with the entrepreneur imposed all the standard provisions to safeguard the interest of both parties. However, special clauses were not many in respective cases.

7.2.3 Monitoring: The monitoring of the cases is analyzed from two aspects. First aspect is the number of clauses relating to monitoring the projects and the behaviour of the entrepreneur during the tenure of GVFL. Second aspect is the number of monitoring events that took place during the same time. The event is defined as the number of actions taken or initiated in compliance with the monitoring clauses of the contract.

There were 104 monitoring clauses—maximum number that a case can have in the contract. These clauses are classified as Core clauses (31), supplement clauses (48) and special clauses/customized clauses (25). Core clauses of the contract are the essential clauses for monitoring. Supplement clauses of the contract are those ones that strengthen the monitoring mechanism to ensure its effectiveness. Special clauses are those customized provisions to each case depending on the nature of the project.

The provisions that help in monitoring the project after the sanction of the funds includes VC as a board member, Interim financial reports, notices, agenda, minutes of the Board meetings, Annual General Meetings on the status of the firms operations, technical, financial and legal inspections, issue of debentures, raising loans, deposits from public, powers to enter into the agreement, changes or delay in the project, end use of the funds, covenants relating to transfer of shares, change in management, actions or decisions taken by the Board of Directors, directions/instructions given by GVFL, legal requirement by SEBI, changes in capital structure, borrowings, listing of shares, control/ownership of assets, buyback by promoters, appointment /removal of directors and other members on the board, voting rights, etc

The monitoring clauses in the contract include provisions

to control the problems of moral hazard. The provisions in these clauses help in monitoring the project after the sanction of the funds. These clauses are maximum in number in the contract and are verv important. Theses are the activities where the role of the VC comes into picture more regularly. These activities help the VC and the promoter to achieve their project objectives, with minimum risk and efforts for the maximum returns. The outcomes of these activities are in the form of divestment of shares, initial public offering or acquisition/merger/takeover by third party.

All the cases had 75 and more clauses relating to monitoring with one exception. Medisurg Surgical Ltd being an exception had five clauses-the least one. Among these, four cases were in the range of 90 and more clauses (Madhulika, Suman Cables, Anjali Biotech, Microtech), five cases in the range of 80-90 clauses (Bals, Shrechem, Abhinav Polyester, Hartec, Beautiful) and two cases: Vikram Industries and Esha with 76 and 77 clauses respectively.

Nine of the thirteen cases had agreed to 31 core-monitoring clauses. Other three cases has less clauses: Campco (24 clauses), Vikram (28 clauses) and Abhinav (30 clauses).

48 supplement clauses were recorded in case of six of the thirteen cases, 47 clauses in two cases (Bals and Abhinav Polyester), 46 clauses in another two cases (Beautiful and Esha), 42 clauses in only one case: Vikram Industries and 28 clauses in Campco. Special or customized clauses were more than 10 in five cases.

In most of the cases, GVFL has verified the physical assets personally by visiting the plant. In some cases, the visit has been made more than twice a year (Anjali Biotech and Beautiful Dekor). In these cases, more frequent visits were required by GVFL officers as they were having problems related to siphoning off money on purchase, deterioration in performance, poor liquidity position to pay dues. In case of MIL, Shrechem, Abhinav Polyester Ltd, Hartec, Esha Cubidor Containers, Microtech Ltd, there was increase in monitoring visits during the last 2-3 yrs of GVFL's tenure. These companies started making losses and due to constant monitoring by GVFL, these companies could able to recover their cash position and at the same time GVFL also was able to recover 50 percent of the amount disbursed. In the remaining three companies: Gujarat Surgico, Bals Ltd and Suman Cables the monitoring visits were very regular after the disbursement of financial assistance. Although these companies also faced problems of product conceptualization, marketing, management team and financial crisis, but with constant monitoring, foreseeing the market conditions, proper distribution and marketing efforts at the right time by GVFL they came out very successfully.

In addition to visits made to the plant, GVFL also monitored the activities of the company through various status/progress reports, letters, Notices, minutes of Board Meeting, Annual General Meetings and annual reports. These were expected to be sent regularly/periodically by all the companies. All these information kept GVFL updated with the activities relating to financial position, problems faced by the promoter on plant location, marketing, competitors, new entrants in the market etc.

It can be seen that on an average monthly two progress/status reports were sent to GVFL. In case of Shrechem Ltd, Hartec Ltd, Anjali Biotech and Microtech Ltd the calling of information was more than twice a month as these companies were engaged in the Biotechnology and Electronic related products which were manufacturing products for the first time in India and required constant study of environment and marketing efforts. Sometimes, the correspondence or monitoring was done weekly, fortnightly, monthly, quarterly and half-yearly.

Thus it can be seen the monitoring activity done by GVFL in all the cases in either way by visiting the plants personally for verification of physical assets or by status reports, letters, notices etc. These help in transparency and decision making of the firm. Almost every alternate month/quarterly the physical visits were made to keep the company on track. In cases where the company had delayed in supplying the information, diverted from the objectives of the project, misused the finances for personal needs or siphoning off the money etc, GVFL has taken strict steps or has filed legal suits against the company.

7.2.4 Disclosure: It includes the legal provisions to furnish GVFL with true and correct information, No conflict with the Memorandum of Association and Articles of association of the company, co has complied with the provision of Sec 81 (1A) of the companies act, the company should not be in arrears of any public demands- income tax, corporation tax etc.

Equity contracts of all the cases contain all the core clauses. Some of these clauses are:

- No conflict between the agreement and MOA & AOA of the company
- The company has complied with the provisions of Sec. 81 (1A) of the companies Act, 1956.
- The company is not in arrears of any public demands- income tax, corporation tax, etc.

7.2.5 Incentivizing, Divestment, IPO, Legal Remedies: It includes the provisions of incentivizing that are performance based by way of assurance for additional funds, divestment, IPO, exit options, sell of shares by promoters, mode and method of purchase of shares, breach of terms and conditions, arbitration, jurisdiction, currency of the agreement as long as the GVFL holds shares in the company etc.

There are clauses that help the VC to provide incentives to the promoters for good performance. It also punishes the promoters for not managing the project efficiently or any illegal activity at the time of disinvestment by sale of equity shares, going for Initial Public Offering etc. Some of the important clauses are:

- Sale of shares by GVFL: GVFL shall always have a) right to reduce or sell the equity shareholding in whole or in part. b) Valuation of the shares by GVFL on the basis of net worth of the company, c) face value plus interest compounded with half yearly rests at the rate of 25 percent per annum from each respective investment/disbursement made by GVFL and /or GVCF 1990.

- Mode and Method of purchase of shares: GVFL shall first offer to promoters in case of sell of its equity and all the expenses regarding transfer fee, stamped duty shall be borne in by the promoters.
- Buyback by promoters: promoters may offer to purchase shares held by GVFL
- The promoters may sell shares held by them
- Right of GVFL to acquire shares from the promoters in case of default and/or loss making
- Reduction in number of directors consequent upon reduction in equity share capital.
- Arbitration (Venue of arbitration is Ahmedabad)
- Currency of this agreement shall be in force so long as GVFL holds shares in the company.
- Jurisdiction (courts at Ahmedabad city only).

Most of the companies had agreed to clauses varying from 23 to 28 with two exceptions. The exceptions were Campco (18 clauses) and Medisurg Surgical (2 clauses). This implies that there were no deficiencies in incentivizing the entrepreneurs.

7.2.6 Performance of Contract: The performance of contract is measured in two ways:- performance by profitability of venture equity given by GVFL (Return in percent per annum on GVFL's funds lent out) in each case and performance in contractual compliance- least or absence of conflict of interest between GVFL and Borrower firm.

Since the venture capitalist is basically concerned with providing financial assistance to the entrepreneurs, financial considerations are of great importance. Major concern areas in this regard are returns from the venture, liquidity and exit mechanism. In the present study, financial considerations have been studied in the form of returns on funds during the tenure of GVFL with the entrepreneur through different instruments of recovery. Here recovery includes principal given to firm.

Total receipts through different recovery instruments were received highest from Medisurg Surgico Ltd of Rs. 237.00 lakh, followed by Madhulika Ceramics of Rs. 165.28 lakh, Suman Cables of Rs. 161.52 lakh and the lowest receipts from Campco Industries Ltd of Rs. 1.13 lakh. However, when we compare the total receipts with the amount disbursed for the financial assistance, only three cases had positive receipts namely: Medisurg Surgical, Suman Cables and Bals Ltd. i.e GVFL was able to recover more than the amount disbursed to them. Suman Cables had excess of Rs. 70.27 lakh (77.01 percent of amount disbursed), Medisurg Surgical had a excess of Rs. 78.5 lakh (49.53 percent of amount disbursed) and Bals Ltd had a excess of Rs. 14.05 lakh (10.52 percent of amount disbursed).

Returns on Investment for GVFL can be calculated in two ways: ROI for GVFL = [(Receipts minus amt given)/amt given by GVFL]. The values obtained to be divided by no of years in tenure (for per annum) and multiply by 100 (for percent) Or ROI for GVFL = [(Receipts/Investment)-1] /no of yrs of tenure (for per annum) multiply by 100 (percent). Using both the methods will give same values. We have used the first method to calculate the ROI for GVFL. Out of thirteen cases, ROI for GVFL is positive for three cases namely: Suman Cables, Medisurg Surgico and Bals Ltd having ROI of 15.4 percent, 9.90 percent and 2.10 percent respectively. In the rest ten cases, the ROI is negative. Madhulika Ceramics Ltd having the lowest negative ROI of –2.71 percent followed by Anjali BioTech (–4 percent) and Shrechem Ltd. (–6.57 percent) and Campco Ltd. having the highest negative ROI of –12.3 percent. Overall there was a negative return on investment from the thirteen cases.

Venture capital-backed projects find dual management on account of venture capitalists participating in the investee company's business. One important aspect in this regard is investor-investee relationships. Investor-investee relationships can be covered under the dimension of status of relationship between the venture capital fund and the Investee Company and causes of conflict.

Status of relationship between Venture Capital and the Investee Company: Involvement of venture capitalists in the investee company's affairs gives a new look to the venture. Both the parties may perceive this aspect differently. A number of studies Tyebjee and Bruno (1984), Sapienza and Timmons (1988), Gordan and Sahlman (1989) have shown that management assistance provided by the venture capitalists are highly valuable in the development and growth of the venture. The results of the studies indicate that the perceptions of the investee companies on the degree of involvement are lower than that of venture capital funds. Pandey and Jang A. (1996) shows that most of the venture capitalists think that their involvement is much more than the investee companies' expectations as they have more valuable ideas than the investee company has. But a good venture is only that in which both parties agree on a common point. Thus, difference of opinion can create major differences among the investor and investee, hence this factor is very important to the study.

7.3 Reasons of Conflict between Venture Capitalist and Entrepreneur

Venture Capital financing differs from more traditional equity financing in that the venture capitalist plays a role in the management of the companies receiving investment i.e. the investee company. The success of any venture depends to a large extent upon the mutual relations between the venture capitalist and the investee company. The success of any venture depends upon the mutual cooperation and trust between the venture capital funds and the investee company. Sometimes, the relations turn sour and conflicts arise between the two causing a threat to the very survival of the venture.

The issues of conflict between venture capitalists and entrepreneurs has been studied under various reasons behind such conflicts as: lack of promoter's attention, different levels of information known to the entrepreneur, siphoning off money, poor and dishonest team or due to violation of legal compliance.

In our sample, despite of having all the core disclosure clauses, out of thirteen, nine cases had conflict of interest due to financial factors i.e. poor and dishonest team, financial constraints, poor financial control system and lack of transparency in financial decisions. Of these seven cases did not have effective professional finance team. In Anjali Biotech, Microtech and Hartec poor performance of the professional team was observed, in Madhulika Ceramics finance executive was appointed, in Suman Cables there was lack of attention paid by the promoters, in Vikram Industries promoters didn't take care of purchase of raw material and in Beautiful Dekor promoters were dishonest and non co-operative. In three cases (Suman cables, Hartec and Beautiful Dekor) siphoning off money from the company's account for personal needs was also recorded. The poor and inadequate financial control system affected only three cases namely; Anjali Biotech, Microtech (anomalies in books of accounts) and Beautiful Dekor (no proper maintenance of records and internal audit). Remaining cases were maintaining the records as desired. There was very poor transparency of financial system in three cases. In Bals Ltd, the promoters were not showing true and fair picture of the company. In Anjali Biotech, the promoters undertook diversification of project in violation of provisions of contract- improper planning and not informing GVFL. The promoters of Beautiful Dekor had absence of transparency in their financial system and records. Marketing factors are essential to be studies by any venture capitalist before putting his funds in any venture.

In our sample, Conflict of interest due to marketing factors was also observed in nine cases. Of thirteen cases, two cases:

Madhulika and Suman Cables Ltd. did not have efficient marketing professional team. Beautiful had dishonest marketing personnel with inefficient marketing team. Distribution network was observed at two levels: wholesalers and retailers. Of thirteen cases, seven had poor distribution network either at a wholesale or retail level. Madhulika Ceramics, Campco, Vikram and Medisurg Surgical had poor dealer's management. Madhulika had an additional problem of reduced dealer. Like wise Anjali Biotech had inefficient representatives. Microtech Ltd had no distribution network and depended solely on defence purchases. Esha had lack of business vision and poor marketing strategy. Five cases had deficient marketing support in terms of weak promotional activities and advertising. These cases are: Madhulika, Abhinav Polyester, Esha, Anjali Biotech and Gujarat Surgico. In addition to this, Abhinav Polyester and Esha suffered from poor market development and Anjali Biotech lacked concept selling to farmers. Low quality products were observed in Esha and Gujarat Surgico. Vikram had poor quality of raw material. Anjali Biotech had low shelf life of its products. Beautiful Dekor had complaints from customers regarding defective moulds and products.

In six cases, apart from different levels of information there was also violation of legal compliance like sale of company without informing GVFL, poor maintenance of statutory records, non-payment of gratuity, fictitious companies as debtors, non-compliance with ROC, irregularities in issuing equity to public, forfeiture of shares, violation of take over code of SEBI etc.

In our sample of 13 cases, three companies have scored the highest index of 6 out of 7. Five companies have scored 5 points, four companies have scored 4 points and three companies have scored index of 1.

In our sample of 13 cases, only one company (Campco Industries Ltd.) has scored the highest score of 14 points and Madhulika Ceramics Ltd. has scored 13 points. Three companies have scored 12 points (Abhinav Polyester Ltd., Microtech Ltd., Hartech Seamless Ltd.,), four companies have scored 11 points (Vikram Industries Ltd., Shrechem Ltd., Anjali Biotech Ltd., Esha Cubidor Containers Ltd.,), three companies have scored 10 points (Bals Ltd., Suman Cables Ltd., Beautiful Dekor Ltd.) and lastly one company Medisurg has scored the lowest of 8 points.

When we compare the points scored by each company with the total returns or the Average rate of return, we find no relationship between them. As the companies having the positive total returns or the average rate of return have a scored 10 or 12 points. But the companies having the same score has negative rate of returns. The characteristics of the firm and the entrepreneur do help the VC in selecting the project but after the sanction of the financial assistance there are some other internal or external factors that are contributing towards the performance or the total returns.

There is lot of variation in the points scored by companies in monitoring clauses. The minimum is 5 and the highest is 96. There was no relation between the clauses and the total returns.

To sum up, the cases are analysed in two parts: Analysing the Charactersistics of the firm as well as the entrepreneur and secondly, analyzing the financial contracts and its impact of the performance of the firm. Most of the companies belong to the family enterprise, set up in 80's and Pre 90's with young Post-graduate promoters in their related area/industry and located in Gujarat. Majority of the promoters had tenure of 5-8 years indicating a good relationship and a proper blending of co-operation and understanding.

In all the cases, the amount sanctioned by GVFL for financial assistance at the time of agreement was fully disbursed by way of equity participation. The total cost of project ranges from Rs. 180 lakh to Rs. 811 lakh. Financial assistance by GVFL is normally recovered by scrutiny fee, sale of equity shares interests, dividends etc. Overall, there was a negative rate of return of 19.29 percent on the total disbursement to thirteen cases. Management fee, paid by the promoters to GVFL is normally 1 percent of total disbursement amount. Most of the companies were in the later and early stage of investment.

Financial factors that affected the performance of the firm include professional team, financial constraints, financial control system, transparency in financial decision etc. Marketing factors that affected the performance of the firm include professional marketing team, wholesaler/retailer distribution network, advertising and promotional activities etc. However, five cases had three/four factors affecting the performance. Business environment factors that affected the performance of the firm include the market conditions, policy changes, technological changes etc. Thus, four cases were affected by at least three business environmental factors.

The equity contracts made between GVFL and entrepreneur include provisions/clauses related to appraisal/screening, self- selection, and monitoring and disclosure compliance. All the cases contain the standard clauses required in the agreement to reduce the moral hazards and adverse selection problems caused due to informational asymmetry and conflict of interest between both the parties.

8

Summary and Conclusions

This chapter provides summary of findings on hypotheses, case analysis, contractual performance, their limitations, policy implications, prospects of Indian Venture Capital, recommendations and future research areas.

8.1 Venture Capital and Information Asymmetric Problem

One of the most important developments in entrepreneurship has been growth of Venture Capital over the past decade. In India, venture capital funded companies are on rise after the introduction of economic reforms. Venture capitalists help the promoter in various ways to nurture companies, providing a network, recruiting key management and building a team, developing financial systems, advising on company law and other legal matters, helping co-investment and arranging working capital facilities from bankers, providing marketing links and contacts, sharing business perspective, helping in long term strategic thinking and planning, helping to create an entrepreneurial climate and devising incentive systems to promote long-term work, and providing support and confidence during bad times.

The concept of Venture Capital as has been taken up in the study includes "investment in the form of equity, quasi–equity and/or a conditional loan, made in new, unlisted, high risk or high-tech firms, stated by technically or professionally qualified entrepreneurs.

The theory of capital market imperfections, the subject matter of chapter on literature review, predicts that, in the presence of asymmetric information and conflicts of interest, some firms will be unable to obtain external finance at the cost of funds set in centralized securities markets. Then the structure of venture capital well suited to addressing problems of informational asymmetry and agency costs that are most pronounced in high-tech industries and young firms. This by no means implies that venture Capital arrangements are devoid of failures or inefficiencies: yet it presents an alternative for financing investment. The performance of venture capital tends to be cyclical. Thus it analyses the structure of venture capital contracts and how such structure might reduce agency costs common in capital markets.

8.2 Research Methodology

A major issue in the design of venture capital contracts is to reduce moral hazard and adverse selection problems by minimizing informational asymmetry and conflicts of interest between the venture capitalist and the entrepreneur.

The research gaps and relevant questions can be listed as below:

- Whether VFs financial contract deal with adverse selection and moral hazard adequately and sufficiently?
- How these contracts affect the firm's performance (Principle Agent Problem)?
- What is its impact on Performance of firms funded by VC?

This study seeks to examine in detail the contracts between VCs and entrepreneurs to determine what provisions are included in these contracts that help in decision making in VC appraisal/screening, self-selection, monitoring, incentivizing and divestment. It is a test of Financial Contracting theory in VC and performance of the firm. Venture Capital structure attempts to reduce moral hazards and adverse selection problems by minimizing informational asymmetry and conflicts of interest between the venture capitalist and the entrepreneur.

To test the agency theory based on the structure of venture capital contracts different hypothesis of relationships between contract and performance tested in the study are:

- H_{10}: Appraisal/screening and self-selection clauses

improve the contractual performance (the repayment & firm's own performance).

- H_{20}: Equity contracts based on monitoring clauses improves the compliance with contractual performance.
- H_{30}: Equity contracts with incentivizing clauses improve the contractual performance.
- H_{40}: Equity contracts with self-selection clauses improve the contractual performance.
- H_{50}: Equity contracts with divesting clauses improve the contractual performance.
- H_{60}: Cases where returns are high, characteristics and clauses are high.

The performance in the above hypotheses can be measured in two ways: firstly, single firm over a period of time, if the case is monitored in successive years and secondly, cross sectional comparison of firm i.e when we move from a poorly monitored firm to a better monitored firm, it must have a corresponding impact from the poor to better contractual performance. In our study, we have adopted the cross-sectional comparison. A longitudinal case study approach has been used to observe the relationship between contractual provision and performance of firm. The decision to use multiple case studies provides a unique opportunity to observe the effects of contracts on the performance at several different stages of development simultaneously.

8.3 Sample and Data

The above hypotheses are tested by analyzing the contracts/agreement (between the VC and the entrepreneur) of the projects that have been funded by a Venture Capital Company (VCC): Gujarat Venture Finance Limited (GVFL). Thirteen firms/projects, funded and subsequently divested fully from the first fund of GVFL (GVCF-1990) are analysed. The nature of these investments was trust fund and close-ended with tenure of 15 years, date of maturity: Nov 2005. Its investment philosophy was to provide financial assistance and hands on management support to innovative and technology based projects and promising returns.

The portfolio management style was to give active management advice. The fund is in its disinvestment phase, with 65 percent of the fund already redeemed to the investors. The different industries in which the investments has been made are related to Biotechnology, Computer Software & Services, Consumer related, Food & food processing, Industrial products & Machinery, Medical, Electronics, Telecom & Data Communications etc. Some of the investments are: Microtech Limited, Medisurg Surgical Ltd., Anjali BioTech (I) Limited, Shrechem Limited, Bals Ltd, Campco industries Ltd, Madhulika Ceramic Industries Limited, etc. The different instruments of finance used in GVCF 1990 fund are Equity Shares, Convertible Preference Shares, Convertible Debentures, Income note loan and other (Temporary loan, Bridge loan). These investments are made in different regions of the country and at different stages (Seed, Star-up, Early and Later). The investment in these projects range from Rs. 209.00 lakh to Rs. 15.60 lakh and the instrument used were equity contracts. In these investments we have mainly concentrated on Contracts which are characterized by: Screening/appraisal, Self-selection, Monitoring, Incentivizing, IPO, Divestment, Legal remedies.

8.4 Case Analysis and Results

Each case has been analysed covering the broad areas: Background of the company, promoters, management, past performance and capital structure, Contract, risk factors involved, product (its production and marketing), project profitability, SWOT analysis, post investment period/financial position, What went wrong and where, Rational behind the sale/divestment, exit and returns to GVFL. All the cases are analysed individually and aggregately. Hypotheses are examined from the data collected.

The cases have been analysed in two parts: Analysing the

Charactersistics of the firm as well as the entrepreneur and secondly, analyzing the financial contracts and its impact of the performance of the firm. The Characteristics of the firm and entrepreneur has been studied by analyzing the profit of entrepreneur, date of incorporation, project location, industry, product, instruments used in the contract, qualification & experience of entrepreneurs, disbursement and share holding of GVFL in project Cost, returns to GVFL, sales performance (expected and actual), Net profit, tenure of GVFL with entrepreneur, expected rate of return, earnings per share, book value, financial and marketing factors of the firms etc.

Profile of entrepreneur: In our sample, nine companies belong to family enterprise and the rest four were first generation entrepreneur having independent business where the promoter is the whole and sole person engaged in developing business. Most of the entrepreneurs were young (age of 30s and 40s) and Post-Graduates in their related area/industry with an experience of one generation (1-2 yrs). Tenure of the company with GVFL has been estimates as the difference between disbursement and divestment year. Majority of the promoters had tenure of 5-8 years indicating a good relationship and a proper blending of co-operation and understanding.

In our sample, eight companies were set-up in 1980s and pre-1990s. On an average every year GVFL received and disbursed two projects. Most of the proposals received financial assistance in the same year when they approached GVFL after the appraisal of project.

Age of the company has been calculated by deducting the year of incorporation from the year company approached GVFL. In our sample there were seven infant companies having age in the range of 0-5 years, four young companies having age of 6-20 years and two very old and mature companies having age of 21 and above. Eight companies were located in Gujarat and rest five in other parts of India: New Delhi, Dadara Nagar, Tamil Nadu and Pune. Most of the companies were engaged in Consumer Related and Industrial products.

In all the cases, the amount sanctioned by GVFL for financial assistance at the time of agreement was fully disbursed by way of equity participation. Madhulika Ceramics (I) Ltd has received the largest amount of Rs. 244.75 lakh and Esha Cubidor Containers Ltd has received the smallest amount in our sample of Rs. 25 lakh. The total cost of project ranges from Rs 180 lakh to Rs. 811 lakh where GVFL's shareholding in the total cost of project was highest in Medisurg Surgical (88 percent of the total equity) followed by Microtech Ltd (49.89 percent) and Suman Cables (34 percent). Management fee, sometimes also referred as scrutiny fee or upfront end charges are paid by the promoters to GVFL is normally 1 percent of total disbursement amount. Most of the companies were in the later and early stage of investment. Financial assistance by GVFL is normally recovered by scrutiny fee, sale of equity shares interests, dividends etc. In three cases GVFL's recovery was more than the disbursement: Medisurg Surgical, Bals Ltd and Suman Cables with the rate of return of 77 percent, 50 percent and 11 percent respectively. In rest ten cases the recovery was smaller than disbursement varying from Rs. 1.13 lakh to Rs. 165.28 lakh. Overall, there was a negative rate of return of 19.29 percent on the total disbursement to thirteen cases.

The actual sales volume/performance was far below the expected volume affecting the net profit of the firm. The shortfall varied from minimum negative 19 percent in Anjali BioTech Ltd to highest negative of 246 percent in Beautiful Dekor Ltd.

Financial factors that affected the performance of the firm include professional team, financial constraints, financial control system, transparency in financial decision etc. Seven cases did not have an effective professional finance team, three had poor performance, lack of attention was paid by promoters, dishonest and non co-operative. Eight cases has severe financial constraints due to cost over-run in implementing the projects, five had a problem of liquidity crunch, in three cases there was a problem of working capital limits and siphoning off money was done. The poor and inadequate financial control system affected only three cases, rest maintained the records. Three cases had poor transparency of financial system where the promoters did not give true & fair picture and violated the provisions of contract. Six cases had problems of legal compliance like poor maintenance of statutory records, financial irregularities, Violation of Companies Act etc.

Marketing factors that affected the performance of the firm include professional marketing team, wholesaler/retailer distribution network, advertising and promotional activities etc. In our sample, five cases did not have effective professional team (inadequate, deficient, dishonest team), seven had poor distribution network either at a wholesale or retail level, five cases had deficient marketing support in terms of weak promotional and advertising activities, seven cases suffered due to poor quality of either product or raw materials& low self life of product. Some other factors affecting the performance were: decline in prices, change in product mix, increase in marketing cost etc. However, five cases had three/four factors affecting the performance.

Business environment factors that affected the performance of the firm include the market conditions, policy changes, technological changes etc. In our sample, nine cases had suffered due to change in market conditions like domestic recession, new entrants, products being export-import oriented substitutes, disintegration of export market, decline in sales, segmented market etc. Four cases faced problems due to change in policy regulations like instability of central government, high excise duty, and imposition of sales tax. Three firms had problems due to technological changes. Six firms also suffered due to other environmental factors like VDIS, sick unit, exchange rate fluctuations, worker absenteeism, transporters strike, NPA, Debt trap etc. Thus, four cases were affected by at least three business environmental factors.

8.5 Financial Contract and Performance

The equity contracts made between GVFL and entrepreneur include provisions/clauses related to appraisal/screening, self- selection, and monitoring and disclosure compliance. Hypotheses are developed based on the clauses/provisions in the contractual agreement and are examined in terms of impact of contractual provisions on the performance of firm. Here it in important to define the two terms: "improvement in performance of contract" and "performance of contract". The improvement in the performance of contract can be examined in two ways: first, the improvement in a case can be measured on specified indicators over the period i.e. if the case is monitored in successive years and secondly, the improvement measured on specified indicators in cross-section of cases at a point of time i.e when we move from a poorly monitored firm to a better monitored firm, it must have a corresponding impact from the poor to better contractual performance. In the thesis first approach is not possible due to data constraints and thus the second approach based on cross section is adopted. The "performance of contract" can again be measured in two ways: - namely, performance in profitability of venture equity given- Return on funds lent out (percent per annum) in each case. Secondly "performance in contractual compliance"- least or absence of conflict of interest between GVFL and Borrower firm".

All the three research questions has been examined and answered in each case separately. Then the hypothesis developed earlier in the chapter of Research Methodology are examined based on the observations and no statistical test has been performed due to the limitations of case study approach and the number of cases (sample) taken for the study.

The answers to the research questions case-wise are as follows:

Case 1: Madhulika Ceramics Industries Ltd. (MCIL): MCIL was engaged in the manufacture of ceramic walls, glazed tiles, and marketed under the brand name of "CERA". Before sanctioning of funds for financial assistance, due diligence was done which includes the appraisal of the company (SWOT, past performance, expected profitability) and self-selection process by GVFL. After observing the salient features of the company: experienced promoters, sound financial position, use of gas-fired kiln technology and geographical advantage, GVFL agreed to finance the project and an agreement was signed between the two parties. GVFL sanctioned Rs. 209.25 lakh to the company in 15.5 lakh equity shares at a premium of Rs. 3.5 per shares with a share holding of 10.2 percent.

During the post GVFL assistance, market for ceramic tiles was growing but due to some internal and external factors, MCIL couldn't satisfy the latent demand of their dealers. The commercial production started late, marketing dealers were appointed selectively and advertising and promotional support was deficient. Product was launched with few designs, light and less gloss, which were not appreciated by the dealers. The external factors like recession in economy, instability of central government, price reduction in housing sector and fierce competition of the tiles market saw declining prices of tiles. When the product did not excite the market sentiments, the dealers lost their interest. The external factors contributed to recessionary demand. The continuous drop in prices of tiles brought the sentiment among the dealers not to stock the materials. The market conditions continued to be low. Looking at the above results, company started reviewing the performance of the company. The activities were geared towards the quality standards, design improvement, distribution strategy by the marketing department.

MCIL couldn't succeed the way the promoters wanted,

resulting in estimated loss of Rs. 55.3m in FY-98. Madhulika group thought of reviewing and restructuring its entire group operations on core competency areas and exit from the others. As an outcome of this exercise, MCIL decided to exit from the tiles business on the consideration of market depression and substantial capital requirement. The promoters and GVFL/CDC started identifying a buyer to take over the entire company. A buyer was identified- Son Earth Ceramics Ltd. (SECL), an aggressive player in the industry and have grown through acquisitions was willing to purchase promoters' holdings in MCIL for the sale of their stake i.e. 69.2 percent @ Rs. 4.55 per share. Thus further acquisitions cannot rule out. In such scenario, in case of future mergers, would further dilute GVFL's holdings in the merged entity. GVFL had two options: Stay with the new promoters or Exit from MCIL. The Board of GVFL decided to go for the option of Non Convertible Debentures (NCDs). After the divestment, GVFL recovered the disbursed amount of Rs. 244.75 lakh through various instruments of recovery.

Research Questions: In case of MCIL, financial contract designed by GVFL for the entrepreneur deals with all the provisions of adverse selection and moral hazard adequately and sufficiently. The problem of adverse selection was mitigated through proper appraisal and self-selection process. After observing the salient features, GVFL sanctioned the financial assistance to meet the capital expenditure on expansion and diversification. During the post GVFL assistance, monitoring of performance was done very carefully. There was no problem of moral hazard caused by the promoters although due to some internal and external factors, MCIL couldn't satisfy the latent demand of their dealers and had to exit from the from the tiles business on the consideration of market depression and substantial capital requirement.

The performance of the firm has been analysed in two ways: 1. Performance of firm Return on funds lent out (percent per annum) and 2. Performance in contractual compliance: least or absence of conflict of interest between GVFL and Borrower firm.

Average Net profit per annum was negative of Rs. 5.57 lakh due to the internal and external factors faced by MCIL. But with the constant monitoring activities both by personal visits paid by the GVFL officers and through calling of information either monthly or whenever required weekly, MCIL was able to save the company from severe losses and could also identify a prospective buyer for its acquisition. GVFL could also recover the amount invested into the company through various instruments, although it was negative. GVFL's ROI was –2.71 percent. During the tenure of 12 years both had maintained good relationship. GVFL's involvement was greater in the venture although both the parties didn't have any major conflict of interest. GVFL always helped the company in solving the marketing problem of poor dealer's management, deficient advertising and promotional activities. Thus, there were no principle-agent problem in the case and the performance was considerably satisfactory.

To sum up, the financial contract of GVFL had adequate provisions and processes to deal with adverse selection and moral hazard problem. Therefore there was no principle agent problem faced by GVFL.

Case 2: Medisurg Surgical Ltd.: M/s Medisurg Surgical was promoted by a first generation entrepreneur, to manufacture Health Care Products in the Mehsana district of Gujarat. These products were manufactured for the first time in India, market price was quite attractive, labour intensive, cheap cost of manufacturing, favourable foreign exchange situation, price benefits being import substitute, international standards. After due appraisal, sensitivity and SWOT analysis, GVFL sanctioned Rs. 134.30 lakh on November 1, 1991.

During the post GVFL assistance, company faced initial problems such as poor market acceptance, irregular sales, persistent losses, which resulted into erosion of liquidity. The company had complaints of leakages and inconsistent dimensions of the product, deficient dealer network and inefficient marketing strategy. GVFL helped the company by introducing with many firms and organizations, informed about technology fairs in order to form dealer network in marketing. The promoters were technocrats with sound product knowledge but lacked marketing and financial know-how. The company had poor accounting policies, improper functioning of quality control department, no provision for TDS, depreciation and dissatisfaction on the part of workers.

Research Questions: The financial contract designed by GVFL for Medisurg Surgical was an exceptional case having less than the required/standard number of clauses. The appraisal clauses that are required at the time of appraising the project, which has approached the VC for financial assistance, can be maximum five core clauses, but in case of Medisurg Surgical there were only three clauses. The two missing clauses are: direct participation in management by VC and staged investment, which are very important for any venture capitalist to safeguard his funds. Self Selection clauses that help in go/no go decision-making along with the Appraisal clauses help in mitigating the problems caused by the adverse selection due to asymmetric information. These include profit participation, Compensation vs. option, subscription by GVFL, progressive release of equity funds, Equity contribution by entrepreneur, Capital structure, Size of board etc. Maximum number of self-selection clauses can be eleven which includes seven core clauses and four special clauses that are particular to case. Medisurg Surgical had only two clauses i.e. one core clause and one special clauses. The six core clauses that are missing were profit participation, compensation vs. option, progressive release of equity funds, Equity contribution by entrepreneur, Capital structure, Size of board.

Each case has been analyzed from two aspects. First aspect is the number of agreement clauses relating to monitoring the projects and the behaviour of the entrepreneur during the tenure of GVFL assistance. Second aspect is the number of monitoring events that took place during the same time. The event is defined as the number of actions taken or initiated in compliance with the monitoring clauses of the contract. Monitoring clauses can be maximum 104 in number, classified as Core clauses (31), supplement clauses (48) and special clauses/customized clauses (25).

After the disbursement of the funds, the personal visits of the GVFL officers to the plant were not regular but after noticing irregularities they started paying regular visits. The information/reports through various status/progress reports, letters, Notices, minutes of Board Meeting, Annual General Meetings and annual reports for transparency in decision making were called quarterly. Similarly the disclosure clauses which includes the legal provisions–to furnish GVFL with true and correct information, No conflict with the Memorandum of Association and Articles of association of the company, company has complied with the provision of Sec 81 (1A) of the companies act, company should not be in arrears of any public demands- income tax, corporation tax etc were only two out of five core clauses. Lastly, Incentivizing, Divestment, IPO, Legal Remedies clauses which includes the provisions of incentivizing that are performance based by way of assurance for additional funds, divestment, IPO, exit options, sell of shares by promoters, mode and method of purchase of shares, breach of terms and conditions, arbitration, jurisdiction, currency of the agreement as long as the GVFL holds shares in the company etc were only two in number out of twenty-eight core clauses.

From the above details we can say that the contract designed by GVFL for Medisurg Surgical was incomplete in terms of standard clauses, which worked as a loophole for the entrepreneur and GVFL faced the problems of moral hazard. The promoters didn't inform GVFL about the cash accepted from Indian Overseas Bank. Mr. Ganesh Talati (promoter) was siphoning cash from Gujarat Surgical. It seemed that the capital investment done by GVFL during initial stages was unnecessary. The forecasted sales figures showed by Mr. Talati were never achieved. The demand for the products is seasonal and proper product planning was not done while forecasting.

Medisurg Surgical Ltd. being financed by GVFL had to function according to the terms of the deal. Any decision to be taken was first supposed to be discussed with GVFL. There were many instances where the pre-determined norms of functioning were not followed: financial irregularities, large dealings in cash, monetary transactions with external investors were not recorded properly and informed to GVFL, sale of assets, divestment process with an NRI investor without GVFL's knowledge. GVFL also started loosing interest in the firm and wanted to divest at an IRR of 18 percent. After negotiations, price of Rs 12 per share was agreed upon.

The performance of the firm on the two parameters: performance by profitability of venture equity given by GVFL (Return in percent per annum on GVFL's funds lent out) and performance in contractual compliance- least or absence of conflict of interest between GVFL and Borrower firm has been satisfactory. Despite of having all the irregularities the net profit of the firms was increasing in the successive years with an average net profit per annum of Rs. 25.92 lakh. Return on investment for GVFL was also positive i.e. the receipts through different recovery instruments were more than the amount disbursed/given by GVFL during their tenure. ROI for GVFL in percentage per annum was 9.91 percent. Medisurg Surgical's expectations were greater than GVFL's during the earlier period of tenure but later on looking at the financial irregularities, siphoning off funds, deficient advertising and promotional activities GVFL appointed a financial executive to which the firm agreed. There was not much conflict of interest between the two parties as GVFL could always resolve the problems.

To sum up, GVFL could divest at the right time in anticipation of the problems of moral hazards and improper /irregularities in maintaining the financial records of the company. Thus GVFL could recover all the funds through its tight monitoring and proper anticipation of problems.

Case 3: BALS: M/s BALS was engaged in manufacture and distribution of Computer hardware and software. The company had introduced a number of innovative products with a Star Exporters status and entered into strategic alliances with many foreign companies. During March 1992, due to the sharp decline in the export sales, government regulations in India, political instability in USSR and unfavourable changes in exchange rates, BALS approached Gujarat Venture Finance Limited (GVFL) for financial assistance and a major change in its strategy. GVFL carried out a due diligence check, apprised the company on its future potential, which looked bright. GVFL invested Rs. 40.00 lakh in the form of Equity and Rs. 58.50 Lakh in the form of Secured Fully Convertible Debentures (SFCDs) on July 10, 1992.

In the post GVFL assistance era, company changed its strategy to tap the Local Area Network and Wide Area Network market. GVFL nominated directors, chairman on the board and set up monitoring committee to look after the progress of the company and also to safeguard its own investment. BALS was later converted into a public limited company. In September 1994, BALS came out with the public issue of Rs. 300 lakh, which was oversubscribed by 12.83 times and shares were listed on the stock exchange at Rs. 30 each.

After liberalization and subsequent opening up of the economy the import duties on computer systems were drastically reduced and competition from foreign manufacturers increased the expenditure on advertisements & promotions. The company had entered into the networking business where its major customers were Government departments, having long drawn repayment procedures. Thus, it resulted in canalization of short-term funds for a longer time due to piling up of inventory. The main reason of failure was technological incompetence as the company's basic strength was in marketing and due to Russian disintegration sales were highly affected. Thus, the company was facing financial crunch although the company had shown profits, they were only book profits as the money invested in business was not generating any returns and instead they were locked up as Debtors.

As per the terms of the Shareholders' Agreement executed with the promoters and the company, GVFL was required to offer the shares obtained on conversion first to the promoters for buyback. However, the promoters were unable to buy back shares from GVFL and therefore a divestment committee was set-up. The divestment committee approved selling of shares at Rs 16 or more per share to maintain an IRR of 37.96 percent. GVFL appointed internal auditors to look into the operations of BALS, as GVFL was not satisfied with the performance of the company. BALS was facing severe liquidity crunch on account of dead stocks and debtors, the recovery of some of which seemed doubtful. BALS had not been able to provide true and fair financial picture to the Board of Directors and the internal auditors appointed by GVFL came out with the conclusion that though the company has been showing profits for the past years it had actually been making losses.

Later, the core promoters gave a commitment to buyback the entire equity held by GVFL-1990 at a price of Rs. 1/- per share amounting to Rs. 12.85 lakh in 6 months time, which was 10 times less than the investment amount of GVCF-1990. Company was also unable to pay the employees salaries. GVFL started selling shares of BALS on August 14, 1997, at the net price of Rs. 5.05 per share and was the only major seller in the market. As part of the divestment exercise GVFL also started to scout for buyers that could bring in additional funds and also new business opportunities. GVFL was also willing to divest some part of its holdings in favour of the strategic buyer.

Research Questions: In case of BALS, financial contract designed by GVFL for the entrepreneur dealt with all the provisions of adverse selection and moral hazard adequately and sufficiently. The problem of adverse selection was mitigated through proper appraisal and self-selection process. After observing the salient features, GVFL sanctioned the financial assistance for expansion. Unfortunately, GVFL while appraising the project failed to foresee the probable changes in economic policy though the wave of liberalization had already started flowing in 1992. Along with this GVFL could also not judge the technological incompetence of the promoter, which later on turned out to be the main reason of downfall of the company. During the post GVFL assistance, monitoring of performance was done very carefully. There was no problem of moral hazard caused by the promoters although the core promoters of BALS were non-technical people who were unable to provide the company with proper vision and the business environment factors that affected the operations of the company.

The performance of the firm has been analyzed in two ways: 1. Performance of firm Return on funds lent out (percent per annum) and 2. Performance in contractual compliance: least or absence of conflict of interest between GVFL and Borrower firm.

Average Net profit per annum was negative of Rs. 41.73 lakh due per annum to the business environment factors faced by BALS. But with the constant monitoring activities both by personal visits paid by the GVFL officers and through calling of information every quarterly, BALS was able to save the company from severe losses and sell the shares in the market. GVFL could also recover the amount invested into the company through various instruments. The total receipts were greater than the amount invested by GVFL for financial assistance. GVFL's ROI was 2.10 percent during its tenure of five years. They both had good relationship. During the earlier years of their tenure, BALS expectations and involvement was higher than GVFL's. GVFL always acted as an advisor rather than a mentor and guide. But later when GVFL anticipated the losses and appointed the internal auditor to review the financial position of the company, both agreed without any conflict of interest. GVFL also helped to scout a buyer for additional funds and business opportunities. Thus, there were no principle-agent problem in the case and the performance was considerably satisfactory.

To sum up, the financial contract of GVFL had adequate provisions and processes to deal with adverse selection and moral hazard problem. Therefore there was no principle agent problem faced by GVFL.

Case 4: Suman Cables Limited: Suman Cables Limited (SCL) was promoted as a Private Limited company, which was the pioneer in the manufacturing of Ultra Fine Magnet wires. The company came to know about GVFL through GIIC and wanted to set up a plant in GIDC Electronics Estate in Ahmedabad. Before sanctioning funds for financial assistance, GVFL made a due diligence, which included the appraisal of the company and self-selection process. After observing the salient features of the company which includes Promoters' sound background, experience, significant exposure, its global collaboration and a history of successful technical innovations, GVFL agreed to finance the project with an agreement signed between the two parties. GVFL sanctioned Rs. 66.25 lakh, which works out to 34 percent of the total equity share capital of the company in March 1994.

During the post GVFL assistance, the company suffered losses due to late commencement of the production, sales below expectations and non-renewal of the long-term order from its collaborator. The Promoters had started giving more importance to one of their other company and became negligent towards SCL. GVFL had insisted several times that one of the sons of the promoter should look after the operations at SCL but the Promoter did not work on the suggestions to improve the productivity of SCL. Eventually it resulted in need of vast amount of money, which forced the promoters to siphon off money from SCL by various abnormal practices. This affected the shop floor people for instance, even though having proper training the technician at the collaborators' plant were unable to deliver the desired quality of product. Thus, the foregoing factors affected the sales severely.

Meanwhile the company was sold to another group without being left to the knowledge of GVFL. This again resulted in making GVFL's investment in trouble. In addition to above some non-compliance issues were noticed by the internal auditors like improper financial recording, lack of proper authorization of vouchers, and issuance of cheques getting dishonoured. Thus considering the above factors GVFL formed a committee to divest its equity partnership from SCL.

Through various rounds of negotiations by the new management of GVFL, it managed to recover nearly double the amount it invested with the IRR of 15 percent. As per shareholders agreement executed between GVFL and promoters on March 6, 1998, GVFL offered its 6.625 lakh equity shares in SCL to promoters @ Rs. 18 per share. The board meeting of SCL on March 21, 1998 brought an end to the negotiation process @ Rs. 18.25 per share.

Research Questions: In case of, Suman Cables the financial contract designed by GVFL for the entrepreneur deals with provisions covering adverse selection and moral hazard adequately and sufficiently. The problem of adverse selection was mitigated through proper appraisal and self-selection process. After observing the salient features, GVFL sanctioned the financial assistance to set up a plant. During the post GVFL assistance, close monitoring of performance was done. But still, due to lack of professional attitude, promoters adopted unethical business practices to cheat the professional team of VC firm, and sold the company without informing GVFL through very mean business tricks. Thus GVFL were left with the option to exit from the venture and the company was sold to a third party.

The performance of the firm has been analyzed in two ways: 1. Performance of firm Return on funds lent out (percent per annum) and 2. Performance in contractual compliance: least or absence of conflict of interest between GVFL and Borrower firm.

Average Net profit per annum was positive of Rs. 59.67 lakh per annum with the help of GVFL who introduced the company with an international quartz watch firm and facilitated the process of obtaining the electronic subsidy from the government. Close monitoring was done by GVFL both by personal visits and acquiring information quarterly, monthly and yearly basis as per the requirement and financial position of the company. GVFL could also recover the amount invested into the company through various instruments, as the total receipts were more than the amount disbursed for the assistance. GVFL's ROI was 15.40 percent (excess of Rs 70.27 lakh). During the tenure of five years both had maintained good relationship. During its course of association with the SCL, GVFL tried to rescue the company in tough periods. It helped to clear the statutory & legal compliances at the inception stage, helped in making tie-ups, granting Bridge loan, pursuing the collaborator to invest into Equity and appointing auditors at its expenses from time to time for helping the company streamlining its systems & procedures. Thus, there were no principle-agent problem in the case and the performance was considerably satisfactory.

To sum up, GVFL did a close monitoring. The bad intentions of the promoters could not remain hidden from GVFL. GVFL at the right time came up with the divestment proposal. It could divest from SCL with good returns even if the liquidity situation of the company was bad and was loaded with debt. The financial contract of GVFL had adequate provisions and processes to deal with adverse selection and moral hazard problem. Therefore there was no principle agent problem faced by GVFL.

Case 5: Campco Industries Ltd.: Campco was engaged in the manufacturing of Engineering Thermoplastic (ETP) Compounds and set up in Dadra Nagar Haveli, Silvasa. The company approached GVFL for expansion of its capacity and to diversify into manufacturing Polypropylene Multi Filament Yarns (PPMFY) for exploiting niche markets. Before sanctioning of funds for financial assistance, due diligence was done which includes the appraisal of the company (SWOT, past performance, expected profitability) and self-selection process by GVFL. After observing the salient features of the company: well-established business, loyal customers, good reputation, qualified technologist/technocrats, track record of innovative products, R&D, joint venture with international company, abundant raw material, and established and registered trademarks, GVFL agreed to finance the project and an agreement was signed between the two parties. On 16th March 1995, GVFL decided to fund the project by the equity participation to the extent of Rs. 88.875 lakh by subscribing 1,18,500 shares of Rs. 10 each with the premium of Rs. 65 which works out to 2.18 percent of the total equity share capital of the company.

During the post GVFL assistance period there was proper flow of information about the happenings of Campco. But slowly information ceased to come from Campco. The position of the company was very pathetic and continuously deteriorating. Campco was facing problems in raising funds, although had higher sales, issued new equity, increase in reserves & surplus, inventory and finished goods stock but at the same time it had losses due to high financial charges. The company was facing marketing, distribution and liquidity constraints. Increase in the polymer prices, wide fluctuation in raw material prices and weak demand of end products the company was not able to pass onto its consumers. CAMPCO could not come out with a public issue in 1995 due to slump in the capital markets & the shift away from small cap companies during the second half of 1995-96.The Company was also facing difficulties with its collaborator.

The auditors of the company in their audit report declared the Company as a Sick Industrial unit. Company approached FIs and Banks for restructuring of their dues, as company had made consistence defaults in repayment of instalments and in payment of interest. GVFL was not able to appoint directors in the board of Campco because it was having only 2.18 percent shareholding. But then also nominees from GVFL attended meetings and kept an eye on the proceedings of the company frequently.

General downward trend in the economy, increase in raw material cost of input, inability to increase product sale prices, continued liquidity and working fund constraints forced GVFL to start the divestment process. The performance of the company was far below the performance as projected during the appraisal. The company had never achieved economies of scale. The exit from CAMPCO by way of an IPO or sale to strategic investors seemed near impossible in the foreseeable future. GVFL had been with Campco for more than 6 years and it was time to divest taking into consideration the normal period for such an investment is around 4-5 years. These issues, coupled with lack of regular information to GVFL, raise considerable concern.

Looking at the above position, GVFL asked Campco to buy back the shares held by GVFL at the price of Rs. 161.19/- per share as the company failed to make the public issue within two years. Campco was not having enough liquidity to buy GVFL's shareholding. Therefore, following two options were suggested: Swap of the shares held by them in Colortek with Campco shares held by GVFL and some amount to be paid in cash to GVFL. And secondly, public issue of Campco as business was showing some improvements. On June 18, 2001, in a meeting at GVFL by both the parties was arranged for divestment proposal where in the Swap of Campco share with Colortek's was decided. After various round of negotiations, on January 9, 2003 the agreement was signed between GVFL & Campco to resolve long-standing problems between them.

Research Questions: In case of Campco, financial contract designed by GVFL for the entrepreneur dealt with all the provisions of adverse selection and moral hazard adequately and sufficiently. The problem of adverse selection was mitigated through proper appraisal and self-selection process. After observing the salient features, GVFL sanctioned the financial assistance to meet the capital expenditure on expansion and diversification. During the post GVFL assistance, monitoring of performance was done very carefully. There was no problem of moral hazard caused by the promoters although financial performance of the company was continuously deteriorating due to under utilization of the plant.

The performance of the firm has been analyzed in two ways: 1. Performance of firm Return on funds lent out (percent per annum) and 2. Performance in contractual compliance: least or absence of conflict of interest between GVFL and Borrower firm.

Average Net profit per annum was negative of Rs. 263.37 lakh per annum due to general downturn in the economy, increase in raw material prices, inability to increase selling price and liquidity constraints. With the constant monitoring activities both by personal visits paid by the GVFL officers and through calling of information either fortnightly or quarterly, GVFL was able to save the company from severe losses and exit at the right time. GVFL could also recover the amount invested into the company through various instruments, although it was negative. GVFL's was –12.34 percent . During the tenure of eight years both has maintained a cordial relation. Most of the time both the parties succeeded to resolve the problem. GVFL helped Campco to take some of the vital strategic decisions, which were necessary for the growth of the company. GVFL had done its best to get proper information from Campco and also maintained the progress of the company through active participation in the affairs of the company through out the investment period. GVFL had advised Campco for strategic tie-up with major foreign companies for increase in revenue from the products, helped in preparing prospectus for IPO and above all added strength to the internal control system by closely monitoring the flow of funds in the company. Thus, there were no principle-agent problem in the case and the performance was considerably satisfactory.

Overall assessment of the investment shows that GVFL, which invested Rs. 88.875 lakh in Campco as a portfolio investment, failed in getting the projected returns on its investment. The decision taken by GVFL was right on the basis of given economic scenario, fluctuations in economy and market conditions due to which Campco made heavy losses. In short, GVFL proved its ability by negotiating on the divestment proposal. Thus, Divestment process taken by GVFL can be seen as profitable for successful ending.

To sum up, the financial contract of GVFL had adequate provisions and processes to deal with adverse selection and moral hazard problem. Close monitoring and active participation in the operations of the company helped GVFL to detect position of the company at the right time. Therefore there was no principle agent problem faced by GVFL.

Case 6: Vikram Industries Limited: M/s Vikram Industries Limited was engaged in the manufacture of Knitted Cotton Socks in Gujarat. The company had approached GVFL in 1994 with a proposal to import advanced computerized socks knitting for Equity participation of Rs. 75.00 lakh in firm allotment category with three years lock-in period. Before sanctioning of funds for financial assistance, due diligence was done which includes the appraisal of the company (past performance, expected profitability, SWOT and sensitivity analysis) and self-selection process by GVFL. After observing the salient features of the company which includes reputed and experienced promoters, latest knitting equipments, large range of socks, reputed consultancy organization for the project formulation and implementation, infrastructure for double capacity and advantage of scale of economy, GVFL agreed to finance the project and an agreement was signed between the two parties.

During the post GVFL assistance, Vikram's performance was affected due to delay in production, cost over-run, slow inflow of orders, poor quality of cotton yarn, careless purchase of raw material, mechanical and technical breakdown and problems of labour absenteeism. GVFL suggested for the viability study of the project. Expenses towards salaries, wages and utilities were high. It was also advised that the company should prepare a budget, monitor its cash flow and appoint an internal auditor to avoid further cash losses. Several consignments could not be dispatched due to transportation strike and change in exchange rate in respect of Foreign Currency Loan for machinery acquired outside India. Delay in product acceptance by overseas customers further slowed the sales. Thus, there was an increase in financial cost and the viability of the venture was adversely affected due to the discrepancies in the purchase orders.

GVFL saw continuous fall in the financial position of the company and decided to divest. GVFL had provided the financial assistance of Rs. 75.00 lakh to Vikram Industries. Looking at a deteriorating condition GVFL divested the shares to a third party at a negotiable price.

Research Questions: In case of Vikram, financial contract designed by GVFL for the entrepreneur dealt with all the provisions of adverse selection and moral hazard adequately and sufficiently. The problem of adverse selection was mitigated through proper appraisal and self-selection process. After observing the salient features, GVFL sanctioned the financial assistance to meet the capital expenditure. During the post GVFL assistance, monitoring of performance was done very carefully. There was no problem of moral hazard caused by the promoters although due to change in government policy, product mix, negligence on the part of promoters and continuous fall in the sales affected the performance of the company.

The performance of the firm has been analyzed in two ways: 1.Performance of firm Return on funds lent out (percent per annum) and 2. Performance in contractual compliance: least or absence of conflict of interest between GVFL and Borrower firm.

Average Net profit per annum was positive of Rs. 14.53 lakh per annum due to marketing and business environmental factors faced by Vikram. But with the constant monitoring activities both by personal visits paid by the GVFL officers and through calling of information quarterly, GVFL was able to save the company from severe losses and could also identify a prospective buyer for the sale of its shares. GVFL could also recover the amount invested into the company through various instruments, although it was negative. GVFL's ROI was –11.22 percent. During the tenure of 12 years both had maintained good relationship. GVFL's involvement was greater in the venture looking at the careless purchase of raw material by the management. GVFL always helped the company in solving the marketing problems of poor dealer network, maintenance of budget, and appointment of internal auditors to safeguard the problems of cash losses. Thus, there were no principle-agent problem in the case and the performance was considerably satisfactory.

To sum up, the financial contract of GVFL had adequate provisions and processes to deal with adverse selection and moral hazard problem. With close monitoring GVFL could save the company from severe losses, find an appropriate buyer for the purchase of shares and exit from the venture. Therefore there was no principle agent problem faced by GVFL.

Case 7: Shrechem Limited: M/s Shrechem Ltd. was engaged in the manufacture of Lactic Acid from Molasses in Tamil Nadu under the assistance of Canara Venture Capital

Fund (CVCF) and TIDCO. To overcome the problem of cost over-run, CVCF and TIDCO requested GVFL in 1991 for providing capital assistance to bridge the gap of Rs. 20.00 lakh in the means of finance. Before sanctioning of funds for financial assistance, due diligence was done which includes the appraisal of the company (SWOT, past performance, expected profitability) and self-selection process by GVFL. After observing the salient features of the company, which includes renowned biotechnologist, innovative products, support for R&D, Marketing, domestic and international demand-supply and plans for IPO, GVFL agreed to finance the project and an agreement was signed between the two parties. On June 29, 1993, GVFL agreed and sanctioned venture capital assistance of Rs. 25.00 lakh to the company by way of equity, based on the appraisal prepared by CVCF. It was also decided that CVCF would take a lead in monitoring of the project.

During the post GVFL assistance period, after the commencement of the production the company faced many serious operational problems. The process technology was reasonably well standardized. But there were difficulties in developing the technology. In its first year of operation the company established product quality with a number of customers and also developed process to make colourless, odourless, heat stable lactic acid but there were cash losses due to lower turnover, lower production, sales, loss of product and leakages from corroded equipments, which eroded the working capital margin. The unidentified impurities in molasses contributed to major problems in purification. The levels of impurities present were very high, requiring repeated purification steps. This was crippling the attainment of the rated production capacity. The process conditions were very corrosive which resulted in damage to plant & machinery that needed repair and replacement. This also resulted in loss of production and not attaining the rated capacity. Since the company was operating at low levels of capacity utilization, the financial costs were not covered.

On May 2, 1995 GVFL sanctioned additional investment of Rs. 19.50 lakh in form of Redeemable Cumulative Convertible Preference Shares (RCCPS) of Rs. 10 each. However the company was unable to achieve targeted levels of production. In the month of November 1996, Canara Bank started adjusting outstanding interest on term loan from the receipts in the current account, which resulted in a tremendous liquidity crunch. The company was also trying to raise funds for payments of bank dues, increasing capacities and supplementing erosion in margin for working capital. It was impossible for GVFL to fund the entire amount and meanwhile the company was declared a NPA. GVFL studied the viability of this proposition and informed the company that it would not be able to sustain payment to the bank, even after raising funds to pay off overdue amounts. Considering the company's tight liquidity position, GVFL disbursed Rs. 10.00 lakh as Optionally Convertible/Redeemable Cumulative Preference shares.

The company was facing severe working capital problems, lacking a clear marketing plan, which was in turn affecting the production and sales of the company. There were statutory compliance to maintain all statutory books and records. The promoters were not showing willingness to return the share application with in the time limit and purchase of stake of either CVCF or GVFL in the range of Rs. 3 per share. The company was tying to explore export avenues and prospective buyers. Alternatives for exit from the company were through Sale of Technology to a prospective buyer in India or Abroad and buyback of shares.

In the months of June 1999, Mr. Prashant one if the promoter of the company proposed to buyback the shares. But CVCF expressed to wait till March 31, 2001 for the exit from the company. On January 4, 2001, Mr. Prashant informed the Board, promoters' plans to offer to GVFL a proposal to buyout its stake for Rs 17 lakh before March 31, 2001, subject to

GVFL's approval. On March 8, 2001, GVFL gave the divestment proposal for buyback of 3,26,800 equity shares and 1,95,000 Preference Shares held by GVFL in Shrechem Ltd to Boston Education & Software Technologies Ltd for appraisal. On March 30, 2001, Mr. Prashant accepted the proposal to buyback of 3, 26,800 equity shares and 1, 95,000 Preference Shares held by GVFL in Shrechem Ltd. On September 12, 2001, GVFL received a one time settlement amount of Rs. 15,65,400 against 3,26,800 equity shares and 1,95,000 CRPS held by GVCF-1990 in Shrechem Ltd and exit from the venture.

Research Questions: In case of Shrechem, the financial contract designed by GVFL for the entrepreneur deals with all the provisions of adverse selection and moral hazard adequately and sufficiently. The problem of adverse selection was mitigated through proper appraisal and self-selection process. After observing the salient features, GVFL sanctioned the financial assistance to over come the problems of cost over-run. During the post GVFL assistance, monitoring of performance was done very carefully. There was no problem of moral hazard caused by the promoters although due to some operational problems the performance was affected.

The performance of the firm has been analyzed in two ways: 1. Performance of firm Return on funds lent out (percent per annum) and 2. Performance in contractual compliance: least or absence of conflict of interest between GVFL and Borrower firm.

Average Net profit per annum was positive due of Rs. 0.03 lakh per annum. With the constant monitoring activities both by personal visits paid by the GVFL officers and through calling of information either fortnightly or weekly, GVFL was able to save the company from severe losses. GVFL could also recover the amount invested into the company through various instruments, although it was negative. GVFL's ROI was –6.57 percent. During the tenure of 8 years both had maintained good relationship. GVFL's involvement was greater in the venture although both the parties didn't have any major conflict of interest. GVFL always helped the company in solving technical problems, maintaining the internal records and raising funds. Thus, there were no principle-agent problem in the case and the performance was considerably satisfactory. During its initial stage the product faced some difficulty in acceptance but later on the marketing problems were taken care of. On account of the delay in quickly getting on to fast track performance the company has accumulated losses due to non-coverage of some fixed costs components. Thus the reason for the erosion in the net worth of the company was not due to any managerial or other problems but due to the circumstances beyond the control of Management.

To sum up, the financial contract of GVFL had adequate provisions and processes to deal with adverse selection and moral hazard problem. Therefore there was no principle agent problem faced by GVFL.

Case 8: Abhinav Polyesters Limited: M/s Abhinav Polyester Limited (APL) was engaged in the manufacture of textured and twisted yarn at Ahmedabad. In 1991, GVFL received a proposal from APL, for equity participation in their proposed expansion and diversification for sizing, warping and weaving of yarn. Before sanctioning of funds for financial assistance, due diligence was done which includes the appraisal of the company (SWOT, past performance, expected profitability) and self-selection process by GVFL. After observing the salient features of the company, which includes four years of existence, good track record and was promoted by professionals, GVFL agreed to finance the project and an agreement was signed between the two parties. On August 25, 1992 the Board of GVFL approved equity participation by way of subscription to 3,00,000 equity shares at a premium of Rs. 7.5 per share aggregating to Rs. 52.50 lakh.

During the post GVFL assistance, the financial performance of the company was encouraging in the face of a general depressive phase in the textile industry with high excise levies in the Union Budget and rising cotton prices. APL had successfully made the public issue @ Rs.17.50 per share, which was fully subscribed. Later the performance of textile industry particularly for texturising, cotton spinning and fabric sectors was affected due to high cotton prices, stiff consumer resistance to price increase, imposition of excise duty in texturising, etc. Company was also facing severe liquidity crunch due to credit squeeze on working capital facilities by company's bankers. As a result the company was forced to approach other institutions/banks for additional working capital/short term borrowings for overcoming liquidity crunch, thereby increasing finance costs. Due to the above reasons profitability i.e. profit margins and EPS were much below the expected levels. GVFL suggested recruiting senior professionals in the areas of Production, Administration, part-time company secretary and marketing arrangements with companies like Mafatlal companies. It was also seen that the sales in the texturing divisions were affected due to transporters strike and text riser's strike. Some legal cases against the company and directors were also brought to the notice of GVFL

In February 1996, GVFL reminded APL of buying back GVFL's shareholding as the lock-in period was expiring in April 1996. The performance of APL was appraised and the share price was worked out to be Rs. 30-31 per share as against the market price of Rs.10-11 per share. In March 1996, GVFL put up an agenda item for divestment from APL. On 6th April 1996, GVFL approved the proposal of buy-back of its shares by the promoters, on the condition of sharing profits with the promoters if the shares were sold by GVFL in the market at a profit. On November 20, 1996, GVFL handed over 1400 shares of APL to the promoters on receipt of Rs. 50,000 from them and simultaneously released 1400 shares held in their name as collateral. This was as per the terms and conditions of the divestment agreement. For the remaining shares, APL was finding it difficult to buyback the shares due to heavy cash losses, operational health and severe sluggishness in the textile market. Owing to such a situation, GVFL had offered to sell those shares to some of the friends of promoters at nominal prices as one time settlement. The promoters were making all possible efforts to motivate people to accept such an offer. The redemption was affected by cash flows of APL and GVFL was forced to accept lower prices per share.

Research Questions: In case of APL financial contract designed by GVFL for the entrepreneur deals with all the provisions of adverse selection and moral hazard adequately and sufficiently. The problem of adverse selection was mitigated through proper appraisal and self-selection process. After observing the salient features, GVFL sanctioned the financial assistance for diversification. During the post GVFL assistance, monitoring of performance was done very carefully. There was no problem of moral hazard caused by the promoters although due to financial, marketing and environmental factors affected the performance.

The performance of the firm has been analyzed in two ways: 1. Performance of firm Return on funds lent out (percent per annum) and 2. Performance in contractual compliance: least or absence of conflict of interest between GVFL and Borrower firm.

Average Net profit per annum was positive of Rs. 74.60 lakh per annum due to constant monitoring activities both by personal visits paid by the GVFL officers and through calling of information fortnightly and monthly. GVFL was able to save its investment from severe losses. GVFL could also recover the amount invested into the company through various instruments, although it was negative. GVFL's ROI was –10.40 percent. During the tenure of five years, both had maintained good relationship. GVFL's involvement was greater in the venture although both the parties didn't have any major conflict of interest. GVFL always helped the company in solving the liquidity crisis, marketing problem of poor dealer's management, deficient advertising and promotional activities. Thus, there were no principle-agent problem in the case and the performance was considerably satisfactory.

Thus, it was a prudent decision by GVFL to divest from APL purely because of business reasons. GVFL did not foresee any significant pick-up in revenue and EPS that would have enabled it to sell the shares at a considerable appreciation compared to the acquisition cost. It was a very open-ended divestment process and it was contingent to the performance of APL as well as the conditions prevailing in the share market. To sum up, the financial contract of GVFL had adequate provisions and processes to deal with adverse selection and moral hazard problem. Therefore there was no principle agent problem faced by GVFL.

Case 9: M/s Anjali Biotech Limited: M/s Anjali BioTech Laboratories Limited was engaged in manufacture of Bio Fertilizer at Pune. The company had marketing tie-up with M/s Zuari Agro Chemicals Ltd which markets Anjali's product under Brand name "BIOPHOS" Neem based Biopesticides. Before sanctioning of funds for financial assistance, due diligence was done which includes the appraisal of the company (SWOT, past performance, expected profitability) and self-selection process by GVFL. After observing the salient features of the company, which includes first generation entrepreneur, technocrat, professionally qualified and experienced entrepreneurs, GVFL agreed to finance the project. On October 6, 1994, GVFL accepted the proposal for setting up a plant to produce 2.50 liters p.a. of Neem based Bio-Pesticides and granted financial assistance by way of subscription to 2, 50,000 equity shares each of Rs 10 at par aggregating to Rs. 25.00 lakh on firm allotment basis.

During the post GVFL assistance, the company's performance in terms of turnover and profits had doubled. In 1996, company came to GVFL with another proposal to expand manufacturing capacities of Bio fertilizers as well as Bioneem plant by addition of balancing equipment for financial assistance of Rs. 30 lakh by way of Fully Convertible Debentures. Later, the company started facing difficulties in both the main products- Biophos and Bioneem due to drop in sales due to poor off-take by Zuari Agro Chemicals, irregular monsoon, labour problems, increase in material cost, employee expenses, selling & distribution expenses, inventory indicating company's affairs were not managed properly. The company progressed diversification project for Bacillus Thuringiensis (BT) based bio-insecticides and Mosquito coil. Looking at the performance of the existing project, commitment by promoters and limited resources, GVFL expressed its serious concern to concentrate on existing projects, which were at critical stage instead of committing additional financial resources for new project. The promoters were keen towards the BT and mosquito project and started working. On proposing to start a new project for manufacture of Mosquito Coils and establishing Anjali Farm Chem. Pvt. Ltd as a SSI unit, GVFL sent a letter to ABIL for violating the agreement and filed a civil suit in civil court.

Looking at the above reasons, on March 4, 2000, a divestment note of Anjali Bio Tech Ltd was prepared and placed before the divestment committee of GVFL. The company was unable to create export market since these products have to undergo an elaborate registration process in each country. Due to deterioration in performance and poor liquidity position, the company was unable to pay dues to IDBI. The company offered its neem plant on job working basis for a nominal charge, which might reduce the cash losses to some extent. However, on the whole, the performance was unlikely to show major improvement over the next 2-3 years. The promoters were technically sound but they lacked focus and were trying to introduce new products before consolidating earlier projects, which affected the performance. Given the above situation, GVFL also tried to explore opportunities for strategic alliance and with the financial position and size of the company, an IPO was unlikely in near future. Considering lack of upside in near future and limitations of exit options, GVFL pursued Buyback by Promoters. After sustained efforts, the promoters agreed to buyback the shares held by GVFL at a price of Rs 4/- per share, by borrowing from co-operative banks. Considering the overall situation, Divestment committee accepted the offer made by the promoters to acquire the holding and to negotiate and finalize the sale at a price of Rs. 4 or above. On March 11, 2000, a meeting was held by the divestment committee of GVFL and approved the divestment of 6.5 lakh shares of Anjali BioTech (India) Limited at Rs. 4 per share.

Research Questions: In case of Anjali BioTech Ltd. financial contract designed by GVFL for the entrepreneur deals with all the provisions of adverse selection and moral hazard adequately and sufficiently. The problem of adverse selection was mitigated through proper appraisal and self-selection process. After observing the salient features, GVFL sanctioned the financial assistance for expansion of the project. During the post GVFL assistance, monitoring of performance was done very carefully. There was no problem of moral hazard caused by the promoters although due to financial, marketing and environmental the performance of the company was affected.

The performance of the firm has been analyzed in two ways: 1. Performance of firm Return on funds lent out (percent per annum) and 2. Performance in contractual compliance: least or absence of conflict of interest between GVFL and Borrower firm.

Average Net profit per annum was positive of 16.43 lakh per annum. With the constant monitoring activities both by personal visits paid by the GVFL officers and through calling of information every fortnightly, GVFL was save the company from severe losses. GVFL could also recover the amount invested into the company through various instruments, although it was negative. GVFL's ROI was –4.00 percent. During the tenure of six years both had maintained good relationship. GVFL's involvement was greater in the venture although both the parties didn't have any major conflict of interest. GVFL always helped the company in solving the marketing problem of poor wholesale dealers, inefficient representatives, poor market development, low shelf life, maintenance of proper financial accounts etc. Thus, there were no principle-agent problem in the case and the performance was considerably satisfactory.

To sum up, the financial contract of GVFL had adequate provisions and processes to deal with adverse selection and moral hazard problem. Therefore there was no principle agent problem faced by GVFL.

Case 10: Microtech Private Limited: M/s Microtech Private Limited was promoted by a second-generation entrepreneur, engaged in manufacture of Special Digital Systems and other high technology electronics items for wide range of industrial applications and set up at Pune. Microtech has successfully developed Flight Data Acquisition & Analysis System (FDAAS) for Defence Aviation for the first time in the country. Microtech approached GVFL with a proposal to develop Systems compatible for defence aircrafts like Civil Aviation and Export. Before sanctioning of funds for financial assistance, due diligence was done which includes the appraisal of the company and self-selection process by GVFL. After observing the salient features of the company, which includes professionally qualified and experienced entrepreneur, customized and cost-effective products, which cannot be copied easily, strong team of detailed technical personnel, good potential for exports and reputation of being a reliable supplier of electronic products, GVFL agreed to finance the project and an agreement was signed between the two parties. GVFL sanctioned equity of Rs. 25.00 lakh and Redeemable Cumulative Preference Shares of Rs. 16.00 Lakh from Gujarat Venture Capital Fund-1990 (GVCF-1990).

During the post GVFL assistance, monitoring committee was formed by GVFL to help the company in policy decision making, feedback on periodic reports, product development, marketing plan, recruitment, etc. which could be complementary to the efforts of promoters. The company was converted into Public Limited: Microtech Limited. Performance of the company was not up to the mark mainly due to interest burden, sales below break-even, increase in term loan, unsecured deposits/loans were repaid, low turnover due to lack of orders that were expected to be received, quality of products etc. There was also high inventory due to import of components in small quantity, which was uneconomical. It was observed that defence products have good market potential; however actual orders take long time to get materialized because of slow decision making process and procedural matters.

After great efforts, Microtech received defence orders and repeated orders. In order to strengthen its existing infrastructure, company recruited personnel for the post of General Manager, Finance Manager & Company Secretary and R&D Engineer.

The major reason for the poor performance was lack of aggressive sales effort by the marketing team. At the same time, the internal auditors observed some anomalies in books of accounts regarding various debit balances; company did not pay statutory dues like PF, ESI, Professional tax and TDS. In order to improve performance and reduce dependence on a single product-FDAAS, GVFL suggested to initiate efforts on development of other products/business line in related area along with its existing business of industrial electronics and marketing to domestic as well as overseas customers, recovery of outstanding dues, introducing system of quarterly targets, budgets for different product for effective monitoring and raising finances for the immediate financial needs of the company.

On September 27, 1997, GVFL met with the promoters with the purpose to know about the proposed buyer and divestment process. Promoters were exploring new business avenues. Looking at the performance of the company, high debtors, inventory, fixed salary expenses, unsecured loans, it was felt that company may not be in a position to service the debts or to meet the liabilities at the present level of operations and will be declared a sick unit or NPA.

Later, a buyer was identified who was trying to obtain all the rights, assets, receivables, equity, Preference shares, dividends and ledger balances due to GVFL, securities held by them, guarantees and other instruments with respect to Microtech Ltd. The essence of the offer was that the investor will step into GVFL's shoes, finally and completely. On December 28, 1999, divestment committee of GVFL approved the divestment of entire stake in M/s Microtech Ltd in favour of the buyer for a consideration of Rs. 7 lakh.

Research Question: In case of Microtech Ltd financial contract financial contract designed by GVFL for the entrepreneur deals with all the provisions of adverse selection and moral hazard adequately and sufficiently. The problem of adverse selection was mitigated through proper appraisal and self-selection process. After observing the salient features, GVFL sanctioned the financial assistance to meet the capital expenditure on expansion project. During the post GVFL assistance, monitoring of performance was done very carefully. There was no problem of moral hazard caused by the promoters although due to various external factors governing acquisition plans of the defence, initial resistance for product acceptance, short life span of CRC and competition from other small manufacturers, Microtech could not stay in the business and had to exit on the consideration of substantial capital requirement.

The performance of the firm has been analyzed in two ways: 1. Performance of firm Return on funds lent out (percent per annum) and 2. Performance in contractual compliance: least or absence of conflict of interest between GVFL and Borrower firm.

Average Net profit per annum was negative of Rs. 9.76

lakh per annum due to government policies, constant R&D and intensive marketing efforts for capturing sizable market share. But with the constant monitoring activities both by personal visits paid by the GVFL officers and through calling of information either monthly or sometimes fortnightly depending on the position and requirement of the company, GVFL was able to save the company from severe losses and could also identify a prospective buyer for its acquisition. GVFL could also recover the amount invested into the company through various instruments, although it was negative. GVFL's ROI was –6.98 percent. During the tenure of eight years both had maintained good relationship. GVFL's involvement was greater in the venture although both the parties didn't have any major conflict of interest. GVFL always helped the company in solving the problems of poor financial accounting, Y2K compliance in-house, distribution and marketing arrangements, appointment of personnel etc. Thus, there were no principle-agent problem in the case and the performance was considerably satisfactory.

To sum up, the financial contract of GVFL had adequate provisions and processes to deal with adverse selection and moral hazard problem. Therefore there was no principle agent problem faced by GVFL.

Case 11: Hartec Seamless Limited: Hartec Seamless Limited (HSL) was engaged in the business of designing, manufacturing and marketing of steel pipes and tubes at Ahmedabad. On August 11, 1992, GVFL received an invitation from promoter of HSL for equity participation of Rs. 25 lakh to meet the long-term working capital requirements and to enlist the shares of the company on the Stock Exchanges. But GVFL did not agree at the first time, as GVFL was more interested in investing in company that can go for some innovation and as they were asking money to fill the working capital gap, it was not possible for GVFL to make the investment in such a situation. On the next approach HSL came –up with the innovative project of manufacture of

Stainless Steel Welded tubes with on line annealing process. Before sanctioning of funds for financial assistance, due diligence was done which includes the appraisal of the company (SWOT, past performance, expected profitability) and self-selection process by GVFL. After observing the salient features of the company which includes virtual monopoly, mastery in technology of redesigning process and machinery, low overheads, high throughput, uses the best available raw material in the world for quality tubes, GVFL agreed to finance the project and an agreement was signed between the two parties. GVFL sanctioned Rs. 37.5 Lakh in the equity share capital of the company in 2,50,000 shares @ Rs.10 per share and a premium of Rs. 5.

During the post GVFL assistance, GVFL kept a constant touch with HSL about almost all the matters. From the very beginning HSL did not comply with GVFL's requirements as prescribed in the shareholders agreement. There was mismatch between the published prospectus and what was desired, funds requirement and means of finance in the prospectus and the appraisal memorandum and sanction letter. Current assets were high, increase in Sundry Debtors and no proper break -up was provided. HSL also violated the spirit of the agreement on many occasions like appointing a director without prior approval of GVFL, opening up of office premises, marketing office, and also change in banks.

Later on hearing that HSL was not going to invest in on-line annealing furnace, GVFL decided to divest from the company and buyback proposal was issued. Buy-back agreement was signed on September 3, 1994 wherein the promoters agreed with GVFL to buy-back 2,50,000 Equity Shares held by GVFL as trustee Manager of GVFC 1990. GVFL also appointed concurrent Auditors but the promoters did not provide enough details as and when required by the appointed auditors. The promoters were consistently requesting for not presenting the cheques given to GVFL as a part of buy-back agreement. But GVFL did not agree to them, as it was required to pay the dues. After some days, both the promoters were arrested for bouncing of the cheque of value 17.5 lakh to GVFL.

There was a continuous increase in amount of Sundry Debtors, promoters were siphoning off the money from the company's account for themselves. When GVFL asked for the list of debtors most of the companies were located in or around Punjab and many of the companies were fictitious as suspected by GVFL. Other irregularities were also shown by the company like they did not hold the board meeting which was gross violation of Companies Act 1956. GVFL also complained to the Registrar of the Companies about these irregularities. GVFL even inspected Company's Record from Roc's office. It was observed that management has defaulted in filling the annual Returns and Balance Sheets, for the respective years within stipulated time.

GVFL also complained GIIC and Canara Bank about the non-payment of dues by HSL. On knowing, GIIC sealed the factory of HSL. Later on February 13, 1996 High court of Gujarat proposed to sell off the surplus assets of the HSL, and to use proceeds of such sales to pay and completely liquidate loan availed by GIIC for the purpose.

One of the promoters had honoured a cheque of Rs. 13 lakh for GVFL. GVFL went for out of the court settlement with one of the promoter and withdrawn the cases against him. The other case against the other promoter are still pending and the promoter is right now absconding from the country.

Research Questions: In the case of Hartech Seamless Steel, financial contract designed by GVFL for the entrepreneur deals with all the provisions of adverse selection and moral hazard adequately and sufficiently. The problem of adverse selection was mitigated through proper appraisal and self-selection process. After observing the salient features, GVFL sanctioned the financial assistance to meet the capital expenditure on expansion and diversification. During the post GVFL assistance, monitoring of performance was done very carefully but still the promoters were involved in the illegal operations and used their assests to construct a money machine.

The performance of the firm has been analysed in two ways: 1. Performance of firm Return on funds lent out (percent per annum) and 2. Performance in contractual compliance: least or absence of conflict of interest between GVFL and Borrower firm.

Average Net profit per annum was positive of Rs. 6.07 lakh per annum. Constant monitoring activities both by personal visits were paid by the GVFL officers and through calling of information fortnightly. GVFL was able to save the company from severe losses and could also exit from the venture through various rounds of negotiations and out of court settlement. GVFL could also recover the amount invested into the company through various instruments, although it was negative. GVFL's ROI was –10.71 percent. During the tenure of five years both had maintained good relationship. GVFL's involvement was greater in the venture due to the irregularities and illegal operations undertaken by the promoters. GVFL always tried to resolve the conflict between the parties and helped the company in solving the problems of financial constraints, legal compliance etc. Thus, there were no principle-agent problem in the case and the performance was considerably satisfactory.

Overall, with constant monitoring GVFL was able to save its investment from severe losses. Looking at the above case, in future GVFL should be choosier about the company to invest in, the appraisal reports should be more strictly scrutinized. Standard formats may be developed by GVFL, which may be used for evaluating any new proposal for investment. This will not only help the approaching company but also GVFL to quickly glance through the reports and their status. GVFL in this kind of investment should be more proactive about the actual status of the customers that companies are serving. In this case when the money is being given for certain purpose like buying any equipment or any such tangible process GVFL can have such clause on the agreement about informing GVFL about the status of the order in each and every step. Also GVFL can have direct contacts with the suppliers of the equipments.

To sum up, the financial contract of GVFL had adequate provisions and processes to deal with adverse selection and moral hazard problem. Therefore there was no principle agent problem faced by GVFL.

Case 12: Beautiful Dekor Limited: M/s Beautiful Dekor Limited (BDL) was engaged in the manufacture Specialty grade decorative laminates. In 1993, the promoters approached GVFL for the equity participation to part finance its expansion project to manufacture Specialty grade decorative laminates. Before sanctioning of funds for financial assistance, due diligence was done which includes the appraisal of the company (SWOT, past performance, expected profitability) and self-selection process by GVFL. After observing the salient features of the company which includes experienced entrepreneurs, established track record in the field of Decorative Laminates, creditworthiness report from bankers, GVFL agreed to finance the project and an agreement was signed between the two parties. GVFL sanctioned Rs. 32.50 lakh on August 23, 1993.

During the post GVFL assistance, GVFL asked to make some changes in the draft prospectus filed with SEBI for public issue of equity shares to the tune of Rs. 236.50 lakh. During the tenure of four years, GVFL's experience has not been satisfactory, as the affairs of the company were not managed in a professional manner. At the time of public issue, considerable grey market activities were noticed and the price of the shares reached unrealistic levels. Later, at the time of allotment of shares for the public issue, the company faced series of litigations and dispute between the promoters and some of the speculators. BDL could not utilize the funds in time, which resulted in cost and time overrun. It was also noticed that the company was not following proper financial discipline, as there were various shortcomings in the company's accounting and control system and violation of FERA provisions. BDL kept on appraising GVFL of the status of the legal cases but did not ever acknowledge any irregularities on its part which were brought to the notice by the tax surveillance report.

It was observed during the course of the investment that details of the agenda of various board meetings and explanations were not sent in advance to the directors. BDL purposely did not want to share information with the investors and provided them only when specifically asked for and that too complete information was never provided. GVFL appointed its nominee director on the Board of BDL to exercise control over the operations of the company. GVFL also placed one of its officers in the share transfer committee of BDL to have control over transfer of shares and identifying irregularities thereof. These observations point to the fact that the promoters were siphoning off money on purchases, which were not even required by the company as also to their apathy towards formalizing strict internal control systems.

Looking at the above reasons, a proposal for divestment of GVFL holding in BDL was placed for consideration. BDL was making losses and facing serious liquidity crisis. GVFL proposed divestment in the scrip by offering shares to the promoters for a one-time settlement. The Board of GVFL on 19th April 1997 approved the proposal for divestment of equity shares in BDL as one-time settlement @ Rs. 7 per share. On May 2, 1997, GVFL returned 3,25,000 shares to BDL for transfer after getting Rs. 22.75 lakh as consideration for sale of shares and withdrew its nominees from the company's board.

Research Questions: In case of BDL, financial contract designed by GVFL for the entrepreneur dealt with all the provisions of adverse selection and moral hazard adequately and sufficiently. The problem of adverse selection was mitigated through proper appraisal and self-selection process.

After observing the salient features, GVFL sanctioned the financial assistance to meet the capital expenditure for expansion of the project. During the post GVFL assistance, monitoring of performance was done very carefully but still the problems of moral hazards were faced by GVFL like deficiency of internal control systems, centralization of purchase activities with MD, non-competitive bidding process, siphoning off the money, etc.

The performance of the firm has been analysed in two ways: 1. Performance of firm Return on funds lent out (percent per annum) and 2. Performance in contractual compliance: least or absence of conflict of interest between GVFL and Borrower firm.

Average Net profit per annum was negative of Rs. 16.45 lakh per annum due to the financial irregularities and discrepancies done by the promoters. But with the constant monitoring activities both by personal visits paid by the GVFL officers and through calling of information fortnightly, monthly, quarterly, half-yearly and yearly as per the requirement and position of the company. GVFL was able to save the company from severe losses and could also exit from the venture at the right time. GVFL could recover the amount invested into the company through various instruments, although it was negative. GVFL's ROI was –7.25 percent. During the tenure of four years both tried to maintained good relationship. GVFL's involvement was greater in the venture. GVFL always helped the company in solving the problems of financial constraints, improper maintenance of records and internal audits. Thus, there were no principle-agent problem in the case and the performance was considerably satisfactory.

Overall, the performance of BDL was not up to the mark since its inception. The irregularities point to the fact that the promoters of BDL were not inclined to work in a transparent and professional manner. GVFL decided to exit from the investment because of the non-cooperation and dishonesty of the promoter and his associates. GVFL tried to bring in proper systems and processes in operations of BDL but sheer lack of support from the promoter-group brought everything to a standstill. Repeated requests from GVFL fell on deaf ears. Corruption became rampant and it added to the owes of other investors as well.

GVFL was hence left with no other option but to recover its investment in BDL the best it could and hence opted for the one-time settlement.

To sum up, the financial contract of GVFL had adequate provisions and processes to deal with adverse selection and moral hazard problem. Therefore there was no principle agent problem faced by GVFL.

Case 13: M/s Esha Cubidor Containers Limited (ECCL): Esha Cubidor Containers limited was engaged in manufacturing and marketing of Rigid Foldable Containers. The Company approached GVFL with a proposal to expand its capacity. Before sanctioning of funds for financial assistance, due diligence was done which includes the appraisal of the company (SWOT, past performance, expected profitability) and self-selection process by GVFL. After observing the salient features of the company which includes experienced technocrats, new concept and technology, product has economic as well as functional advantage over conventional and has also received good market response and favourable economy of scale, GVFL agreed to finance the project and an agreement was signed between the two parties. GVFL sanctioned Rs. 25 lakh @ Rs. 10 per share, as a co-promoter on firm–allotment basis.

During the post GVFL assistance, GVFL did close monitoring which included regular visits to the company, attending the board meeting, asking for the balance sheet and P&L accounts looking in to the debtors list and age cycle analysis. GVFL was also asking for the periodical reporting of cash flow, P&L and Financial positions, checked for the order position with quantity, amounts, payment terms and delivery schedule. Public Issue of 27,20,000 equity shares was issued by the company, which was fully subscribed. The company was concentrating on market development and in the absence of large bulk orders it could not receive substantial orders and was going slow on the expansion plans. The company them started developing market, adding new products so as to effectively utilize its infrastructure and generate economic sales volume in order to meet its debt obligations.

GVFL insisted to recruit marketing and financial professionals to support its development efforts and handling of secretarial and accounting matters. The performance of the company slowly started getting repeat orders in a small quantity. In order to improve the performance, company decided to opt for diversification into manufacture of transparent packaging. GVFL advised the company to increase its focus on export market development as well as try to consolidate its present customer base in domestic market. It was suggested that company should take a cautious approach for taking up transparent packaging project and commit funds only after receiving initial feedback with respect to suitability of indigenous materials and product acceptance in the domestic market.

The overall performance of Esha was observed for buyback of the GVFL shares. The company was facing problems of very slow product acceptance, low capacity utilization, cash losses, frequent power failure and high turnover of the factory staff and performance was much below the projections. The company's diversification plan into the other packaging products did not materialized. The promoters were also not interested in the business and had applied for a new business. It is also observed that the relation between the two promoters strained over a period. Considering the above-mentioned points, it was felt that the performance of the company will not improve significantly in near future. Even if the company turns around, it would take long time before it can wipe out its accumulated losses. The scrip was trading at low price and the volume was also low. The possibility of the strategic tie up or sell was negligible, as the company was not offering synergy to the other existing packaging firm.

Looking at all these factors GVFL decided to divest from the company. GVFL had two options: either divests through stock exchange or through negotiation deal with the promoter. The buyback can be made on the basis of inter se transfer between the core-promoters and GVFL. After considerable persuasion, on 12th March 1997, Esha Cubidor agreed to buyback the share at Rs. 4.10 per share as against the market price of around Rs. 1 or 2 per share. The promoters requested to allow purchase in four instalments, which GVFL had accepted. GVFL received payments aggregating to Rs. 10,24,500.

Research Questions: In case of Esha, financial contract designed by GVFL for the entrepreneur deals with all the provisions of adverse selection and moral hazard adequately and sufficiently. The problem of adverse selection was mitigated through proper appraisal and self-selection process. After observing the salient features, GVFL sanctioned the financial assistance to meet the capital expenditure on expansion plans. During the post GVFL assistance, monitoring of performance was done very carefully. There was no problem of moral hazard caused by the promoters although due product failure and poor marketing & advertising efforts, performance of Esha never matched with projected one.

The performance of the firm has been analysed in two ways: 1.Performance of firm Return on funds lent out (percent per annum) and 2. Performance in contractual compliance: least or absence of conflict of interest between GVFL and Borrower firm.

Average Net profit per annum was positive of Rs 10.25 lakh per annum due to constant watch on the activities of the company. But with the constant monitoring activities both by personal visits paid by the GVFL officers and through calling of information either quarterly and half-yearly, GVFL was able to save the company from severe losses. GVFL could also recover the amount invested into the company through various instruments, although it was negative. GVFL's ROI was –11.70 percent. During the tenure of five years both had maintained good relationship. GVFL's involvement was greater in the venture although both the parties didn't have any major conflict of interest. GVFL always helped the company in strategic decisions like diversification issues, changing product mix, deciding target market and recruiting professionals. To increase the product acceptance and sales, GVFL introduced the company with prospective clients. GVFL guided Esha Cubidor in initiating the legal process. Finally with GVFL's guidance company was able to recover the money. Thus, there were no principle-agent problem in the case and the performance was considerably satisfactory.

The key factors for the poor performance were new product, company failed to generate repeat and big orders, was not able to support customization, never approached government agencies and organizations, lack of marketing strategy and business vision. In case of Esha Cubidor the company was never forming the component of forward or backward integration for any client. The promoters of the company preferably should have only one business. The promoters of the Esha Cubidor had other factories also. So later on they were not visiting the office regularly and their interest in the business was also reduced.

To sum up, the financial contract of GVFL had adequate provisions and processes to deal with adverse selection and moral hazard problem. Therefore there was no principle agent problem faced by GVFL.

8.6 Contractual Performance

Results on each hypothesis are as follows:

H_{10}: Appraisal/screening and self-selection clauses improve the contractual performance (the repayment & firm's own performance).

In our sample, appraisal clauses include the activities

required at the time of appraisal and are maximum five in number. These Clauses include primary information like: Project in which the company is presently engaged/desires to start or the proposed expansion or diversification and the location of the proposed plant, financial plan (includes the cost of the venture and its means of financing), staged investment, management fee, and lastly direct participation in management by VC. Most of the cases were subjected to all the core clauses relating to appraisal in their contracts except Medisurg Surgical had the lowest of three clauses. Thus, the hypothesis is valid as per the clauses/provisions available in the contract.

H_{20}: Equity contracts based on monitoring clauses improves the compliance with contractual performance.

The monitoring clauses in the contract include provisions to control the problems of moral hazard. The provisions in these clauses help in monitoring the project after the sanction of the funds. These clauses are maximum in number in the contract and are very important. Monitoring of the cases has been done from two aspects: Firstly, the number of clauses relating to monitoring the projects and the behaviour of the entrepreneur during the tenure of GVFL. Secondly, number of monitoring events that took place during the same time. The event is defined as the number of actions taken or initiated in compliance with the monitoring clauses of the contract.

The maximum numbers of monitoring clauses in our contract are 104, which has been further classified as Core clauses (31), Supplement clauses (48) and special/customized clauses (25). The provisions that help in monitoring the project after the sanction of the funds includes VC as a board member, Interim financial reports, notices, agenda, minutes of the Board meetings, Annual General Meetings on the status of the firms operations, technical, financial and legal inspections, issue of debentures, raising loans, deposits from public, powers to enter into the agreement, changes or delay in the project, end use of the funds, covenants relating to transfer of shares, change in management, actions or decisions taken by the Board of

Directors, directions/instructions given by GVFL, legal requirement by SEBI, changes in capital structure, borrowings, listing of shares, control/ownership of assets, buyback by promoters, appointment /removal of directors and other members on the board, voting rights, etc. All the cases had 75 and more clauses relating to monitoring with one exception of Medisurg Surgical Ltd. Nine of the thirteen cases had agreed to 31 core-monitoring clauses, six cases to 48 supplement clauses recorded and five cases to more than 10 special or customized clauses.

To gain further insight into the intensity of performance reviews by the venture capital funds, the number of visits to the investee company can be an important guide. In our sample, GVFL has verified the physical assets personally by visiting the plant. The number of visits vary in all the cases: regular visits, frequent visits, during last 2-3 years of GVFL or twice a year depending on the requirements and problems faced by respective firm. It is evident that Indian venture capital firms are in favour of regular and continuous monitoring of activities of investee company.

Monitoring events for transparency in decision making through calling of information/ reports, letters, notices, minutes of Board Meeting, annual General Meeting etc which are sent periodically by all the companies. In a study conducted by Gorman and Sahlman (1989) regarding the US economy, it was concluded that US venture capitalists spent about half their time monitoring investments. Scottish based firms, Hatherly (1994) found that less emphasis was put on more formal monitoring and more emphasis on trust, openness and mutual support between the venture capitalist and the investee company. In our sample, on an average monthly two-progress/ status reports were sent to GVFL. In some cases it varied from more than twice a month, weekly, fortnightly, monthly, quarterly reports depending on the financial position, problem faced by the promoter, competitors etc. Thus, monitoring activity done by GVFL in all the cases in either way by visits to the plants or by calling of information or status report was regular and helped in minimizing the problems faced by the company. Thus, the hypothesis is valid as per the clauses/provisions available in the contract.

H_{30}: Equity contracts with incentivizing clauses improve the contractual performance.

The provisions of incentivizing are performance based by way of assurance for additional funds, exit options, sell of shares by promoters etc. It also punishes the promoters for not managing the project efficiently. Some of the important clauses are: sale of shares by GVFL, mode and method of purchase of shares, right of GVFL to acquire shares from the promoters in case of default and/or loss making etc. Most of the companies has agreed to clauses varying from 23 to 28 with two exceptions: Campco (18 clauses) and Medisurg Surgical (2 clauses). This implies that there was no deficiency in incentivizing the entrepreneurs. Thus, the hypothesis is valid as per the clauses/provisions available in the contract.

H_{40}: Equity contracts with self-selection clauses improve the contractual performance.

Self-selection clauses along with the appraisal clauses help in mitigating the problems caused by the adverse selection due to asymmetric information. They help in go/no go decision-making. The provisions include profit participation, Compensation vis-à-vis stock option, subscription by GVFL, progressive release of equity funds, Equity contribution by entrepreneur, Capital structure, Size of board etc. Maximum number of self-selection clauses in the contract is eleven and none of the cases recorded the highest one. Most of the cases contain all the core clauses in their contract with one exception of Gujarat Surgical. The maximum special clauses were four that were observed in Microtech only. Other had two or less special clauses. Thus, GVFL's contact with entrepreneur imposed all the standard provisions to safeguard the interest of both parties, validating our hypotheses of self-selection.

H_{50}: Equity contracts with divesting clauses improve the contractual performance.

Divesting clauses help the VC to exit from the project in case of any problem faced by the company, which can't be mitigated or due to some illegal activities carried by the firm. Most of the companies agreed to all the clauses relating to divestment. Thus, it validates our hypotheses.

H_{60}: Cases where returns are high, characteristics and clauses are high.

In our sample, the results do not support the above hypotheses i.e cases where returns are high or returns are low, characteristics and clauses are high.

Overall, the financial contracts between the VC and the entrepreneur designed by GVFL helped to reduce the moral hazards and adverse selection problems caused due to informational asymmetry and conflict of interest between both the parties.

8.7 Control Areas of Venture Capital Company

Hands-on approach as witnessed by venture capital industry abroad as well as in India demands active participation of venture capitalist in the investee company. This involvement can be in form of assistance so as to create a higher value-added investment for the investees so that better investment performances can be ensured and a competitive edge is created by creating value to the investees.

Sweeting and Wong (1997) found that venture capitalists structure their investments in such a way so as to maintain firm control over the investee company. Sahlman (1990) finds that the deal structure is basically contained in the stock purchase agreement, which to a large extent forms the basis of governance to the relationship between the venture capitalist and the investee. In a study of Scottish institutions known to fund management Buy-outs, identifies a range of controls to be exercised by investors upon investees by means of venture agreements. These identified control areas include control over dividends payments levels, participation in mergers, sale of assets, debt/gearing levels, capital expenditure, management remuneration, working capital maintenance and hiring of employees. However, by definition, venture capitalists cannot be generally considered to 'control' their investees in any strict legal sense as this would bring their investees under the category of subsidiaries.

In our sample, the various control areas for the VC were: Dividend payment levels, participation in mergers, sales of assets, capital expenditure, management remuneration, working capital maintenance and hiring of employees. The maximum weight age has been to control over working capital maintenance and hiring of employees.

8.8 Limitations

The study reported here is necessarily limited by a number of constraints: Information on venture capital industry in India is not available publicly. The agreements made between the parties, post disbursement financial performance, divestment process, and negotiations etc. are very sensitive in nature as they may affect the position of the entrepreneur in the market. Also due to financial and time constraints, the present study/thesis concentrates only on one VCC: Gujarat Venture Finance Limited. GVFL extended active co-operation, provided invaluable insights into entrepreneurial behaviour, direct access to data, all the files of the entrepreneurs required for the research. Other VCs might be possible in large study.

It consists of 13 cases fully divested and has completed the life cycle. In other cases, some were in the divestment process, returns were yet to be received, some were having the legal litigations, looking for a prospective investor to acquire the firm or the project was still undergoing its life cycle.

The inability to verify outcomes makes it difficult to write contracts that are contingent upon particular events. This inability makes external financing costly. Investors/VCs find it difficult to verify that certain actions have been taken or certain outcomes have occurred-even if they strongly suspect the entrepreneur has followed a certain action which was counter to their original agreement, they cannot prove it in a court of law. The agreements in our study are all equity contracts and no debt or hybrid contracts. As the GVCF-90 was the first fund that GVFL had floated, to minimize their risk, equity contracts were used. All contracts are standardized contract and not customized to suit the entrepreneur and risk.

Funds were sanctioned to private sector only and not to a heterogeneous sector. Therefore the results will have to be taken with these limitations

8.9 Implications

The present study has its implications for VCs, entrepreneurs and government policy makers. For the Venture capitalist: The role of investors in screening, financing, and over-seeing a company is very important in the dramatic growth of the private equity industry.

The implications of the study are also of concern to the entrepreneurs seeking venture capital, the Indian individuals who are professionally in position to play the role of intermediaries between venture capital seekers and potential venture capital purveyors

For the economy, the national and regional policy–makers: The effectiveness of venture capital arrangements in reducing agency costs suggests that its scope could be expanded to other high-risk environment, like emerging markets in developing countries. Not only would venture capital be more suitable for financing development, it would also help developing countries avoid financial crises similar to the world debt crisis that many developing countries currently are suffering. Venture Capital therefore, helps promote growth while maintaining financial stability: which are necessary requirements for any successful development plan.

8.10 Prospects of Indian Venture Capital

Indian venture capital has a long way to go. Started just a

decade ago, venture capital financing activity is catching fire on the Indian market scene. Although presently at nascent stage, the future can be quite challenging for venture capital industry in India. No doubt, it is a late entrant in India in the field of industrial financing and is in its infancy stage, it has tremendous potential for growth. The present liberalized economic environment and steps taken by government to make it more conducive for the growth of VC industry tend to pose some challenges before the players so as to draw their attention towards reappraising their strategic positions in light of such threats caused to VC industry in India. So managing future challenges is also an important part of management of venture capital funds. 'How to manage future challenges"? i.e Identification of sources of competitive threats, consideration of various alternatives for facing such threats, areas of specialization, forms of diversification strategies, and factors critical in view of future prospects of Indian Venture Capital industry as perceived by the venture capital funds in India.

Indian venture funds will have more challenges as noted in the findings. The challenges can be in form of increasing bargaining power of institutional investors, future profit uncertainties, entry of new parties/competitive threat, availability of substitute products to venture capital finance and difficulty in raising new funds. In India, since the venture capital industry is still at the nascent stage, no bargaining power of Investee Company exits. However, competitive pressure may exist on account of entry of new players, as India is becoming a lucrative place for both domestic and offshore funds.

In view on Indian venture capital Industry becoming more challenging, an attempt can be made to find out the strategic choices individual venture capital funds are going to make to face the same. Ansoff's 'growth matrix' (Corporate strategy-1968) can be used to clarify the range of product/market opportunities available to the individual firms.

Quadrant I - Product Development: Firms can go for

sectoral, geographical or stage financing specialization argu... the advantage of greater industry specific or local knowledge.

Quadrant II - Market Penetration: It advocates for market penetration that parallels recent trends in the US venture penetration sector. The higher the funds under management, the larger the number of deals to be supported which means more profitability.

Quadrant III - Market Development: It encompasses new market segments, new uses for existing procedures or geographical expansion. Since the first two can be fitted becomes the sole option available to the venture capitalist.

Quadrant IV - Diversification: It speaks of diversification strategy. Although most risky because of inherent uncertainty on both axes i.e. new markets and new products, many economies of the world are opting for it. Diversification can be backward, forward, horizontal or a combination of these strategies adopted simultaneously.

In view of the above discussion, keeping in view the challenges posed to Indian VC industry, one of the most important courses to face competitive threat can be differentiation between individual venture capitalist's product or services. Alternatively, venture capital funds can go for specialization regarding investment in any particular industry on account of their in-depth knowledge about the same on the basis of experience gained from previous investments or provide financing through any particular instrument of financing because of similar reasons.

Another aspect of management of funds can be 'core competency factor'. A core competency factor is that factor which enables any company to have a competitive edge over its competitors. A key distinguishing characteristic of venture capital compares to the other forms of funding is its ability to provide money as well as business and management skills to the investee company to maximize the value of the firm so that a greater than normal capital gain can be reaped. This is especially true of venture capitalists who have some field of specialization- industry, stage of financing and instrument of financing.

Their specialization is in the structuring of equity-based venture deals, not in the segmentation of companies, locations or sectors to which their funds are applied. They manage their portfolios in such a way so as to reap the rewards by investing in a number of industries through various instruments in various stages.

In future, Indian market is going to be quite challenging for venture capitalists. According to this growth matrix, venture capital funds should go in for diversification strategies in case of new markets and new products.

8.11 Recommendations

Some of the suggestions for the venture capitalists are as follows:

- **VCFs Can Partake Various Forms of Funds:** Venture capitalists should also look beyond seeding or funding companies, and often moves to rescuing faulting companies with good potential. It is suggested that venture capital companies be encouraged to establish Distress Funds/Turnaround Funds for helping ailing companies.
- **Intricate Linkages with NRI Community:** Non Resident Indians are amongst the more positioned foreign communities in other countries, especially North American and parts of Europe. The constituents are known for their respected standing in professional world as well as personal wealth. It is suggested that industry in India should take steps to forge more intricate ties with NRI community that can lead to not only greater investments flowing to Indian ventures, but also lead to assistance in venture development and probability of reverse brain drain.
- **Sources of Collection of Information Regarding Investee Company:** Board meetings and company visits are the two most preferred sources of information about

the investee company. The problem with these sources is that they tend to give the information that is projected or desired rather than actual which creates gap between level of informational known to the entrepreneur and the venture capitalist. Besides, formal performances measures include ROI projections, net profits i.e parameters largely financial in nature and the ones that are given after taking the most optimistic scenario into consideration. Therefore, venture capitalist should take into consideration other sources of information so as to obtain a fair picture of the performance of the company.

- **Performance Measures of Investee Company:** The most important control checks used by venture capitalist are mainly financial in nature like projected ROI, net profits and market shares. As a venture, it is very important for the venture capitalist to take in consideration various non-financial factors. Thus, it becomes imperative for the firms to also look into non-financial factors, as they are very vital for success of these kinds of ventures.
- **Checking the Status of the Investment Made by Venture Capitalist:** Any venture capitalist strategically invests his money into various ventures bearing various characteristics. Therefore, time-to-time appraisal of such investments should be done so as to ensure conformance to the strategy drawn. Thus, reappraising the status of the portfolio forms a very important aspect of the management of the venture capital.
- **Conflict Management:** Venture capital financing differs from traditional equity financing in that the venture capitalist plays a role in the management of the companies receiving investment i.e. the investee-company. The success of any venture depends to a large extent upon the mutual relations between the venture capitalist and the investee company. The basic issues of conflict arise due to ambiguity in the roles of both the venture capitalist and the entrepreneur in the functioning. One of the strategies that

can be implemented in this regards is staging the capital committed. It implies that the venture capitalist commits only a fraction of the capital needed for the ultimate development of the project. Subsequent financing is then tied to the successful completion of the intermediate objectives. Staging the capital commitment creates an abandonment option and thereby increases the value of the investment. Further, an entrepreneur's decision to accept such a contract will provide information about the entrepreneur's beliefs in his or her own estimates and in the time and cost required to develop the first stage. Subsequent capital commitments will then benefit from additional information. The venture capitalist will be able to reduce risk before the second round of financing, and if all goes well, the entrepreneur may benefit from increase in valuation, leading to less dilution of his or her ownership interests in subsequent rounds. Hence, stage capital commitments keep the entrepreneur focused on the task at hand and may motivate a more rapid pace of activity.

Suggestions for the Entrepreneurs/Firms:

- **Introduction to Entrepreneurial Course Components:** Business Schools in India must come forward with course components on entrepreneurship and venture development. It would be great facilitator in exposing budding entrepreneurs and business management practitioners to dynamics of developing a venture.
- **Venture Investment Fairs:** It is suggested that a series of venture investment fairs must be organized in all parts of the country. The objective is to bring together venture capitalists and entrepreneurs on the same platform in a business environment for results.

Suggestions for National and Regional Policy-makers

- **Eliminate Anomalies in Taxation:** Most of the venture capitalists in India share concern with regard to taxation practices prevailing upon them. Globally, venture funds and other funds incur minimum or no tax liability on their capital gains as empirical studies have shown that venture capitalists create high value addition for an economy and society. It is therefore, suggested that venture fund capital gains be treated at least at par with mutual funds.

- **Encourage Participation of Provident Funds, Pension Funds etc:** Government of India could catalyse large inflow of venture capital funds by permitting Provident Funds and Pension Funds to invest a certain portion of their incremental inflows in venture capital and other such activities. This would not only lead to larger proliferation of domestic venture capital activity, but also results in realizing exponentially larger returns on asset base. This automatically permits larger retention capacity to government offers.
- **Early Implementation of OTCEI Plans:** The Government of India should issue earliest permission for implementation of trading of unlisted securities on over the counter exchange of India. This could also be a key to having a vibrant pre-IPO market in India.
- **Exit Options:** Exit options to investors and promoters are a key to successful venture capital partnership. This is integral to realizing gains from a successful company. It is suggested that Government of India should allow a liberal exit framework at par with that prevalent in USA.

8.12 Guidelines for Future Research

The subject is very rich and there are plenty of areas that are worth exploration. Research on venture capital is in its infancy. The problems encountered are not simple. Realistic treatment of the issues in venture capital research will require innovations approaches. The above research has been a small effort in this direction. One extension of the current research is to study the projects funded by different VCs & their different schemes in India. Bygrave and Timmons (1992) provide policy recommendations for expending the industry in the U.S.

Sagari (1992) explores government policies towards risk capital in different developing countries and point to necessary ingredients for venture capital to grow in such countries.

Further research could also be carried out for industry-wise comparison between Private sector, Public sector & others, continental/region wise comparison (Asian, American, African, European, Australian). Its scope can also be seen in other areas like River-linking projects (Garland project), port-development (Adani Group in Dahej, Gujarat).

The above study has only been carried out in perspective of the venture capitalist and the views of investee company have not been taken into consideration. Future research can be carried out so as to gain an insight into their viewpoints. To what extent control by the venture capitalist firm is acceptable to them? What is their perception about the different roles played by the venture capitalist? Do they believe that venture capitalist firms add value to their venture by providing expertise and skills other than financial in nature? Do they consider them as their strategic partner or still believe to be providers of only capital? All the above factors when considered would be able to present a better picture of the venture capital management scenario and thus, help in devising better strategies for management of the venture capital funds.

Finally, it might be insightful to examine the effects of venture capital funding on financial constraints for companies after going public. Such research would help to evaluate the effect of "initial conditions" on the performance and accessibility to capital markets of venture-backed companies.

Do Venture Capitalists add value within the portfolio firm? Venture capitalist as a intermediary, a related issue that has not been resolved is whether or not venture capitalists add value within a portfolio firm. Do companies perform better when venture capital is present than when it is absent, all else equal.

The above-recommended strategies are basically

generalized strategies for the management of the venture capital funds, but do not take into consideration the fact that funds across different industries behave differently due to the effect of other factors present. Does the evaluation remains same across all industries or it differs across high technology or low technology oriented industries? Thus, for proper management of venture capital funds, it becomes imperative to study the different factors affecting funding of varied sectors and how do they in counter affect the management of venture capital funds.

Alternative organizational forms and Venture Capital Performance: There are various types of venture capital organizations. Therefore, agency conflicts and their solution in one kind of venture capital firm do not apply fully to other forms. Because venture capitalists operating within different organizational forms differ in their relationships with their principal investors. Therefore, further research can be carried out so as to study the differences in different kind of firms and thus, to check how organizational form is associated with performance.

Appendix

Appendix

Securities and Exchange Board of India (SEBI): Venture Capital Fund Regulations, 1996

SEBI has been a regulatory body for venture capital companies or funds with effect from January 25, 1995. It issued certain guidelines on December 4, 1996 which defines venture capital fund as "fund established in the form of a company or trust which raises moneys through loans, donations, issue of securities or units as the case may be, and makes or proposes to make investments in accordance with these regulations". The Guidelines are listed below:

Registration of Venture Capital Funds

Application for Grant of Certificate

1. Any company or trust proposing to carry on any activity as a venture capital fund on or after the commencement of these regulations shall make an application to the Board for grant of a certificate.
2. Any company or trust, who on the date of commencement of these regulations is carrying any activity as a venture capital fund without a certificate shall make an application to the Board for grant of a certificate within a period of three months from the date of such commencement: Provided that the board, in special cases, may extent the said period up to a maximum of six months form the date of such commencement.
3. An application for grant of certificate under sub-regulation (1) or sub-regulation (2) shall be made to the Board in Form A and shall be accompanied by a non-refundable application fee of Rs. 25,000 by way of bank draft issued in favour of SEBI at Mumbai.

4. Any company or trust referred to in sub-regulation (2) who fails to make an application for grant of a certificate within the period specified therein shall cease to carry on any activity as a venture capital fund.
5. The Board may in the interest of the investors issue directions with regard to the transfer of records, documents or securities or disposal of investments relating to its activities as a venture capital fund.
6. The Board may in order to protect the interests of investors appoints any person to take charge of records, documents, securities and for this purpose also determine the terms and conditions of such an appointment.

Eligibility Criteria: For the purpose of the grant of a certificate by the Board the applicant have to fulfil in particular the following conditions, namely

If the application is made by a company:

- memorandum of association as has its main objective, the carrying on of the activity of a venture capital fund;
- it is prohibited by its memorandum and articles of association from making an invitation to the public to subscribe to its securities;
- its director or principal officer or employee is not involved in any litigation connected with the securities market which may have an adverse bearing on the business of the applicant;
- its director, principal officer or employee has not at any time been convicted of any offence involving moral turpitude or any economic offence;
- it is a fit and proper person;
- if the application is made by a trust, the instrument of trust is in the form of a deed and has been duly registered under the provisions of the Indian Registration Act, 1908 (16 of 1908) ;
- the main object of the trust is to carry on the activity of a venture capital fund;
- the directors of its trustee company, if any or any trustee is

not involved in any litigation connected with the securities market which may have an adverse bearing on the business of the applicant;

- the directors of its trustee company, if any, or a trustee has not at any time, been convicted of any offence involving moral turpitude or of any economic offence;
- the applicant is a fit and proper person;
- the company or trust has not been refused a certificate by the Board or its certificate has been suspended or cancelled.

Furnishing of Information, Clarification: The Board may require the applicant to furnish such further information as it may consider necessary.

Consideration of Application: An application which is not complete in all respects shall be rejected by the Board: Provided that, before rejecting any such application, the applicant shall be given an opportunity to remove, within thirty days of the date of receipt of communication, the objections indicated by the Board: Provided further that the Board may, on being satisfied that it is necessary to extend the period specified in the first proviso, extend such period by such further time not exceeding ninety days.

Procedure for Grant of Certificate

- If the Board is satisfied that the applicant is eligible for the grant of certificate, it shall send intimation to the applicant.
- On receipt of intimation, the applicant shall pay to the Board, the registration fee of Rs. 500,000 payable by way of bank draft in favour of SEBI at Mumbai.
- The Board shall on receipt of the registration fee grant a certificate of registration in Form B.

Conditions of Certificate: The certificate granted shall be *inter alia,* subject to the following conditions, namely:

- the venture capital fund shall abide by the provisions of the Act, the Government of India Guidelines and these regulations;
- the venture capital fund shall not carry on any other

activity other than that of a venture capital fund;

- the venture capital fund shall forthwith inform the Board in writing if any information or particulars previously submitted to the Board are found to be false or misleading in any material particular or if there is any change in the information already submitted.

Procedure where Certificate is not Granted

- After considering an application if the Board is of the opinion that a certificate should not be granted, it may reject the application after giving the applicant a reasonable opportunity of being heard.
- The decision of the Board to reject the application shall be communicated to the applicant within thirty days.

Effect of Refusal to Grant Certificate

- Any applicant whose application has been rejected shall not carryon any activity as a venture capital fund.
- Any company or trust whose application for grant of certificate has been rejected by the Board shall, on and from the date of the receipt of the communication cease to carry on any activity as a venture capital fund.
- The Board may in the interest of the investors issue directions with regard to the transfer of records, documents or securities or disposal of investments relating to its activities as a venture capital fund.
- The Board may in order to protect the interests of the investors appoint any person to take charge of records, documents, securities and for this purpose also determine the terms and conditions of such an appointment.

Investment Conditions and Restrictions

Minimum investment in a venture capital fund

- A venture capital fund may raise monies from any investor whether Indian, foreign or non-resident Indian.
- No venture capital fund set up as a company or any scheme of a venture capital fund set up as a trust shall accept any investment from any investor which is less than

five lakh rupees: Provided that nothing contained in sub-regulation (2) shall apply to investors who are (a) employees or the principal officer or directors of the venture capital fund, or directors of the trustee company or trustees where the venture capital fund has been established as a trust; or (b) non-resident Indians; or (c) persons or institutions of foreign origin.

Restrictions on Investment by a Venture Capital Fund. All investments made or to be made by a venture capital fund shall be subject to the following restrictions:

1. the venture capital fund shall not invest in the equity shares of the company or institutions providing financial services;
2. at least 80 percent of funds raised by a venture capital fund shall be invested in

- the equity shares or equity related securities issued by a company whose securities are not listed on any recognised stock exchange: Provided that a venture capital fund may invest in equity shares or equity related securities of a company whose securities are to be listed or are listed where the venture capital fund has made. these investments through private placements prior to the listing of the securities;
- the equity shares or equity related securities of a financially weak company or a sick industrial company, whose securities mayor may not be listed on any recognised stock exchange.

Explanation: *For* the purposes of this regulation, a "financially weak company" means a company, which has at the end of the previous financial year accumulated losses, which has resulted in erosion of more than 50 percent but less than 100 percent of its net worth as at the beginning of the previous financial year;

- providing financial assistance in any other manner to companies in whose equity shares the venture capital fund has invested under sub-clause (i) or sub-clause (i), as the case may be.

Explanation: *For* the purposes of this regulation, "funds raised" means the actual monies raised from investors for subscribing to the securities of the venture capital fund and includes monies raised from the author of the trust in case the venture capital fund has been established as a trust but shall not include the paid up capital of the trustee company, if any.

Prohibition on listing - No venture capital fund shall be entitled to get its securities or units, as the case may be, listed on any recognised stock exchange till the expiry of three years from the date of the issuance of securities or units, as the case may be, by the venture capital fund.

General Obligations and Responsibilities

Prohibition on Inviting Subscription from the Public: No venture capital fund shall issue any document or advertisement inviting offers from the public for the subscription or purchase of any of its securities or units.

Private Placemen: A venture capital fund may receive monies for investment in the venture capital fund through private placement of its securities or units.

Placement Memorandum

- The venture capital fund established as a trust shall, before issuing any units, file witl1 the Board a placement memorandum which shall give details of the terms subject to which monies are proposed to be raised from investors.
- A venture capital fund established as a company shall, before making an offer inviting any subscription to its securities, file with the Board a placement memorandum which shall give details of the terms subject to which monies are proposed to be raised from the investors.

Contents of Placement Memorandum

The placement memorandum referred to in sub-regulation (1) of regulation shall contain the following,

namely:

- details of the trustees or trustee company of the venture capital fund; .
- details of entitlement on the units of the trust for which subscription is being sought;
- details of investments that are proposed to be made;
- tax implications that are likely to apply to investors;
- manner of subscription to the units of the trust;
- the period of maturity, if any, of the scheme;
- the manner, if any, in which the scheme is to be wound up;
- manner in which the benefits accruing to investors in the units of the trust are to be distributed;
- details of the asset management company, if any, and of fees to be paid to such a company.

The placement memorandum referred to in sub-regulation (2) above shall contain the following namely:

- details of the securities that are being offered;
- details of investments that are proposed to be made;
- details of directors of the company;
- tax implications that are likely to apply to investors;
- manner of subscription to the securities that are to be issued;
- manner in which the benefits accruing to investors in the securities are to be distributed; and
- details of the asset management company, if any, and of fees to be paid to such a company.

Circulation of Placement Memorandum: The placement memorandum may be issued for private circulation only after the expiry of twenty-one days of its submission to the Board: provided that if, within twenty-one days of submission of the placement memorandum, the Board communicates any amendments to the placement memorandum, the venture capital fund shall carry out such amendments in the placement memorandum before such memorandum is circulated to the investors.

Changes in the placement memorandum to be intimated to the Board Amendments or changes to any placement memorandum already filed with the Board can be made only if

- a copy of the placement memorandum indicating the changes is filed with the Board; and
- within twenty-one days of such filing, the Board has not communicated any objections or observations on the said amendments or changes.

Maintenance of Books and Records

- Every venture capital fund shall maintain for a period of ten years books of accounts, records and documents which shall give a true and fair picture of the state of affairs of the venture capital fund.
- Every venture capital fund shall intimate the Board, in writing, the place where the books, records and documents referred to in sub-regulation (1) are being maintained.

Power to Call for Information

- The Board may at any time call for any information from a venture capital fund with respect to any matter relating to its activity as a venture capital fund.
- Where any information is called for under sub-regulation (1) it shall be furnished to the Board within fifteen days.

Submission of Reports to the Board

The Board may at any time call upon the venture capital fund to file such reports as the Board may desire with regard to the activities carried on by the venture capital fund.

Winding up

A scheme of a venture capital fund set up as a trust shall be wound up,

- when the period of the scheme, if any, mentioned in the placement memorandum is over;

- if it is the opinion of the trustees or the trustee company, as the case may be, that the scheme shall be wound up in the interests of investors in the units;
- if seventy-five percent of the investors in the scheme pass a resolution at a meeting of unit holders that the scheme be wound up ; or
- if the Board so directs in the interests of investors.

A venture capital fund set up as a company shall be wound up in accordance with the provisions of the Companies Act. 1956 (1 of 1956).

The trustees or trustee company of the venture capital fund set up as a trust shall intimate the Board and investors of the circumstances leading to the winding up of the scheme under sub-regulation (1).

Effect of Winding up

- On and from the date of intimation, no further investments shall be made on behalf of the scheme so wound up.
- Within three months from the date of intimation the assets of the scheme shall be liquidated, and the proceeds accruing to investors in the scheme distributed to them after satisfying all liabilities.

Inspection and Investigation

Board's Right to Inspect or Investigate: The Board may appoint one or more persons as inspecting or investigating officer to undertake inspection or investigation of the books of accounts, records and documents relating to a venture capital fund for any of the following reasons, namely

- to ensure that the books of account, records and documents are being maintained by the venture capital fund in the manner specified in these regulations;
- to inspect or investigate into complaints received from investors, clients or any other person, on any matter having a bearing on the activities of the venture capital fund;
- to ascertain whether the provisions of the Act and these

regulations are being complied with by the venture capital fund; and

- to inspect or investigate *suo moto* into the affairs of a venture capital fund, in the interest of the securities
- market or in the interest of investors.

Notice before Inspection or Investigation

- Before ordering an inspection or investigation the Board shall give not less than ten days notice to the venture capital fund.
- Notwithstanding anything contained in sub-regulation (1), where the Board is satisfied that in the interest of the investors no such notice should be given, it may by an order in writing direct that the inspection or investigation of the affairs of the venture capital fund be taken up without such notice.
- During the course of an inspection or investigation, the venture capital fund against whom the inspection or investigation is being carried out shall be bound to discharge its obligations as given below.

Obligations of Venture Capital Fund on Inspection or Investigation by the Board

- It shall be the duty of the venture capital fund whose affairs are being inspected or investigated, and of every director, officer and employee thereof, of its asset management company, if any, and of its trustees or directors or the directors of the trustee company, if any, to produce before the inspecting or investigating officer such books, securities, accounts, records and other documents in its custody or control and furnish him with such statements and information relating to the venture capital fund, as the inspecting or investigating officer may require, within such reasonable period as the inspecting officers may specify.
- The venture capital fund shall allow the inspecting or

investigating officer to have reasonable access to the premises occupied by such venture capital fund or by any other person on his behalf and also extend reasonable facility for examining any books, records, documents and computer data in the possession of the venture capital fund or such other person and also provide copies of documents or other materials which, in the opinion of the inspecting or investigation, as the case may be.

- The inspecting or investigating officer, in the course of inspection or investigation shall be entitled to examine or to record the statements of any director, officer or employee of the venture capital fund.
- It shall be the duty of every director, officer or employee, trustee or director of the trustee company of the venture capital fund to give to the inspecting or investigating officer all assistance in connection with the inspection or investigation, which the inspecting or investigating officer may reasonably require.

Submission of Report to the Board

The inspecting or investigating officer shall, as soon as possible, on completion of the inspection or investigation submit an inspection or investigation report to the Board: Provided that if directed to do so by the Board, he may submit an interim report.

Communication of Findings, etc. to the Venture Capital Fund

- The Board shall, after consideration of the inspection or investigation report or the interim report communicate the findings of the inspection officer to the venture capital fund and give him an opportunity of being heard.
- On receipt of the reply if any, from the venture capital fund, the Board may call upon the venture capital fund to take such measures as the Board may deem fit in the interest of the securities market and for the due compliance

with the provisions of the Act and these regulations.

Procedure for Action in Case of Default

Suspension of Certificate: The Board may suspend the certificate granted to a venture capital fund where the venture capital funds:

- contravenes any of the provisions of the Act or these regulations;
- fails to furnish any information relating to its activity as a venture capital fund as required by the Board;
- furnishes to the Board information which is false or misleading in any material particular;
- does not submit periodic returns or reports as required by the Board;
- does "not co-operate in any enquiry, inspection or investigation conducted by the Board;
- fails to resolve the complaints of investors or fails to give a satisfactory reply to the Board in this behalf.

Cancellation of Certificate: The Board may cancel the certificate granted to a venture capital fund

- when the venture capital fund is guilty of fraud or has been convicted of an offence involving moral turpitude; "
- The venture capital fund has been guilty of repeated defaults of the nature. Explanation - In this regulation, "fraud" has the same meaning as is assigned to it in section 17 of the Indian Contract Act, 1972 (9 of 1872) ; or
- Contravenes any of the provisions of the Act or these regulations.

Manner of Making Order of Cancellation or Suspension

No order of suspension or cancellation of certificate shall be made by the Board, except after holding an enquiry.

Manner of Holding Enquiry before Suspension or Cancellation

- For the purpose of holding an enquiry the Board may

appoint one or more enquiry officers.

- The enquiry officer shall issue to the venture capital fund, at its registered office or its principal place of business, a notice setting out the grounds which on action is proposed to be taken against it and calling upon it to show cause against such action within a period of fourteen days from the date of receipt of the notice.
- The venture capital fund may, within fourteen days from the date of receipt of such notice, furnish to the enquiry officer a written reply, together with copies of documentary or other evidence relied on by it or sought by the Board from the venture capital fund.
- The enquiry officer shall give a reasonable opportunity of hearing to the venture capital fund to enable him to make submission in support of its reply made under subregulation (3).
- Before the enquiry officer, the venture capital fund may appear through any person duly authorised by the venture capital fund: Provided that not lawyer or advocate shall be permitted to represent the venture capital fund at the enquiry: Provided further that where a lawyer or an advocate has been appointed by the Board as a presenting officer under sub-regulation (6), it shall be lawful f6r the venture capital fund to present its case through a lawyer or advocate.
- Enquiry officer may, if he considers it necessary, ask the Board to appoint a presenting officer to present its case.
- The enquiry officer shall, after taking into account all relevant facts and submissions made by the venture capital fund, submit a report to the Board and recommend the penal action, if any, to be taken against the venture capital fund as also the grounds on which the proposed action is justified.

Show-cause Notice and Order

- On receipt of the report from the enquiry officer, the Board shall consider the same and may issue to the venture capital fund a show-cause notice as to why the penal action as proposed by the enquiry officer should not be taken against it.

- The venture capital fund shall, within fourteen days of the date of the receipt of the show-cause notice, send a reply to the Board.
- The Board, after considering the reply, if any, of the venture capital fund, shall, as soon as possible pass such order as it deems fit.

Effect of Suspension and Cancellation of Certificate

- On and from the date of the suspension of the certificate, the venture capital fund shall cease to carryon any activity as a venture capital fund during the period of suspension, and shall be subject to such directions of the Board with regard to any records, documents or securities that may be in its custody or control, relating to its activities as venture capital fund, as the Board may specify.
- On and from the date of cancellation of the certificate, the venture capital fund shall, with immediate effect, cease to carryon any activity as a venture capital fund, and shall be subject to such directions of the Board with regard to the transfer of records, documents or securities that may be in its custody or control, relating to its activities as venture capital fund, as the Board may specify.

Publication of Order of Suspension or Cancellation

The order of suspension or cancellation of certificate passed may be published by the Board in two newspapers.

Securities and exchange board of India (foreign venture capital investors) regulations, 2000. The gazette of India extra ordinary part ii section 3 sub-section (ii) published by authority Mumbai the 15th day of September, 2000 notification Securities and exchange board of India (foreign venture capital investors) regulations, 2000

S.O. 832 (E) In exercise of the powers conferred by sub-section (1) of Section 30 of the Securities and Exchange Board of India Act, 1992 (15 of 1992), the Securities and Exchange Board of India hereby makes the following regulations namely:

Preliminary

Short title and commencement

- These regulations may be called the Securities and Exchange Board of India (Foreign Venture Capital Investor) Regulations, 2000.
- They shall come into force on the date of their publication in the Official Gazette.

Registration of Foreign Venture Capital Investors

Application for grant of certificate: For the purposes of seeking registration under these regulations, the applicant shall make an application to the Board in Form A along with the application fee as specified in Part A of the Second Schedule to be paid in the manner specified in Part B thereof.

Eligibility Criteria: For the purpose of the grant of a certificate to an applicant as a Foreign Venture Capital Investor, the Board shall consider the following conditions for eligibility, namely:

- the applicants track record, professional competence, financial soundness, experience, general reputation of fairness and integrity.
- Whether the applicant has been granted necessary approval by the Reserve Bank of India for making investments in India;
- whether the applicant is an investment company, investment trust, investment partnership, pension fund, mutual fund, endowment fund, university fund, charitable institution or any other entity incorporated outside India; or
- whether the applicant is an asset management company,

investment manager or investment management company or any other investment vehicle incorporated outside India;

- whether the applicant is authorised to invest in venture capital fund or carry on activity as a [foreign venture capital investors];
- whether the applicant is regulated by an appropriate foreign regulatory authority or is an income tax payer; or submits a certificate from its banker of its or its promoter's track record where the applicant is neither a regulated entity nor an income tax payer.
- the applicant has not been refused a certificate by the Board.
- whether the applicant is a fit and proper person.

Applicability of Securities and Exchange Board of India (Criteria for Fit and proper Person) Regulations, 2004

The provisions of the Securities and Exchange Board of India (Criteria for fit and proper person) Regulations, 2004 shall, as for as may be, apply to all applicants or the foreign venture capital investors under these regulations"]

Furnishing of Information, Clarification

The Board may require the applicant to furnish such further information as it may consider necessary.

Consideration of Application

An application which is not complete in all respects shall be rejected by the Board:

Provided that, before rejecting any such application, the applicant shall be given an opportunity to remove, within thirty days of the date of receipt of communication, the objections indicated by the Board.

Provided further that the Board may, on being satisfied that it is necessary to extend the period specified above may extend such period not beyond ninety days.

Procedure for Grant of Certificate

- If the Board is satisfied that the applicant is eligible for the grant of certificate, it shall send an intimation to the applicant.
- On receipt of intimation, the applicant shall pay to the Board, the registration fee specified in Part A of the Second Schedule in the manner specified in Part B thereof.
- The Board shall on receipt of the registration fee grant a certificate of registration in Form B.

Conditions of Certificate

The certificate granted to the foreign venture capital [investor] under regulation 7 shall be inter-alia, subject to the following conditions, namely:-

- it shall abide by the provisions of the Act, and these regulations;
- it shall appoint a domestic custodian for purpose of custody of securities;
- it shall enter into arrangement with a designated bank for the purpose of operating a special non-resident rupee or foreign currency account.
- it shall forthwith inform the Board in writing if any information or particulars previously submitted to the Board are found to be false or misleading in any material particular or if there is any change in the information already submitted.

Procedure where Certificate is not Granted

- On considering an application made under regulation 3, if the Board is of the opinion that a certificate should not be granted, it may reject the application after giving the applicant a reasonable opportunity of being heard.
- The decision of the Board to reject the application shall be communicated to the applicant.

Effect of Refusal to Grant Certificate

Any applicant whose application has been rejected under regulation 9 shall not carry on any activity as a Foreign Venture Capital Investor.

Investment Conditions and Restrictions

Investment Criteria for a Foreign Venture Capital Investor: All investments to be made by a foreign venture capital investors shall be subject to the following conditions: -

1. it shall disclose to the Board its investment strategy.
2. it can invest its total funds committed in one venture capital fund .
3. it shall make investments as enumerated below:

- at least [66.67 percent] of the investible funds shall be invested in unlisted equity shares or equity linked instruments [of Venture Capital Undertaking].
- not more than [33.33 percent] of the investible funds may be invested by way of:

4. subscription to initial public offer of a venture capital undertaking whose shares are proposed to be listed
5. debt or debt instrument of a venture capital undertaking in which the [foreign venture capital investor] has already made an investment by way of equity.
6. [preferential allotment of equity shares of a listed company subject to lock in period of one year].
7. [the equity shares or equity linked instruments of a financially weak company or a sick industrial company whose shares are listed].

Explanation 1: For the purpose of these regulations, a "financially weak company " means a company, which has at the end of the previous financial year accumulated losses, which has resulted in erosion or more than 50 percent but less than 100 percent of its net worth as at the beginning of the previous financial year."

[Special Purpose Vehicles which are created for the purpose of facilitating or promoting investment in accordance with these Regulations].

Explanation: the investment conditions and restrictions stipulated in clause (c) of regulation 11 shall be achieved by the Foreign Venture Capital Investor by the end of its life cycle".

[It shall disclose the duration of life cycle of the fund].

General Obligations and Responsibilities

Maintenance of books and records

- Every Foreign Venture Capital Investor shall maintain for a period of eight years, books of accounts, records and documents which shall give a true and fair picture of the state of affairs of the Foreign Venture Capital Investor.
- Every Foreign Venture Capital Investor shall intimate to the Board, in writing, the place where the books, records and documents referred to in sub-regulation (1) are being maintained.

Power to Call for Information

- The Board may at any time call for any information from a Foreign Venture Capital Investor with respect to any matter relating to its activity as a Foreign Venture Capital Investor.
- Where any information is called for under sub-regulation (1) it shall be furnished within the time specified by the Board.

General Obligations and Responsibilities

1. Foreign Venture Capital Investor or a global custodian acting on behalf of the foreign venture capital investor shall enter into an agreement with the domestic custodian to act as a custodian of securities for Foreign Venture Capital Investor.
2. Foreign Venture Capital Investor shall ensure that domestic custodian takes steps for,-

- monitoring of investment of Foreign Venture Capital

Investors in India
- furnishing of periodic reports to the Board
- furnishing such information as may be called for by the Board.

Appointment of Designated Bank

Foreign Venture Capital Investor shall appoint a branch of a bank approved by Reserve Bank of India as designated bank for opening of foreign currency denominated accounts or special non-resident rupee account.

Inspection and Investigations

Board's Right to Inspect or Investigate: The Board may, suo-moto or upon receipt of information or complaint, cause an inspection or investigation to be made in respect of conduct and affairs of any foreign venture capital investor by an Officer whom the Board considers fit for any of the following reasons namely:

- to ensure that the books of account, records and documents are being maintained by the foreign venture capital investor in the manner specified in these regulations.
- to inspect or investigate into complaints received from investors, clients or any other person, on any matter having a bearing on the activities of the foreign venture capital investor;
- to ascertain whether the provisions of the Act and these regulations are being complied with by the foreign venture capital investor; and
- to inspect or investigate suo-moto into the affairs of a foreign venture capital investor in the interest of the securities market or in the interest of investors.

Obligation of Foreign Venture Capital Investor on investigation or inspection by Board

- It shall be the duty of every Foreign Venture Capital Investor in respect of whom an inspection or investigation has been ordered under regulation 16 and any other person associated who is in possession of relevant information pertaining to conduct and affairs of such Foreign Venture Capital Investor including asset management company or fund manager, to produce to the Inspecting or Investigating Officer such books, accounts and other documents in his custody or control and furnish him with such statements and information as the said Officer may require for the purposes of the inspection or investigation.

It shall be the duty of Foreign Venture Capital Investor and any other person associated who is in possession of relevant information pertaining to conduct and affairs of the Foreign Venture Capital Investor to give to the Inspecting or Investigating Officer all such assistance and shall extend all such co-operation as may be required in connection with the inspections or investigations and shall furnish such information sought by the Inspecting or Investigating Officer in connection with the inspections or investigations.

- The Inspecting or Investigating Officer shall, for the purposes of inspection or investigation, have power to examine on oath and record the statement of any person responsible for or connected with activities of Foreign Venture Capital Investor or any other person associated having relevant information pertaining to such Foreign Venture Capital Investor.
- The Inspecting or Investigating Officer shall, for the purposes of inspection or investigation, have power to get authenticated copies of documents, books, accounts of Foreign Venture Capital Investor, from any person having control or custody of such documents, books or accounts.

Submission of the Report

The Inspecting or Investigating Officer shall on completion of inspection or investigations, submit a report to the Board.

Board's Right to Issue any Direction to Foreign Venture Capital Investor

The Board may after consideration of the inspection or investigation report and after giving a reasonable opportunity of hearing to the Foreign Venture Capital Investor, require it to take such measure or issue such directions as it deems fit in the interest of capital market and investors, including directions in the nature of:

- requiring the person concerned to dispose of the securities or disinvest in a manner as may be specified in the directions;
- requiring the person concerned not to further invest for a particular period;
- prohibiting the person concerned from operating in the capital market in India for a specified period.

Procedure for Action in Case of Default

Board's right to suspend or cancel certificate of registration: Without prejudice to the appropriate directions or measures under regulation 19, it may after consideration of the investigation report, initiate action for suspension or cancellation of the registration of such Foreign Venture Capital Investor:

Provided that no such certificate of registration shall be suspended or cancelled unless the procedure specified in regulation 23 is complied with.

Suspension of Certificate

The Board may suspend the certificate where the Foreign Venture Capital Investor:

- contravenes any of the provisions of the Act or these regulations;
- fails to furnish any information relating to its activity as a Foreign Venture Capital Investor as required by the Board;
- furnishes to the Board information which is false or misleading in any material particular;

- does not submit periodic returns or reports as required by the Board;
- does not co-operate in any enquiry or inspection conducted by the Board;

Cancellation of Certificate

The Board may cancel the certificate granted to a Foreign Venture Capital Investor:

- when the Foreign Venture Capital Investor is guilty of fraud or has been convicted of an offence involving moral turpitude;
- Explanation: The expression "fraud" has the same meaning as is assigned to it in section 17 of the Indian Contract Act, 1872. (9 of 1872);
- the Foreign Venture Capital Investor has been guilty of repeated defaults of the nature mentioned in the regulation 21; or
- Foreign Venture Capital Investor does not continue to meet the eligibility criteria laid down in these regulations;
- contravenes any of the provisions of the Act or these regulations.

Manner of Making Order of Cancellation or Suspension

No order of penalty or cancellation of certificate shall be imposed on the Foreign Venture Capital Investor except after holding an enquiry in accordance with the procedure specified in the regulation 24.

Manner of Holding Enquiry before Suspension or Cancellation

- For the purpose of holding an enquiry under regulation 23, the Board may appoint one or more enquiry officers.
- The enquiry officer shall issue to the Foreign Venture Capital Investors, at its registered office or its principal place of business or its agent or representative in India, a notice setting out the grounds on which action is proposed

to be taken against it and calling upon it to show cause against such action within a period of fourteen days from the date of receipt of the notice.

- The Foreign Venture Capital Investor may, within fourteen days from the date of receipt of such notice, furnish to the enquiry officer a written reply, together with copies of documentary or other evidence relied on by it or sought by the Board from the Foreign Venture Capital Investor.
- The enquiry officer shall give a reasonable opportunity of hearing to the Foreign Venture Capital Investor to enable him to make submissions in support of its reply made under sub-regulation (3).
- Before the enquiry officer, the Foreign Venture Capital Investor may appear through any person duly authorised by the Foreign Venture Capital Investor:
- Provided that no lawyer or advocate shall be permitted to represent the Foreign Venture Capital Investors at the enquiry:
- Provided further that where a lawyer or an advocate has been appointed by the Board as a presenting officer under sub-regulation (6), it shall be lawful for the Foreign Venture Capital Investor to present its case through a lawyer or advocate.
- The enquiry officer may, if he considers it necessary, ask the Board to appoint a presenting officer to present its case
- The enquiry officer shall, after taking into account all relevant facts and submissions made by the Foreign Venture Capital Investor, submit a report to the Board and recommend the penal action, if any, to be taken against the Foreign Venture Capital Investor as also the grounds on which the proposed action is justified.

Show-cause Notice and Order

- On receipt of the report from the enquiry officer, the Board shall consider the same and may issue to the Foreign Venture Capital Investor a show-cause notice as to why the penal action as proposed by the enquiry officer or such appropriate action should not be taken against it.

- The Foreign Venture Capital Investor shall, within fourteen days of the date of the receipt of the show-cause notice, send a reply to the Board.
- The Board, after considering the reply, if any, of the Foreign Venture Capital Investor, shall, as soon as possible pass such order as it deems fit.

Effect of Suspension and Cancellation of Certificate

- On and from the date of the suspension of the certificate, the Foreign Venture Capital Investor shall cease to carry on any activity as a Foreign Venture Capital Investor during the period of suspension, and shall be subject to such directions of the Board with regard to any records, documents or securities that may be in its custody or control, relating to its activities as Foreign Venture Capital Investor, as the Board may specify.
- On and from the date of cancellation of the certificate, the Foreign Venture Capital Investor shall, with immediate effect, cease to carry on any activity as a Foreign Venture Capital Investor, and shall be subject to such directions of the Board with regard to the transfer of records, documents or securities that may be in its custody or control, relating to its activities as Foreign Venture Capital Investor, as the Board may specify.

Publication of Order of Suspension or Cancellation

The order of suspension or cancellation of certificate passed under regulation 25 may be published by the Board in two newspapers.

Action against Intermediary

The Board may initiate action for suspension or cancellation of registration of an intermediary holding a certificate of registration under section 12 of the Act who fails to exercise due diligence in the performance of its functions or fails to comply with its obligations under these regulations.

Provided that no such certificate of registration shall be suspended or cancelled unless the procedure specified in the regulations applicable to such intermediary is complied with.

[**Appeal to Securities Appellate Tribunal**]

Any person aggrieved by an order of the Board under these regulations may prefer an appeal to the Securities Appellate Tribunal in accordance with section 15T of the Act.]

Bibliography

Bibliography

1. Admatı, A. R. and P. Pfleiderer (1994). "Robust Financial Contracting and the Role of Venture Capitalists." The Journal of Finance Vol. XLIX (2): pp. 371-402.
2. Akerlof, G. (1970). "The Markets for Lemons: Quality uncertainty and the Market Mechanism." Quarterly Journal of Economics Vol. 84(3): pp.s488-500.
3. Amit, R., J. Brander, et al. (1998). "Why do Venture Capital Firms Exist? Theory and Canadian Evidence." Journal of Business Venturing 13(6, 01-November): pp. 441-466.
4. Amit, R., L. Glosten, et al. (1990a). "Does Venture Capital Foster the Most Promising Entrepreneurial Firms?" California Management Review 32(pp.102-111).
5. Apax Partners, *Unlocking global Value Report*, 2006
6. Barry,C.B. (1994). "New Directions in research on venture capital finance." Financial Management 23(3): 3-15.
7. Bergemann, D. and U. Hege (1998). "Venture Capital Financing, Moral hazard, and learning." Journal of Banking & Finance 22(6-8, 15-August): pp. 703-735.
8. Bergemann, D. and U. Hege (2002). "The Financing of Innovation Learning and Stopping." Yale University: pp. 1-40.
9. Bester, H. (1985). "Screening versus Rationing in Credit Markets with Imperfect Information." American Economic Review 75: pp.850-855.
10. Black, B. and B. Gilson (1998). "Venture Capital and the Structure of Capital Markets: Banks versus Stock Markets." Journal of Financial Economics Vol. 47: pp. 243-277.
11. Bloomberg.com, *Blackstone, Still Seeking a Deal, Plans $500 Million India Fund,* June 12 2006
12. Bowden, R. J. (1994). "Bargaining, size, and return in venture capital funds." Journal of Business Venturing 9(4): pp.307-331.
13. Bygrave, W. and J.Timmons (1992). Venture Capital at the Cross Roads.
14. Brunswik, E. 1956. Perception and the Representation Design of Experiments. University of California Press.
15. Bygrave, W. D. 1987. Syndicated investments by venture capital firms: a networking perspective. Journal of Business Venturing, 2(2): 139-154.

16. Carroll, J. S. & Johnson, E. J. 1990. Decison research : a field guide.: Applied Social Research Methods Series: Sage Publications.
17. C. Cheung for Bloomberg, *China May Draw $6 billion in Private Equity in 2006, May 12th 2006 China Daily at* http://www.chinadaily.com.cn/bizchina/2006-05/12/content_588156.htm
18. Calomiris, C. and G.Hubbard (1990). "Firm Heterogeneity, Internal Finance, and 'Credit Rationing'." The Economic Journal 100: pp. 90-104.
19. Carpenter, R. (1992). An Empirical Investigation of the Financial Hierarchy Hypothesis: Evidence from Panel Data. Working paper no. 164, Department of Economics, Washington University.
20. Carter, R. and H. V. Auken (1994). "Venture Capital Firms' preferences for Projects in Particular Stages of Development." Journal of Small Business Management 32: pp.60-73.
21. Chan.Y (1983). "On the Positive Role of Financial Intermediation in Allocation of Venture Capital in a Market with Imperfect Information." Journal of Finance 38: pp.1543-1568.
22. Citigroup, Y. Huang and C. Tan, *Asia-Pacific Economic Strategy*, June 2006
23. Cyert, R. M. & March, J. G. 1963. A Behaviourial Theory of the Firm: Prentice Hall.
24. Davis, E. (1992). Debt, Financial Fragility, and Systemic Risk.
25. Dossani, R. and M. Kenney (April 4, 2001). Creating an Environment: Developing Venture Capital in India.
26. Dawes, R. M. 1979. The robust beauty of improper lianera models in decision making. American Psychologist, 34(7): 571-582.
27. Dawes, R. M., Faust, D., & Meehl, P. E. 1989. Clinical versus acturial judgment. Science, 24(3): 1668-1674.
28. Duncan, R. B. 1972. Characteristics of organizational environments and perceived organizational uncertainty. Administrative Science Quarterly, 17: 313-327.
29. Economist Intelligence Unit, *Foresight 2020: Economic, industry and corporate trends*, March 2006.
30. Elango, B., Fried, V. H., Hisrich, R. D., & Polonchek, A. 1995. How venture capital firms differ. Journal of Business Venturing, 10(Issue 2, -March-1995): 157-179.

31. Ernst and Young, Transition: Global Venture Capital Insight Report 2006
32. Ernst & Young, Renewal and new frontiers, 2005
33. Fazzari, S. and B.Peterson (1993). "Working Capital and Fixed Investment: New Evidence on Financing Constraints." Rand Journal of Economics 24: pp. 328-342.
34. Fazzari, S., R. G. Hubbard, et al. (1988). Financial Constraints and Corporate Investment, Brookings Papers on Economic Activities no.1: pp. 141-195.
35. Fenn, G. W., Liang, N., and, & Prowse, S. 1995. The economics of the private equity market. Washington, DC:: Board of Governors of the Federal Reserve System.
36. Fiske, S. T. & Taylor, S. E. 1991. Social Cognition: Random House.
37. Fladmoe-Lindquist, K. (1996). "International franchising: capabilities and development." Journal of Business Venturing 11(Issue 5, -September-1996): 419-438.
38. Flannery, M. (1986). "Asymmetric Information and Risky Debt maturity Choice." The Journal of Finance 41: pp. 19-37.
39. Freear, J., J. E. Sohl, et al. (1994). ""Angels and non-angels: Are there differences?"" Journal of Business Venturing 9(2): 109-124.
40. Fenwick & West LLP, F.M. Greguras and S. R. Gopalan, *Update to Structuring Venture Capital and other investments in India*
41. Fried, V. H. & Hisrich, R. D. 1994. Toward a model of venture capital investment decision-making. Financial Management, 23(3): 28-37.
42. Gibbon, R. (1992). Game theory for applied Economics.
43. Gibson, L. and S.Blake (1992). ""Venture capital and Economic Development"." Economic Development Review 10: pp. 41-46.
44. Gompers, P. and J. Lerner (1996). "The Use of Convenants: An Empirical Analysis of Venture Partnership Agreements." Journal of Law and Economics Vol. XXXIX(October): pp.463-498.
45. Gompers, P. and J. Lerner (2001). "The Venture Capital Revolution." Journal of Economic Perspectives Vol. 15(2): pp. 145-168.
46. Gorman, M. and W. Sahlman (1989). ""What do Venture Capitalists Do?"" Journal of Business Venturing 4: pp.231-248.
47. Goldman Sachs Global Economics Group, *The World and the*

BRICS Dream, February 2006

48. Grant Thornton, *Dealtracker Annual Issue*, 2006
49. Grant Thornton, Dealtracker June 2006
50. Gupta, A. K. & Sapienza, H. J. 1992. Determinants of Venture Capital Firms' Preferences Regarding the Industry Diversity and Geographic Scope of Their Investments. Journal of Business Venturing, 7(5, New York; Sep 1992): 347-363.
51. Hall, H. J. 1989. Venture capitalist decision-making and the entrepreneur: an exploratory investigation. University of Georgia, Athens.
52. Hall, J. and C. W. Hofer (1993). "Venture capitalists' decision criteria in new venture evaluation." Journal of Business Venturing 8(1).
53. Harsanyi, J. (1976). ""Games with Incomplete Information Played by 'Bayesian' Players Part I. The Basic Model"." Management Science 14: pp. 159-182.
54. Harsanyi, J. (1995). ""Games with Incomplete Information"." American Economic Review 85: pp. 291-303.
55. Hermalin, B. (1986). "Adverse Selection and Contract Length". memo, MIT.
56. Hoshi, T., A. Kashyap, et al. (1991). ""Corporate Structure, Liquidity, and Investment: Evidence from Japanese Panel Data"." Quarterly Journal of Economics 106: pp. 33-60.
57. Hisrich, R., D., & Jankowicz, A. D. 1990. Intuition in venture capital decisions: an exploratory study using a new technique. Journal of Business Venturing, 5(1): 49-62.
58. Hitt, M. A. & Tyler, B. B. 1991. Strategic decision models: Integrating different perspectives. Strategic Management Journal, 12: 327-351.
59. S. Howes, *Will India become an economic superpower*, March 2005
60. http://www.worldbank.org
61. http://www.abvcap.com.br
62. http://www.asiape.com, with special material sent by Ryan Tang on request
63. Indian Venture Capital Association, *PE and VC Investment Trends 2005*, personal copy
64. Indian Venture Capital Journal, *The BPO Opportunity*, Issue Nr.1 2006
65. The Indian Express, *Private equity bemoans price of Indian*

developers, 30 June 2006

66. Indiaenews.com, *India, China have great potential in private equity investment*, May 06 2006 http://indiaenews.com/2006-05/6918-india-china-potential-private-equity-investment.htm
67. I. Kannan for Moneycontrol.com, *India Attractive for late & early stage pvt equity*, May 23 2006,http://news.moneycontrol.com/india/news/business/private equitiesuniversitychicago/indiaattractiveforlateearlystagepvtequity/23/53/article/215980
68. Jovanovic, B. (1982). "Selection and the Evolution of Industry." Econometrica Vol.50: pp. 649-670.
69. Kirilenko, A. A. (2001). "Valuation and Control in Venture Finance." The Journal of Finance Vol. 56(2): pp.565-587.
70. Klein, L. (1990). "Financial Options for Economic Development." The Pakistan Development Review Vol. 30: pp. 369- 393.
71. KnowledgeManagement-India (2002). http://210.212.218.42/sectors/venturecapital.html.
72. K. Can and S. Jan, *Risk Management in Private Equity Funds: a Comparative Study of Indian and Franco-German Funds*, Journal of Developmental Entrepreneurship May 2006
73. Kreps, D. (1990). A Course in Microeconomic Theory, Princeton University Press.
74. Kunze, R. (1990). Nothing Ventured, Harper Collins Publishers.
75. Khan, A. M. 1987. Assessing venture capital investments with noncompensatory behavioral decision models. Journal of Business Venturing, 2(3): 193-204.
76. Knight, R. M. 1994. Criteria used by venture capitalists: a cross cultural analysis. Paper presented at the Proceedings of ASAC.
77. Lenzi, R. (1992). "Non-traditional Sources of Economic Development." Economic Development Review Vol. 10: pp. 11-19.
78. Lerner, J. (1994b). "The syndication of Venture Capital Investments." Financial Management Vol. 23: pp. 16-27.
79. Lerner, J. (1995). "Venture Capitalists and Oversight of Private Firms." Journal of Finance Vol. 50(5): pp.301-318.
80. Lucas, R. (1978). "On the Size Distribution of Business Firms." Bell Journal of Economics Vol 9: pp. 508- 523.
81. MacMillan, I., L. Zeman, and P. Narsimha (1987). ""Criterion Distinguishing Successful from unsuccessful Ventures in the

Venture Screening Process"." Journal of Business Venturing 2: 123-137.

82. MacMillan, I. C. S., Robin; Subba Narasimha, P. N.;. 1985. Criteria Used by Venture Capitalists to Evaluate New Venture Proposals. Journal of Business Venturing, 1(1): 119-129.
83. Mattesini, F. (1993). Financial Markets: Asymmetric Information and Macroeconomic Equilibrium, Dartmouth Publishing Co.
84. Merrill Lynch, R. Varma and S. Sharma, *India Economics*: *RBI raises rates unexpectedly*, June 2006
85. Milgrom, P. and J. Roberts (1992). Economics, Organization & Management, Prentice Hall.
86. Minsky, H. (1982). Can it Happen Again? Essays on stability and Finance. M.E. Sharpe.
87. Mintzberg, H., Raisinghani, D., & Theoret, A. 1976. The structure of unstructured decision processes. Administrative Science Quarterly, 21(2): 246-275.
88. Morgan, D. (1991). New Evidence Firms are Financially Constrained. E. Review. Federal Reserve Bank of Kansas City. Vol. 76: pp. 37-45.
89. Myers, S. and N. Majluf (1984). "Corporate Financing and Investment Decisions when Firms have Information that Investors Do not have." Journal of Financial Economics Vol.13: pp. 187-221.
90. Nasscom. (2000). "http://www.nasscom.org/business_in_india/vc_scenario.asp."
91. Neher, D. (1997). Stage Financing: An agency perspective, Boston University.
92. Newell, A. & Simon, H. A. 1972. Human problem solving: Englewood Cliffs, NJ: Prentice Hall Inc.
93. Nisbett, R. E., Borgida, E., Crandall, R., & Reed , H. 1976. Popular induction: Information is not necessarily normative.: Cignition and social Behaviour. Erlbaum.
94. NVCA; National Venture Capital Association. http://www.nvca.org.
95. Pandey, I. M. (1996). "Venture capitalists' Evaluation criteria in a Developing Country: Case of India." International Journal of Development banking 14(1).
96. Pandey, I. M. (1996). "Venture Capital-The Indian Experience." Prentice hall of India- Private limited, New Delhi- 110 001.

97. Pandey, I.M. and Jang, A., (1996), "Venture Capital for Financing Technology in Taiwan." Technovation 16, pp.499-514.
98. Petersen, B. (1992). "Roundtable on US Risk Capital and Innovation." Journal of Applied Corporate Finance Vol. 4: pp. 48-78.
99. Poindexter, J. B. (1976). "The Efficiency Of Financial Markets: The Venture Capital Case." Dissertations Institution: New York University, Graduate School Of Business Administration; 0868
100. Pratt's (Ed.). 1995. Pratt's guide to venture capital sources: Securities Data Publishing , Inc.
101. P. Smith for Financial Times, *Buy-out groups set to drive private equity,* May 12 2006
102. Poza, E. (1989). Smart Growth, Jossey-Bass Publishers.
103. PriceWaterhouseCoopers, *The Evolution of BPO in India*, April 2005
104. PriceWaterhouseCoopers, *Destination India: A Brief Overview of Tax and Regulatory Framework*, December 2005
105. PriceWaterhouseCoopers, J. Haksworth, *The World in 2050*, March 2006
106. PriceWaterhouseCoopers, *Global Private Equity Report 2005*
107. PriceWaterhouseCoopers, *M&A Bulletin India 2005*
108. Rafiq Dossani, M. K. (April 4, 2001). "Creating an Environment: Developing Venture Capital in India." BRIE Working Paper 143.
109. Rasmussen, E. (1990). Games and Information, Basil Blackwell.
110. Ray, D. M. (1991). "Venture Capital and Entrepreneurial Development in Singapore." International Small Business Journal 10(1): 11-26.
111. Ray, D. M. a. T., Dominique V (1993). "Venture Capital in Japan." International Small Business Journal 4: 39-56.
112. Robinson, R. B. (1987). ""Emerging strategies in the Venture Capital industry"." Journal of Business Venturing 2: 53-77.
113. Rosman, A. and H.O'Neill (1993). "Comparing the Information Acquisition Strategies of Venture Capital and Commercial Lenders." Journal of Business Venturing Vol. 8: pp. 443-460.
114. Rothschild, M. and J. Stiglitz (1970). "Increasing Risk:I, A Definition." Journal of Economic Theory Vol. 2: pp. 225-243.
115. Riquelme, H. & Rickards, T. 1992. Hybrid conjoint analysis: an estimation probe in new venture decisions. Journal of Business

Venturing, 7(6): 505-518.

116.Roberts, E. B. 1991. High stakes for high-tech entrepreneurs: understanding venture capital decision making. Sloan Management Review, 32(2): 9-20.

117.S. Anand for Finance Asia, *Private Equity firm attracts India BPO specialist, May 10 2006*

118.Sagari, S. B. and G. Guidotti (1991a). Venture Capital: Lessons from the developed world for the developing markets. International Finance Corporation,, Discussion paper No.13.

119.Sagari, S. B. and G. Guidotti (1991b). "Venture capital operation and their role in less developed markets." The World Bank Working paper No. WPS 540.

120.Sahlman, W. (1988). "Aspects of Financial Contracting in Venture Capital." Journal of Applied Corporate Finance Vol. 1: pp. 23-36.

121.Sahlman, W. (1994a). "Insights from the Venture Capital Model of Project Governance." Business Economics July: pp. 35-37.

122.Sahlman, W. A. (1990). "The structure and governance of venture-capital organizations." Journal of Financial Economics Vol. 27(2, 01-October).

123.Sandberg, W. E., Schwelger, D. M., & Hofer, C. W. 1987. Determining venture capitalists' decision criteria: the use of verbal protocols. Frontiers of Entrepreneurship Research: 392-407.

124.Sandberg, W. R., Schweiger, D.M., and Hofer, C.W. (1988). "The use of verbal protocols in determining venture capitalists' decision processes." Entrepreneurship Theory and Practice (Winter): 8–20.

125.Sapienza, H. J. (1992). "When Do Venture Capitalists Add Value?" Journal of Business Venturing Vol. 7: pp.9-27.

126.Schaller, H. (1993). "Asymmetric Information, Liquidity Constraints, and Canadian Investment." Canadian Journal of Economics Vol. 26: pp. 552-574.

127.Scherer, F. (1984). Innovation and Growth: Schumpeterian Perspectives, MIT Press.

128.Schilit, W. K. & Chandran, J. 1993. The venture capital decision process : a reappraisal. Entrepreneurship, Innovation, and Change, 2(4): 359-382.

129.Silver, A. D. 1985. Venture capital: the complete guide for investors: John Wiley and Sons.

130.Simon, H. A. 1955. A behavioural model of rational choice. Quarterly Journal of Economics, 69· 99-118.

131.Slovic, P. & Lichtenstein, S. 1971. Comparison of Bayesian and regression approaches to the study of information processing in judgment. Organizational Behaviour and Human Performance, 6: 649-744.

132.Stewart, T. R. 1988. Judgment analysis: procedures: In Brehmer, B., and Joyce,c (Eds.) Human Judgment: The SJT View Elsevier.

133.Stiglitz, J. and A. Weiss (1983). "Incentive effects of Termination: Application to the Credit and Labour Markets." American Economic Review Vol. 73: pp. 393-410.

134.Stiglitz, J. and A. Weiss (1987). "Credit rationing with Many Borrowers." American Economic Review Vol. 77: pp. 228-231.

135.Stiglitz, J. and A. Weiss (1981). "Credit Rationing with Imperfect Information." American Economic Review Vol. 71: pp. 393-410.

136.Strong, K. C. 1992. A cognitive model of down structuring strategy. Ph.D. Dissertation, University of Colorado.

137.S.Sheth for DNA India, *Private equity is now a $4billion gusher,* May 07 2006 http://www.dnaindia.com/report.asp?NewsID=1028220&CatID =4

138.S. Vallikappen and N. Lakshman for DNA Money, *Non-traditional private equity is streaming in,* June 28 2006

139.Timmons, J. A., Muzyka, D.F., Stevenson, H.H., and Bygrave, W.D. (1987). "Opportunity recognition: The core of entrepreneurship." Frontiers Of Entrepreneurship Research: 109–123.

140.Timmons, J. A. 1994. New venture creation: Entrepreneurship for the 21st century. Homewood, IL: Irwin.

141.Times News Network, *Pharma to see growth in private equity deals,* May 27 2006

142.Townsend, R. (1979). "Optimal Contracts and Competitive Markets with Costly State Verification." Journal of Economic Theory Vol. 21: pp. 265-293.

143.Trester, J. J. (1997). "Venture Capital Contracting under Asymmetric Information." Journal of Banking & Finance Vol. 22: pp. 675-699.

144.Tversky, A. & Kahneman, D. 1974. Judgment under uncertainty:

Heuristics and biases. Science, 185: 1124-1131.

145. Tyebjee, T. T. a. B. (1984). "A model of Venture Capitalist Investment Activity." Management Science 30(9): 1051-1066.

146. V. Venugopal for Business Standard, *Firms swerve into private equity lane,* June 12 2006, http://www.business-standard.com/common/storypage.php?autono=94597

147. Warne, F. K. (1988). Essays On The Venture Capital Market. Doctoral Dissertation, Yale University.

148. Wharton Private Equity Review, *Finding Value in a crowded market*, 2006

149. Weinberg, J. (1994). "Firm Size, Finance, and Investment." Economic Quarterly Vol. 81(Federal Reserve bank of Richmond): pp. 19-40.

150. Wetzel, W. E. J. (1983). "Angels and Informal Risk Capital." Sloan Management Review Vol.24: pp. 23-24.

151. Whited, T. (1992). "Debt, Liquidity Constraints, and Corportae Investment: Evidence From Panel Data." The Journal of Finance Vol 47: pp. 1425-1459.

152. Williamson, S. (1986). "Costly Monitoring, Financial Intermediation, and Equilibrium Credit Rationing." Journal of Monetary Economics Vol. 18: pp. 156-179.

153. Y. A. Pitawalla for Fortune Magazine, *Indian Real Estate: Boom or Bubble?,* July 2006, pp. 14-15

154. Zacharakis, L, A., & Meyer, G. D. 1998. A lack of insight: Do venture capitalists really understand their own decision processes? Journal of Business Venturing, 13(1): 57-76.

155. Zacharakis, A. L. 1995. The venture capital investment decision. Dissertations, Institution: UNIVERSITY OF COLORADO AT BOULDER

156. ZACHARAKIS, A. L., Meyer, G. D., & DeCastro, J. 1999. Differing perceptions of new venture failure: A matched exploratory study of venture capitalists and entrepreneurs. Journal of Small Business Management, 37(3): 1-14.

157. Z. Shenshen for Shangai Daily, *Venturecapital firm bullish on cyberland China,* May 17 2006

158. Zopounidis, C. (1994). ""Venture Capital Modeling: Evaluation Criteria for the appraisal of Investments"." The Financier ACMT 1(2): 54-64.

Index

Index